DOLLARS
AND
COMMON SENSE

TAKING CHARGE OF
YOUR INVESTMENTS
IN THE
TUMULTUOUS 21ST CENTURY

PETER G. ANDRESEN

TIMEWALKER
PRESS

Dollars and Common Sense

Publisher's Cataloging-in-Publication Data
Andresen, Peter Garth.

Dollars and common sense : taking charge of your investments in the tumultuous 21st century / written by Peter G. Andresen.
    p. cm.
    ISBN 978-0-615-53783-2 (pbk.)
    ISBN 978-0-98542385-9-4 (Kindle)
    ISBN 978-0-98542385-0-1 (iPad ebook)
    ISBN 978-0-98542385-1-8 (Nook)

Includes index.
1. Investments. 2. Finance, Personal. 3. Portfolio management. 4. Saving and investment. 5. Asset allocation. 6. Mutual funds. 7. Bonds. 8. Stocks. I. Dollars and common sense : taking charge of your investments in the tumultuous twenty-first century. II. Title.

HG179 .A53 2012
332.024 --dc23
                                          2012936329

Acknowledgements

Thanks to the people who made this book possible.

Proofreaders and Editors:
Erin Brown
Eric Andresen
Susanne Andresen
Laurie Classen

Index: Rose Ippolito
Cover design: Gaelyn Larrick
Interior design: Bram Larrick
Book Shepherd & Publicist: Stephanie Barko
Administration: Renee Guyton

The lessons included in this book: the clients of Andresen & Associates

From the Author

What you are about to read is a book about how to become financially secure, even wealthy. By "wealthy" I mean a life which encompasses the abilities to sleep well at night, have enough reserves to meet family expenses even during emergencies, enjoy some decent vacations, contribute to your children's college education, retire gracefully, and hopefully leave at least a small bequest to your family. I am not talking about celebrity-level wealth. I am not talking about financial miracles or day-trading in your basement. For all that you will need to look elsewhere.

I am talking about potentially accumulating millions of dollars during your lifetime. Read this book, and live it for three decades or more, and you will probably find yourself to be a millionaire at some point in your life.

But "wealth" to me also means living a life free of investment fear, phobias, and mythology. It also means living a rich life regardless of your financial success. In particular, this book is about basic investing techniques, focusing on how to invest successfully for the rest of your life. Because I'm more interested in long-term, permanent success, this book does not contain the newest investment fad, or specific instructions on how to deal with today's market.

In fact, one of the reasons I wrote this book is that there really isn't a secret method to tell the future. There is no newest, better method. Instructions for today's market will usually fail when tomorrow dawns. So this is a book to show you how to invest successfully regardless of market conditions for decades to come.

This is also a book to assist you when you work with an investment advisor, to show you what "good" looks like. You face two choices: to do it yourself or to work with a professional. This book is intended to help you make the best choice, and succeed regardless of which path you choose.

In this book, I focus on the time-tested investment tactics which have worked for us at our investment advisory firm. Using these techniques, my clients and I have thrived for decades. And we have done so with much less angst and turmoil than many investors seem to experience.

I have included a small glossary in the back of this book, to help you with basic terms. Please look there whenever you encounter a concept or a word which is new to you. You will also find appendices which address several specific topics that I thought would be pertinent to many of you..

What you are about to read are my opinions and my suggestions based on my more-than-twenty-year successful career as a self-employed investment advisor. I have no idea how you will employ these concepts, or the details of your portfolio. So do your own research as directed in this book.

Now go be rich.

Pete Andresen — January 31, 2012

Ten Commandments of Investing for Success in the 21ˢᵗ Century

Everything in this book orbits around these ten concepts. We'll explain all this throughout the book. But meanwhile, here's the outline.

1. Times of economic and physical hardship are an inevitable part of life. They pass.
2. Budget, reduce or avoid debt, and save to succeed.
3. Manage your own irrational mind.
4. Be cautious with your investments:
   a. Use a discount brokerage
   b. Select actionable, relevant financial information
   c. Select good professional help.
5. Invest only in mutual funds:
   1. Cash and money market funds
   2. Bond mutual funds
   3. Diversified asset allocation mutual funds
   4. Stock mutual funds
   5. International mutual funds

We will cover mutual funds and mutual fund types in five chapters.

6. Diversify through asset classes to reduce risk to your perceived tolerance.
7. Rebalance your portfolio annually <u>between and within</u> asset classes.
8. "Weed the garden" annually to find the best possible mutual funds.
9. Recognize and avoid investment bubbles by recognizing mania and overvaluation.
10. Repeat steps 1 through 9 to succeed with time, discipline, and consistency.

Here we go.

Table of Contents

Chapter 1

Times of Economic and Physical Hardship are Inevitable

*Life is like an onion: You peel it off one layer
at a time, and sometimes you weep.*
—Carl Sandburg

Section 1.1: If my Old House Could Talk

Lesson #1: Times of economic hardship are an inevitable part of life. We will all live through market downturns, recessions, and wars. With good investing techniques, we can thrive despite hard times.

To invest successfully, you need to understand the way the world of money works. Then we'll delve into investments themselves. And one of the many dimensions of the world of money is time.

Unless you win the lottery or inherit, almost all successful investing requires a long time…10 to 30 years or longer. Yet almost all of us think and invest in very short-term vistas. In other words, most of us don't have a grasp of the time horizon required for successful investing.

But if successful investing means that you will be involved in investing for decades, it also means that your investing experience will inevitably incorporate good times… and bad.

Any investing…any SUCCESSFUL investing…should be planned with the realization that <u>unexpected hard times are inevitable</u>.

The challenge is that hard times come so unexpectedly and hopefully so infrequently that it's easy to assume that they won't happen at all. But in the span of a lifetime, <u>hard times are inevitable</u>.

We all have examples of this challenge in our own family histories. Talk to the older members of your family about this issue and you'll find that every life has its hard times, even if the behavioral or emotional scars aren't public.

I can see one validation of this simply by looking up from the desk where I am writing. I work in my great-grandfather's home, which he built in 1894.

If we measure the human lifespan as between 80 to 100 years, then this house is about 1 ½ life-spans old. During that time, the occupants of this house have witnessed the Spanish American War, the panic of 1907, World War I, the Great Depression, World War II, Korea, Vietnam, the Oil Embargo, Watergate, the 1987 stock market crash, several Middle Eastern wars, the Tech collapse, uncountable family dramas, and the Financial Panic of 2008 with its current stumbling recovery.

During each of these crises, the people living in this neighborhood responded as people do: with short-term thinking. They envisioned world-ending catastrophes with the onset of each new challenge.

For example, during the Great Depression in the 1930's one of the neighbors dug up his yard so that he could grow vegetables when the economy failed. We live in one of the most agriculturally productive places in the world, the Salinas Valley. But the social mood was so dismal in the 1930's that this neighbor became convinced that farming would fail as well.

Immediately following the Pearl Harbor attacks in 1941, my grandmother had all her dogs euthanized so that they would not be eaten by invading Japanese troops. And this was in coastal California.

During the 1960's, the height of the Cold War, one neighbor put in a complete bomb shelter. It's still there: nobody can figure out how to demolish the thick concrete walls.

Later, in the inflationary 1970's, as Vietnam was ending badly, another neighbor converted his savings and his investments into gold coins and stored them in his basement. They were still there when he died in relative penury a few years ago, having missed one of the greatest economic booms in history.

All these examples seem ludicrous to us now, in hindsight, but the reality is that during hard economic times the social mood becomes bleak. In fact, something resembling all these examples can be found in every neighborhood in America.

While all this was going on, let's take a look at the REAL return on investments. During this time, what was the performance of the average investment? For example, what was the overall performance of stocks?

For the entire 20th Century, 100 years which includes the Financial panic of 1907 and World War I, the stock market delivered about 12% a year, while bonds produced about 5%. The American financial engine of the 20th Century was a marvel. (Fig.1-1)

So why not just put all your money in a stock market index fund and walk away?

Because when hard times arrive, they tend to arrive unexpectedly, after a period of plenty. And when they arrive, they can be brutal and last longer than most people can stand…up to ten years.

Following the boom years of the 1920's, one of our neighbors lost not only his home but his 8,000 acre cattle ranch as well by embracing too much risk in the stock market and going into debt to fund his lifestyle. At the time he was a bank president.

Seventy years later, the tech bubble of the 1990's created many millionaires as tech stocks went up relentlessly. One of them lives down the street from me currently: he is now a former millionaire because he had all his money in tech stocks when the market collapsed in 2000.

As I write this, in 2010, the street is dotted with "for-sale" signs as people lose their homes after over-borrowing in the roaring 2000's.

Study after study has discovered that despite financial markets which provide marvelous gains over the long run, many if not most investors have lost money when they put their own nest eggs into these same financial venues.

These losses happen because investors have misperceptions about how real-world investing actually works. And, more importantly, people do not manage their own minds to create success.

During economic booms, people forget that bad times happen.

When hardships strike, we tend to forget that these inevitably end as well.

We need to embrace an investment style which protects us from both extremes of experience and behavior.

Ibbotson® SBBI®
Stocks, Bonds, Bills, and Inflation 1926–2010

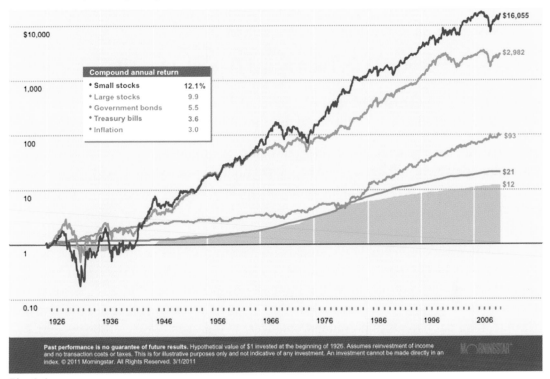

Compound annual return	
• Small stocks	12.1%
• Large stocks	9.9
• Government bonds	5.5
• Treasury bills	3.6
• Inflation	3.0

Fig. 1-1

Here are financial market performances from 1926---before the Great Depression---through 2010, after the Financial Panic of 2008. As you can see, investing in the stock market has been a very successful effort over the very long term

That ---precisely---is why I wrote this book.

If my home could talk, it would add that time, discipline, and consistency pay off.

In other words, when you think life is dreadful, if you respond with the application of time, discipline, and consistency, you quite possibly may be planting the seeds for future success.

This is even true if you are broke, ill, or dying: your behavior, your financial planning, and your time, discipline, and consistency may easily prove a legacy to your descendants.

History tells us that even the worst of financial panics in American history have lasted 10 years or less.

If you look back through history, you will realize that the American people have been challenged before, time and time again. Creative destruction and financial mistakes are a key albeit unpleasant component of the American system.

My ancestors who lived in this home thrived DESPITE events like the Great Depression. If they could do it, you and I can as well.

It will be possible to become wealthy beyond your wildest expectations in the 21st Century, if your playbook includes some basic rules.

- Some of the best experiences of life, and some of the best opportunities, take place in the most difficult of times.
- We want to LEARN from our recent history so that we don't repeat common

investors' mistakes again. After all, learning from hardships has always been a key component of successful people.

• Like our ancestors, we can go on to wealth if we stay calm and employ time, discipline, and consistency to our advantage..

Section 1.2: The Flawed Financial Model

Lesson #2: The "borrow and spend" model of American society doesn't work. If we want to succeed, it's time for us to do something different.

What follows is a necessary telling, simply to establish that we are emerging from a multi-decade financial mistake. As the philosopher George Santayana said, "Those who cannot learn from history are doomed to repeat it." Since we don't want to do that, a bit of history is in order.

In short, we've been on a thirty-year binge of public and personal overspending. As the elites of Washington and Wall Street have transformed into a private clique bent on power and wealth, the American middle class has been misled and ripped off.

Part of our insanity has been the mass delusion that financial and personal risk have somehow gone away. The result is that many of us are much poorer, in terms of lifestyle, than our parents and grandparents were at our ages. We've all been conned… by our own society. Essentially, we've conned ourselves.

Here's how it happened.

The people who fought in World War II grew up during the Depression, and fought a world war that was by no means a sure victory. They looked disaster straight in the eye, and won. A result of that was that the World War II generation was in general forever cautious, forever conservative financially.

The baby boomers, people like me who were born after World War II, from 1943 to 1957, grew up in a society immersed in the post traumatic stress disorder of World War II. We grew up with civil defense alerts wherein we ducked under our school desks to avoid the expected Soviet A-bombs. We came of age when fighting communism was everything. We were told that the Reds in the east comprised the greatest threat. And our parents were very, very frugal because of their own Great Depression childhoods.

Of course we rebelled against such restraints. In the 1960's it seemed that wealth was blooming all around us despite the World War II generation's fears. And finally, amazingly, the Soviet Union crumbled unexpectedly away in 1991. It seemed to us that our generation's more optimistic version of reality was in fact correct.

So the baby boomers reacted to the fall of the Soviet Union with an irrational holistic swing to complacency. Such complacency was probably inevitable. After all, the Great Depression and World War II were only history to us. And most of us…certainly the most chic of us…had evaded the war in Vietnam. With the crumbling of the vaunted Russian communist bloc it was natural to be less fearful.

Heady with anticipation of a "peace dividend", most of us eagerly sought to prove, or at least to believe, that all the economic fears of our childhood were so many imaginary boogiemen.

The seeds of this flight of imagination had been sown much earlier: in 1948,

MIT economist Paul Samuelson published his seminal textbook **Economics** which employed mathematics and statistics to quantify and model what had been simply a dismal exercise in sociology. In other words, **Economics** succeeded in quantifying what was heretofore considered unquantifiable.

So after 1948, the financial world began to change. In our search to prove what we wanted to believe, that we could control economic risk, we educated and paid legions of baby boomer economists to tell us that we were much too sophisticated to replicate the conditions of a major financial melt-down.

The rise of computers gave us the capacity to create complex mathematical models of human behavior, and defend these theories with vast oceans of data. What we didn't fully grasp is that it is routine to detect statistical trends without causality, or causality which is so random as to be useless for predicting.

It was entirely possible to sell the newly-minted concept of the Efficient Market Hypothesis or the Capital Asset Pricing Model, since only people with time and energy to examine the data could say that the emperor had no clothes.

Economics and finance became dominated by "quants", highly-paid professionals who made big bucks crunching numbers. From the point of view of Wall Street and the academics, this was wonderful. Society's increasing worship of digital models of all sorts created the perception that economics was mysterious and arcane.

Therefore they, the highly paid experts, were essential. It was quite possible, even normal, to build a high-paying job on Wall Street spinning numbers. Simply the act of crunching numbers itself generated a mystical force, and gave authority to the results.

I suppose we could term this the arrogance of the new. If you have family photo albums from the 1970's, find one of your relatives wearing platform shoes and you will see this in action.

Thus, if you studied finance and investing in college since 1970, you were required to embrace a curriculum based on the premise that all these new ideas really worked. The college graduates from these programs then went out, got hired by the best firms and governments, and rebuilt our financial system around these theoretical ideas. Of course relatively few of these concepts had been genuinely tested in the real world.

Part of this process was that Wall Street and the banking sector changed our minds about debt.

The World War II generation and their ancestors—your ancestors—regarded debt as a reckless vice.

Since 1970, however, Wall Street and the banks have tirelessly promoted the perception that the portion of our homes which we own beyond the bank mortgage is "equity", to be "put to work" with second mortgages and HELOC's (Home Equity Lines Of Credit).

Cheered on by the banks and "experts", many of us have become indebted up to our eyeballs. The banks have made money on this. Consumers have been left with big SUV's, big houses, big toys, and big debt.

As you can see, the percentage of household income consumed by debt grew and grew, to a level which would have been seen by the World War II generation as either hilarious or alarming. (Fig 1-2)

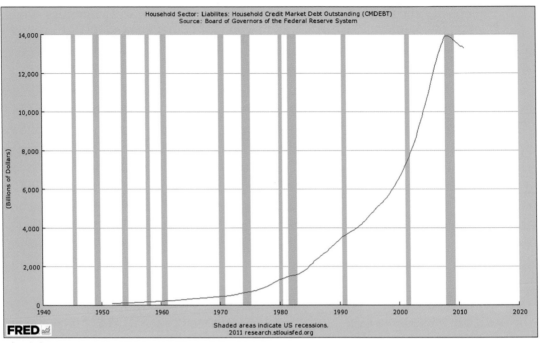

Fig. 1-2

Government spending has also ballooned. As I write this, politicians of all persuasions are milking votes by transferring our private debt to the public. It's easy to gain power if you can just promise more goodies than the next guy. So we really haven't stopped overspending. We've just changed from a private to a public credit card.

In either case, the embrace of debt was the result of our society---that would be us--embracing a fantasy.

The core of 2008's financial explosion was thus constructed as early as 1970.

There were those who spoke out. Nassim Nicholas Taleb wrote his books on the Black Swan, the effects of the unexpected. Robert Schiller wrote about Unbridled Exuberance. So we were warned, but their voices were drowned out in a sea of marketing disguised as advice. After all, who wants to hear bad news when life is good?

Then things began to unwind.

First we had the technology crash in 2000. Tech stocks had been puffed up to unreal values, and the world trumpeted the "New Economy" where growth of market share trumped earnings. That "New Economy" investment model lasted less than six years.

Then of course we had 9/11. Our sense of complacency burned up in jet fuel in one morning. When we lost our sense of physical safety, we began to wonder about the rest.

The booming real estate market broke in 2007. The first crack was the rising number of sub-prime mortgages in default. Then real estate speculators rushed for the exits, and the prices of homes began to plummet.

The mortgage breakdown happened next. There was literally no market for sub-prime mortgages which had been cut up and reshaped into Frankenstein creations.

Thus, in 2008, as the entire mortgage-backed securities market came crashing down, the stock market, the oil market, the gold market, and the real estate market imploded as well. It was a perfect storm. There was nowhere to hide, except Treasury bonds.

The result was that this downturn punished hard working responsible investors in 2008. It gored Main Street as well as Wall Street. If you saved diligently in your self-funded retirement plan, then much of your diligence was undone by market losses. If you invested in "safe" large corporations such as the auto manufacturers or the banks, your investments declined catastrophically. If you diversified and held a variety of different investments according to any of the most popular investing theories, then the theory didn't work. If you owned a home, instead of renting, then you lost much of its value as well.

The bottom line is that the rules of the last 30 years don't appear to have worked. How humbling to discover that the World War II generation was right after all!

Section 1.3: Kleptocracy

Lesson #3: Elites look after themselves, not you.

In the latter half of the 20th Century, we also experienced a profound cultural shift. Society was transformed from a largely rural and older population to a younger and more urban population.

That was accompanied by a shift away from the rural social expectation of independence, wherein government is "bottom up" and individuals are largely responsible for their own care. As people became more urban, government began to play a larger role in their lives.

By the end of the 20th Century, it was largely implicitly assumed that our government would take care of us. Of course politicians flogged this concept mercilessly. More dependence on government equals more government, more government spending, and more control.

So why hasn't the government delivered more?

In his book, "Guns, Germs, And Steel", Dr. Jared Diamond defines the concept of "Kleptocracy". The kleptocracy model posits that the elites in power within <u>any</u> society siphon off a certain portion of national economic output for their own agenda. They inevitably place their own needs first.

Experts, political leaders, and elites also, if only implicitly, ensure their own enrichment.

Researchers are just beginning to recognize the pervasive nature of this behavior. From Native American societies in 17th century Virginia to Soviet Russia in 1954, to the US in 2011, elites <u>always</u> organize society to their increasing benefit, and often make decisions which benefit themselves in the short run but hurt society in the long run.

They will do this until the people providing the benefits get fed up, remove the current government, and start the inescapable cycle again.

This is not your legendary third-world corruption. We are not talking about criminal behavior. We are addressing the natural tendency of people throughout history and world wide to enrich themselves in money and power as much as possible.

Kleptocracy is why religious organizations, charities, large corporations, and small businesses tend to create cadres of overpaid self-absorbed executives, more interested with feathering their own nests than serving customers, parishioners, or clients. It's just a natural human tendency.

You can also see this natural human tendency at work in the following graph. We are making more, earning more, but we aren't getting wealthier. Part of this is social:

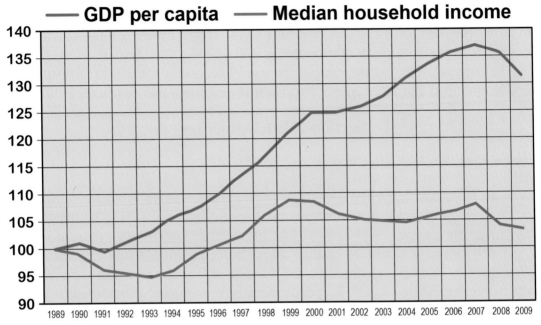

Fig. 1-3

we live in smaller family units than we did, and thus there is less economic sharing. Part of this is that we are brainwashed into spending more than we earn. And part of this, as you can see, is that the elites are gaming the system. (Fig. 1-3)

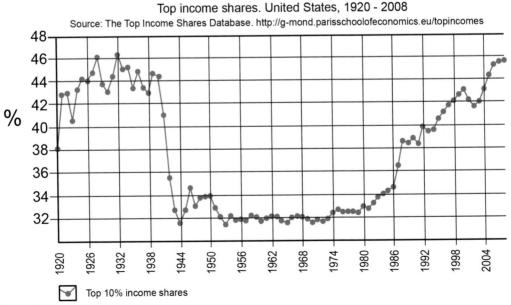

Fig. 1-4

As you can see GDP per capita is growing. But median family income is not increasing as rapidly. This is somewhat due to our own choices: smaller family size, more divorce, more drug addiction, and deferred or under-employment. Whether all these social changes generate more values than they cost is not the venue of this book. Regardless, there is another factor at work here: Kleptocracy is creating a climate wherein there is an increasing amount of wealth in the hands of a few.

In 1970 the highest-earning 10% of Americans received about 33% of the national income. In 2007 the highest-earning 10% of Americans received almost 50% of the national income. As you can see, this is in line with the old "robber baron" era of American wealth, in the 1920's. (Fig. 1-4)

Before you get too red in the face, the wealthiest Americans also pay the bulk of the taxes. For example, as you can see, the top 10% paid 71% of income taxes in 2007. The lowest 50% of earners paid only 2.9%. [Internal Revenue Service] (Fig. 1-5)

If I was a visiting Martian completely unschooled in human behavior, I might perceive that the richest Americans support the rest of us, and pay the politicians, and we sit in docility, clamor for benefits, hope to win the lottery, and accept the status quo.

Wall Street is not immune to kleptocracy at all. No organization populated by humans is immune. But Wall Street now manages the capital flows of the world. Therefore, Wall Street, although comprised of an oligarchy of large private firms, is a species of de-facto government.

Famed mutual fund manager Jean-Marie Eveillard has long said that Wall Street is a vast machine bent on ripping us off. He's right, but not due to intent. It is simply

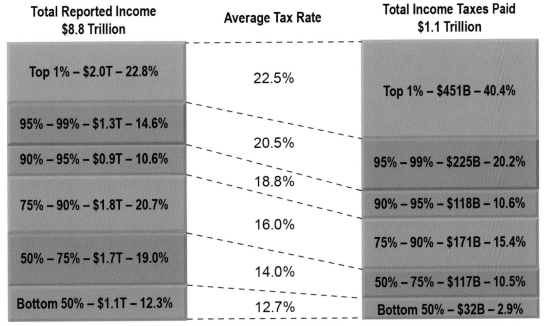

Fig. 1-5

the nature of systems that elites will gradually bend the rules to enrich themselves, all quite legally.

So why don't we do something about this? When we are experiencing good times economically, we feel somewhat satiated. Elites can advance their plans for self-enrichment without a lot of fuss. Thus societies tend to deregulate excessively during the good times. People feel good about life when the economy is booming, and they tend to feel irrationally trusting.

In contrast, scams are revealed in hard times when investors begin to ask questions. Certainly when that happens, scammers go to jail, governments are voted out, and financial advisors find themselves replaced. That's when we feel most repulsed by the financial excesses of the super-rich, and we tend to be punitive.

At that point, change feels good, just, and permanent. Probably, however, real change is illusory, and the effects of the kleptocracy cycle merely begin anew as we replace old elites with new. The new elites are eventually, inevitably, caught up by the natural drive for kleptocracy. And the cycle begins again.

Thus, hitching our financial wagon to promises made by elites will probably prove frustrating. New elites will replace the old agenda with a new agenda. Inexorably, that agenda will gradually become as inward-looking as the old.

But beyond today and tomorrow, we need to take responsibility for ourselves. The kleptocracy model tells us that delegating our personal well being to others is a textbook opportunity to be abused.

While employing financial professionals is often essential, you can't delegate ultimate responsibility to Wall Street or Washington. Bottom line: It's your money. It's your life. Take command.

Section 1.4: Expect Unforeseen Change

Lesson #4: Unforeseen change plays a major role in all our lives. But we don't live with that reality in mind.

People tend to think that the world is unchanging. It isn't. The fabric of our universe is constantly in flux.

For example, in the past three decades we have experienced AIDS, the invention of DVD's, a giant tsunami in Southeast Asia, personal computers, and 9/11. And these are only a few of the big changes.

We are able to identify themes. For example, we can probably guess with some accuracy that the pace of technology will increase, jets will continue to replace propeller-driven aircraft, and the Internet will have an increasing impact.

But obviously there is much we cannot predict.

As Nassim Nicholas Taleb points out in his books, "The Black Swan" and "Fooled By Randomness", we emotionally consider rare catastrophic events as impossible, but they are nonetheless catastrophic when they occur.

It isn't the day after a disaster that will cause us to forget caution, it's the next decade, and the decade after that. It is a natural aspect of human thought that people in San Francisco expect life to unfold as it did yesterday and not as it did on April 14th, 1906, the day of the San Francisco earthquake.

This belief, that things will continue as they are, played a major role in our 2008 financial panic. In the years preceding, our entire financial system was based on the expectation that our investment theories, based on the Capital Asset Pricing Model, would work. For the most part, we remained in a happy state of ignorance about the changes taking place in our financial system…until it broke.

Why did this happen? Because thoughtful, educated investors followed the investing guidelines of the last 50 years…and things changed in a week.

Section 1.5: The Tumultuous 21st Century

Lesson #5: 21st Century financial markets may be even more volatile than markets in the 20th Century. We need to diversify our investments much more than was thought necessary in the past, to reduce our dependence on any one investment type.

A prudent thinker can quickly realize that the future is going to be less predictable than what they teach us in grade school. Of course, a great deal of your life is within your control, or reading this book would be meaningless.

On the other hand, some circumstances that affect your future financial success are to a large degree a matter of luck. For example, if you are struck by a meteor tomorrow, it will probably reduce your future earnings power. Unless, of course, you write a best-selling inspirational book about it.

This is why investing is such a challenge. You don't know at any time what amount of knowledge and control you really have. Sometimes you have more control, and sometimes less.

The solution is to act as though you are informed, but to invest as though you are not. In other words, invest with the understanding that you may face a crisis with the investments you have now, not the investments you would choose if you knew hardship was just around the corner.

Let's simplify this even more: **The first requirement of successful investing is to admit that we don't truly know what will happen next.** This flies in the face of society's behavior, but it is nonetheless true.

As a nation, we reward politicians and "experts" who tell us what we want to hear, and punish those who do not. As a result, society is seldom prepared for challenge, even when it is possible to foresee it. If society cannot warn and prepare us for crises, then you and I as individuals need to behave differently. Part of that is being willing to speculate…dream if you will…about what will happen in the 21st Century.

One catalyst for this kind of proactive thinking is personal study. Books such as "The Next 100 Years" by George Friedman and "The Post American World" by Fareed Zakaria should provoke you to insight.

When you study the future, remember we are all guessing. You don't want to guess when you invest because the cost of guessing wrong is too high. But you CAN and

SHOULD invest with cautious discipline and a consistent plan.

What should we expect in the 21st Century?

1. Completely unforeseen events and technological change will have immense impact. There it is again: we don't really know what will happen.

2. Turbulent business cycles will continue as always, and will be enlarged by the Internet. The Wall Street oligarchs and the big banks will continue to "game" the system. We may easily face big global recessions, and big global growth periods.

3. It is very possible that we may have global affluence beyond our wildest dreams. We don't know. But we have to realize that the unknown is not all bad news. Based on past history, we can postulate that investing solely and completely for Armageddon will probably yield paltry results.

4. You are likely to be unemployed at some point, or if you are self-employed, your business may temporarily have less revenue than before. Inevitably, your path to wealth will be bumpy.

5. Very unexpected geo-political events such as war and trade conflicts will temporarily ravage the financial markets. We may face simmering 30-year long low level police actions. Or we may face something truly catastrophic, bigger even than World War II. We simply do not know. Interestingly, the financial markets have survived disasters and wars and gone on to thrive, time and time again.

6. Will this be the American Century #2? The reality is that the United States is beginning the century as the dominant global power. Leadership is ours to lose.

7. Knowledge will continue to disseminate throughout the globe. The results will be the rise of a global middle class sharing some similar values and technology, and explicitly competing for mastery. You will compete for your job against a person in Sydney, Bombay, or London as much as you will compete against the person down the street. Education will continue to morph into a lifetime experience.

8. We will probably be engulfed by an information tsunami. This has already happened. Check your email to see what I mean.

As Laurence Gonzales pointed out in his superb book, "Deep Survival", more complexity in a system creates more variables. These variables may create a sense of security, yet they may actually be adding risk as well. That seems to be happening now.

We don't know what kind of changes will happen in the next 10, 20, 30, or 50 years, but we can expect big change, and we should plan our lives and invest with that in mind.

Review: The Lessons of Chapter 1

Lesson #1: Times of economic hardship are an inevitable part of life. We will all live through market downturns, recessions, and wars. With disciplined habits of saving and spending, and with good investing techniques, we can thrive despite hard times.

Lesson #2: Even if you DID make big mistakes financially in the past three decades, you did so because our society unknowingly fostered a flawed financial model. It doesn't work. It's time for us to do something new.

Lesson #3: Because of the human characteristic of kleptocracy, you shouldn't rely on government and Wall Street to protect you. Take charge of your own financial life.

Lesson #4: Unforeseen change plays a major role in your life. You need to live and invest with the expectation that change will happen and you won't be able to accurately predict it. Therefore you need to invest in many more unrelated investment classes than anyone thought before.

Lesson #5: 21st Century financial markets will probably be even more volatile. You need to diversify your investments much more than was thought necessary in the past, to reduce your dependence on any one investment type.

Chapter 2

Budget, Avoid Debt, and Save

Anybody who has ever been in business, anybody who has ever paid bills, anybody who has ever lived in a serious adult life knows that indebtedness is a killer.
—Frank Lautenberg

Section 2.1: Your Grandparents Were Right

Lesson #6: Change your spending habits to reduce debt, and to save.

One of the interesting things about really big crises, such as civil wars, earthquakes, pandemics, and financial collapses, is that they often occur at longer intervals than the normal human lifespan. As a result, we don't feel a compelling need to prepare for them, because they aren't part of our normal life experiences. Likewise, we often drift into social behaviors which aren't sustainable in the very long run.

During the last 30 years of the 20th Century, life was sublimely easy in the United States, in long-term historical terms. As a result, our concepts of spending and indebtedness gradually morphed as marketers convinced us to consume more and save less. As you can see, the average savings rate of American citizens has plummeted in the last few decades. Only the shock of the Financial Panic of 2008 was able to stimulate Americans to save anything at all. (Fig. 2-1)

So, if saving seems hard for you, it's natural: for many Americans, saving is an unnatural act. And of course, that's why most Americans are not wealthy.

Our grandparents and parents were much better savers. That's because the Great Depression, World War II, and having the millions of children which comprise the Baby Boom made them that way. They had the spending habit beat out of them.

If you can't save, you can't become financially secure. If you can't alter your spending habits, you will find it much more difficult to recover from financial losses. It's that simple.

It is also an unavoidable reality that the sooner you begin saving, the sooner you are likely to be wealthy. Here's a graph which shows you how much you need to save to be a millionaire by age 65. As you can see, if you are 25, you need to save $381 per month to accumulate $1,000,000 under long-term conditions. Under the same conditions, a 55 year old must save $5,778 per month. For most people in the real world, that's very challenging. But it's still doable, as many people on the verge of retirement prove to us every year. (Fig. 2-2)

When I show this graph to people they often say that inflation will make $1,000,000 less valuable in twenty or thirty years. That's absolutely correct. It is also correct that whatever its spending power, $1,000,000 will certainly buy more than zero dollars.

In other words, as you can see, if you are younger, start saving now. If you are older, save as much as possible. Something is always better than nothing.

Any other plan is just an excuse.

Most Americans Are Not Saving Enough for Retirement
Personal savings rate 1947–2010

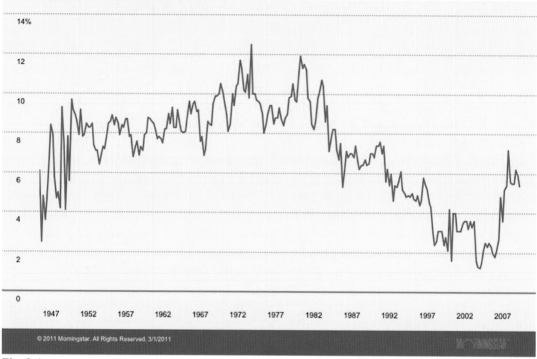

Fig. 2-1

The Earlier You Start Investing, the Easier It Is to Reach Your Goals
Monthly savings needed to accumulate $1 million by age 65

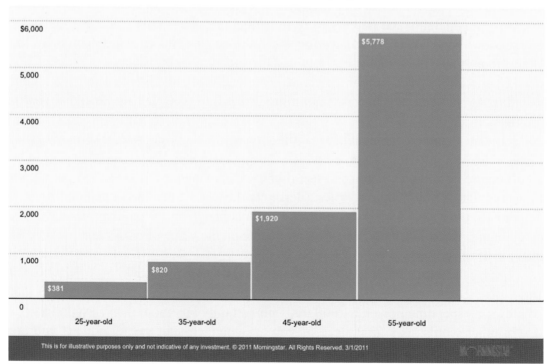

Fig. 2-2

To some degree, wealth is a measure of a person's self-discipline. When you meet a rich person, you know one thing for sure. You may not know how he or she acquired wealth, but you can be sure that so far at least this person has been able to avoid the temptation to spend the wealth. That's a lot in itself.

Believe it or not, one key to staying rich is to learn to be happy regardless of circumstances. How's that for a contradiction?

Study after study has revealed what they don't teach you in school: people have to consciously choose to be happy regardless of money. Beyond a certain amount of income and affluence, the value per dollar of additional wealth adds less and less satisfaction.

It is one of life's ironies that the more obsessed with money a person is, and the more his or her happiness is dependent upon wealth, the more he or she will be impacted by financial turmoil. The stress of this impact actually degrades his or her ability to invest successfully in a crisis. The more hungry and fearful a person is concerning money, the more she or he is likely to take irrational, reactive investment risks.

OK, ready for the punchline? The people who spend their whole life frantically chasing money seldom find it. They are too busy chasing the next big "get rich quick" deal to gather the smaller nuggets at their feet.

When people like this DO find money, they often blow it quickly. That's because they are possessed with the illusion that spending equals happiness. They are like dieters who think only of food.

Believe me, Greta Garbo was right when she said, "I've been rich, I've been poor. Rich is better." Wealth is good stuff. More money is better. But money does not EQUAL contentment, or health, or love.

Conversely, many of the holistically rich people I know cultivated their sense of well-being before they became rich, and they nurture it now to remain wealthy.

Budgeting adds to your sense of control and well-being. It has a reputation of being an unpleasant exercise in parsimony. In reality it is a precursor to financial success.

Most people regard budgeting as a dreadful chore. But it gets a bad rap when it comes to difficulty and to its value. It isn't as hard to do as it sounds, and it adds A LOT of calmness to your life.

OK, I'll admit it: to me it still sucks, even after all these years. But it's as essential as flossing your teeth if you wish to become wealthy. And if you don't floss your teeth… well, good luck with that.

Before you can change your spending and saving habits, you need to know where you want to go, and first you need to know where you are going at present. You need to know how much you are spending now. Only then can you make any decisions about your income.

Budgeting is an ongoing process. You will find that you will be most successful when you do a little of it weekly. Annual budgets tend to get negated as soon as they are made. Life does that to us all. Still, the plan may be neutralized by life, but the planning itself is absolutely necessary, because the act of budgeting causes you to think about your spending in the first place. It's worth the effort.

The absence of credit cards and home-equity loans is one major reason why the World War II generation was so good at saving. They had no internet, no debt pushers banging down their doors, and much less stuff out there to buy. They simply couldn't borrow money if they wished to do so. In that one respect, saving was easier for them than it is for you. If you feel that it was easier for them, in this one respect you are completely right.

If you find yourself ensnared in excessive debt, you may need help to get out. This book is not about debt reduction. Suffice it to say that the only way to get out of crushing debt, aside from bankruptcy or another legal solution is to treat your debt like an enemy.

No reasonable investment can make you the same rate of return as what you pay on an accumulating credit card balance. For example, if the stock market historically yields 10%, but your credit card charges a compound rate of 14% annually, you will lose money forever by saving instead of paying off your credit card. Therefore credit cards MUST be paid off monthly.

If you find yourself rolling your accumulated credit card debt into your home mortgage every few years, this is a sign that you are spending too much. Attend local classes, study, and if possible find a local non-profit consumer credit counseling agency.

The socially-dominant wisdom is that people build their credit by maintaining credit card balances. This is toxic urban mythology. In fact, the best way to build credit is to evolve a large net worth, pay bills on time, and carry a small amount of debt in the form of a mortgage. Maintaining a rolling credit card balance is ALWAYS a bad idea.

Major monthly commitments---the auto, the credit cards, and an oversized mortgage---are wealth-busters. To avoid debt you have to avoid the spending habits of the past few decades and build back a sense of frugality. That is very much easier said than done.

One great place to get more budgeting advice is at your local consumer credit counseling service. You might also simply find a basic budgeting class or program on-line, and dive in. It'll be chaos at first. But you'll make it work with time, discipline, and consistency. And see my recommended reading list at the back of this book for more recommendations for budgeting and saving advice.

Saving is quite a challenge. Staying out of debt, when so many are trying to get you into debt, is also a challenge. Yet to attain any sort of financial freedom, you have to save AT LEAST 10% and better yet 20% of your gross income. Some of this will be in your retirement plans, so you will hardly notice it. Some of it will be in personal accounts exposed to taxation. Of course this is hard, and at first you may find you can't bring yourself to meet that 10% goal. Apply time, discipline, and consistency to the challenge, keep getting back in the game, and you will find that you've made it happen. Meanwhile, saving anything is better than saving nothing. Even saving 1% is a victory. Go right at it.

Understand that we all want to spend. Delayed gratification is hard for anyone, regardless of whether you are 2, 20, or 60 years old. We don't ever outgrow our susceptibility to advertising and social pressures. Exalt your effort for frugality and saving. This is as much a perceptual lifestyle change as it is anything else.

If you do this, and invest moderately, you will inevitably grow wealthier.

Section 2.2: Pools of Money

Lesson #7: To be a genuinely successful saver, your eventual goal is to deposit money monthly to each of four accounts. You will also create a hoard of enough cash to survive seven days. If you can't do all this in the beginning, keep working at it. You will get there with time, discipline, and consistency. The four accounts are:

1. **A bank cash/checking account for daily and short-term spending.**
2. **A bank savings account with between 6 month's to one year "safe money" for emergencies, big ticket items, and special events.**
3. **One or more retirement plans, including IRA's.**
4. **One or more taxable long-term discount brokerage investment accounts.**

Here is how to save:

1. Open a payroll deduction into your bank checking account. This will be where ALL your routine cash flow comes from. Budgeting will be easier since aside from big-ticket annual purchases ALL your spending money will come from here. This account's value will rise or fall depending on recent spending activity.
2. Open a payroll deduction into your bank savings account. For most of us, this is a simple savings account, perhaps with checking access, at a local bank. You want to gather at least 6 month's expenses in very liquid low risk investments. This means that you will invest only in the bank's savings offerings, or certificates of deposit up to 3 months maturity.

   Fill this savings account by having a bit taken out of your paycheck each month, and then ignore that money as much as possible. You can gather assets for expected vacations and holidays by saving more than your six month's expenses in that same account. But here's the deal: you need six months of expenses in the bank, and you want to keep that for emergencies.

   If you find that you make your contribution into your savings account but your account value continuously drops, it's a bit like seeing an extra high water bill. You know there's a leak in the system somewhere. DO NOT allow this account to dwindle. Take immediate action to identify and correct the cause of overspending.

   Pre-2008, most investment advisors, including me, would have subscribed to the idea that you can have your six month's expenses in the form of long-term mutual fund investments. We found out the hard way that financial markets can collapse simultaneously and more rapidly than we all expected. So keep this money in the bank, regardless of how attractive the financial markets seem.
3. Enroll in your company's 401(k) or 403(b) retirement plan and have a portion of your paycheck automatically invested via payroll deduction. If you don't have access to a 401(k) or 403(b), invest in an individual retirement account (IRA).

Since your 401(k) or 403(b) money is pre-tax, and thus results in lower withholding, most people who partake in these plans scarcely even realize the money is gone. The money contributed to a company-sponsored retirement plan is deducted from your gross income, so it represents hidden treasure. That should be enough to make you smile right there.

To turn your smile into a genuine grin, consider that many companies offer a contribution match. That is, they add to the money you put in. The result can be a portfolio on steroids. Check out the graph on the following page. A company-sponsored match should bring you to invest like a koi comes to fish food.

If you don't have any access to these plans, consider an IRA. These may or may not allow a tax deduction for the money you contribute. What is most important is that while your money is in an IRA or a 401(k) or a 403(b), it grows tax-deferred. You <u>do not</u> pay capital gains taxes or income taxes on investments which make money while they are in your plan. You DO pay ordinary income taxes on any money you take OUT of the plan.

Figure 2-3 shows what tax deferred growth does to your investment returns

Some people say that they don't want to save in a retirement plan because taxes will be higher in the future anyway.

But when you are retired, in an uncertain future time, you will face two alternative scenarios:

A. You are making less money than you did when you were employed, in which case you need that retirement plan payout as income.

B. You have been a successful investor and you are making more money than you did when you were working. Thus, although your taxes on your retirement plan are high, you don't care.

Meanwhile, <u>you genuinely don't know which of these alternatives you will face,</u> and you can't afford to guess. So even if your menu of investments in your retirement plan isn't the best, the mechanics of savings which they offer you are usually unbeatable.

Sit down with your tax expert and consider the "Roth IRA", which allows you to save money AFTER TAX but allows you to take the money out TAX FREE!

If you are self-employed, ask your tax expert about a "SEP" or "SIMPLE IRA". Either will serve as the retirement plan you need to ensure your continued prosperity.

These tax-deferred retirement plans are where you will invest in your mutual funds with lots of potential tax exposure. As you will see, these represent one of the two core venues of your investment plan.

4. Your final payroll deduction should be to your other primary long-term investing venue: a discount brokerage taxable investment account. Why? As Forrest Gump famously said, "Life is like a box of chocolates. You never know what you are going to get". Sometimes you will either face unusual but risky buying opportunities or the opportunity to invest elsewhere if you can provide the capital. Sometimes you will find that your needs and desires change, and the primary source of funding for your dreams will be this non-retirement account.

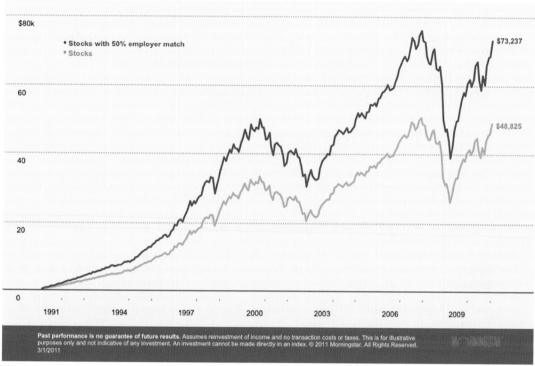

Enhancing Your Wealth: Employer Match
Hypothetical value of $100 invested each month 1991–2010

Fig. 2-3

Obviously, this money is to be invested and liquidated or spent only as a last resort.

Investing in mutual funds outside of your retirement plans allows you to invest in mutual funds which may lose money to the point you want to take a tax loss by "swapping" when you "weed the garden". This is a procedure I will explain later. What is important to know now is that you can't do that inside a retirement plan.

Also, your goal is to invest in mutual funds with less potential taxable exposure than the funds in your retirement plan so that you can take advantage of capital gains laws when they are available. Sometimes it is less expensive after taxes to liquidate funds in a taxable account and pay the capital gains taxes, rather than take a payout from a retirement plan and pay taxes on the proceeds as ordinary income.

A final reason for a long-term investment venue outside of your retirement plans is that you face a penalty for taking money out of most retirement plans prior to age 59 ½ . At present that fine is 10%. Yet many of us will want to change our lives before age 59 ½. The funding for that may come from your taxable discount brokerage account.

5. Finally, we come to our cash hoard, literally buried treasure. This money is important because bad things happen to good people, and sometimes the banks are closed when they do.

My suggestion that you assemble a cash hoard comes from my region's experience with earthquakes. I have experienced one major quake in Los Angeles, and my family and clients experienced a big jolt closer to home in 1989.

With the power out for five days, some of my clients who had millions of dollars in net worth and a large stash of gold coins for society-wide melt-down found that they could not buy food. They could not use their credit cards, because the computer networks and phone lines were down. So they were reduced to spending cash on hand, eating whatever remained of food at home, or hoping the National Guard had an additional MRE. Nobody died, or suffered malnutrition, but there were a few missed meals. With one more number on the Richter scale, it could have been much worse.

One challenge with cash is that it invites spending. In my home $20 bills literally grow wings and fly out the door. It is much too tempting to grab one when a good movie comes to town. Successful hoarders find that large denomination bills don't work well because there are no cash registers in a disaster. One individual in New Orleans carefully saved 10 $100 bills, over a period of a year. When Katrina came to visit, he found that nobody would cash his bills because nobody had cash to make change, and nobody had a non-electric cash register.

It is better to ask your local bank to provide you with bundles of $2 bills, which you will be very reluctant to spend. If you see your teenager paying the pizza man with a fistful of Jeffersons, you will know that the stash has been plundered.

You might also try dollar coins, which are heavier but more resistant to damage. I used these when I unexpectedly went into the military reserve during the first Gulf War. I became well-known at the base dining facility as the man with the Susan B. Anthony's. Still, I had cash, which was better than many other suddenly-recalled reservists.

Another challenge of cash is that it invites theft. You will need to be inventive. It is absolutely worth the effort and cost to lock up your cash in a small concealed safe. The details are up to you. It is also very important that as few people as possible know about your cash. It's only 7 days worth of money—hardly the crown jewels—but a known quantity of cash of any size is a magnet for home burglary. The less said, the better.

One final word about budgeting, spending, and saving: it is always imperfect. Dwight Eisenhower once said, "In preparing for battle I have always found that plans are useless but planning is indispensable." Budgeting is just like that, so don't allow yourself to obsess about it. Keep it flexible and understand that mistakes are normal. What matters most of all is that you are thinking about spending before you do it, and avoiding reactive or addictive consumption.

Likewise, your savings efforts will have gaps, fits, and starts. Give yourself a break. Press on, regardless. The only time in life you have genuine control is right now.

Review: The Lessons of Chapter 2

Lesson #6: Change your spending habits to reduce debt, and to save.

Lesson #7: To be a genuinely successful saver, your eventual goal is to deposit money monthly to each of four accounts. If you can't do all this in the beginning, keep working at it. You will get there with time, discipline, and consistency. The four accounts are:

1. A bank cash/checking account for daily and short-term spending.
2. A bank savings account with six month's to one year's "safe money" for emergencies, big ticket items, and special events. You will also create a hoard of enough cash to survive seven days.
3. One or more retirement plans, including IRA's.
4. One or more taxable long-term discount brokerage investment accounts.

Chapter 3

Manage Your Own Irrational Mind

How few there are who have courage enough to own their faults,
or resolution enough to mend them.
—Benjamin Franklin

In Chapter 1, I wrote about the reality that hardship is a natural and unavoidable part of life. Change is relentless. Big infrequent events shape our lives much more than we realize. Just ask the dinosaurs.

I also wrote about the reasonable expectation that the 21st Century will be even more volatile, at least from the vantage point of technological change.

In Chapter 2, I showed you that you must budget, avoid debt, and save to succeed. It's unavoidable: to succeed, you must spend less than you earn.

If this is so obvious, why doesn't everyone just do it?

Answer: few people can master their own irrational minds.

Most people are normal. Most people run their financial lives with their emotions, thinking viscerally and reactively. Because we are genetically engineered for a Pleistocene-era existence of hunting and gathering, we invest as though we were facing down a saber-tooth tiger on the African veldt. After all, that's what we evolved to do: think very, very short-term.

As I wrote in Chapter 1, change is a wildly-fluctuating constant. But in this chapter I am going to write about what does NOT change: the human mind, and how we react to change, stress, and the unpredictable future.

Section 3.1: Competence by Proxy

Lesson #8: Competence by proxy is a normal irrational behavior by which you diffuse your responsibility for making decisions. It leads you to perceive that risk is lower and your control is greater than they actually are.

Competence by proxy is a normal irrational behavior by which you and I avoid responsibility for making decisions. We all experience this kind of irrational thinking. The best investors realize it. The rest of us just enjoy the ride.

That is, we gather an irrational sensation of security and control by assigning fictional competence to others, and then create a sense of our own competence by our imagined affiliation with them.

You can see this weekly: when a market expert recommends a stock, it soars. When a famous market guru recommends selling a stock, it plummets.

Yet studies indicate that such a maven on average knows no more about the future than you do. After all, if all the experts were such competent prognosticators, how was it that they were largely blindsided by the Financial Panic of 2008?

Another example of competence by proxy is when you receive a stock market tip from someone you respect, or at least perceive as wealthy. Many people in this situation will buy the stock. Yet such recommendations fail routinely.

Diffusion of responsibility is the classic, school-book psychological behavior which motivates competence by proxy.

Responsibility causes stress. The more critical or vital the decision, the more stressful it is.

A classic <u>financial</u> example of diffusion of responsibility occurred in 2008 when the Bernie Madoff Ponzi rip-off was revealed to a stunned investment community in New York City.

A Ponzi scheme is when the fraudster pays back early investors with the money from later investors, creates a fake high return by providing large cash flows to investors, and draws in new money.

A financial crisis will inevitably reveal Ponzi schemes when investors begin to ask for their money back. Bernie Madoff was able to keep it going for decades, and…here's the important part…he was able to attract celebrity money and evade detection for a long time.

He did this by appealing to people's irrational attraction to celebrities as a form of competence by proxy. In other words, as one ripped-off investor said later, it just felt safer when famous people were involved. People assumed that wealthy celebrities could and would pay for exceptionally competent investment advice. So not only was there a visceral sense of competence assigned to the celebrities, there was also an implied level of competence assigned to the professionals servicing the rich and the famous. Literally billions of dollars were caught up. While some individuals gave warning, even the government financial regulator, the Securities & Exchange Commission, was too swept away in the elitism of it all to take the warnings seriously.

Mentally enlisting celebrities or "experts" via competence by proxy **creates** diffusion of responsibility because the investor perceives that he or she is no longer totally responsible for the particular investment decision. If the chosen investment goes up, the investor is free to take total psychological credit. If the investment goes down, the investor can blame the "expert". Thus investors feel more confident, hence "competence by proxy".

Employing competence by proxy like this is a short-term win/win psychologically. But it is too often a lose/lose financially. Study after study has revealed that trying to pick individual stocks as an amateur investor is a loser's game.

Pandering to your desire to pick individual stocks keeps the media rich. It keeps the brokerages rich. But it doesn't work for you, at least not in the long-term.

The only way that you, or any of us, can avoid "competence by proxy" behavior is to remain aware that you will have a natural tendency to seek the confirmation of others. Keep in mind that a powerful consensus opinion about the direction of financial markets is almost always eventually WRONG!

When markets are soaring, you WILL feel the urge to buy, buy, buy, and you must intentionally dispute that urge. You WILL feel the need to flee, to sell out, and to simply sink to the floor in despair when markets drop suddenly. Only by overtly rejecting such impulses and discarding the accompanying panic, can you separate yourself from the herd.

You have to CHOOSE to IGNORE your own emotions as much as possible.

Section 3.2: Ego Extrapolation

Lesson #9: Ego extrapolation is another normal irrational behavior by which you reduce internal stress while investing. When you extrapolate your ego, you extend your competence from one aspect of your life to all others, including investing.

If you are a world-class brain surgeon or a professional baseball player or a famous actor, you may tend to believe that you are also a savvy investor. The greater your self-perception of professional competence, the more at risk you are for ego extrapolation.

In reality, the investing disasters of doctors, famous performers, and sports stars are the stuff of legends.

It is natural, normal, and even healthy, to have a robust sense of self confidence. Extrapolation emerges when you extend your ego into capacities which NOBODY possesses.

For example, as we saw in Chapter 1, NOBODY knows what will happen in the future. But if you have a solid sense of well-being about any aspect of your life, and feel that you possess genuine expertise in that area, then you may extend that feeling of control into predicting the path of markets, and gambling with your money as a result.

This happens frequently to many people. It usually doesn't create a successful outcome.

Investment brokerages make most of their money from active traders.

In reality, the majority of active traders do not outperform a portfolio of mutual funds of equivalent risk. Many active traders work very hard to break even.

If an active trader sits down and reflects, he or she is likely to choose a less turbulent form of investing. To avoid such an onset of rationality, brokerage advertisements feature actors who appear to be competent, successful, beautiful people, and imply that such accomplished professionals are also competent at investment management. They are aiming straight at your vulnerability for ego extrapolation.

Likewise, financial magazines become successful by appealing to your ego. Most of what you read in financial magazines does not really increase your ability to invest successfully. Instead these articles artificially increase your sense of control.

When you unconsciously weave ego-gratification into your investment plan, you may rapidly find yourself investing for entertainment rather than simply to make money. This is another normal behavior, but it carries with it the increasing risk that you will trade simply to create good feelings. As you can see, this has the potential to morph into something akin to a spending or gambling addiction.

Of course it is possible to be a world-class brain surgeon <u>and</u> a competent investor. But to do so requires that you squelch any illusions of automatic expertise. You became a world-class brain surgeon or a world-class auto mechanic through years of training and experience. Why should any other complex skill be any different?

Simply keep in mind that you might not be as competent and rational as you think you are. A strategy which restrains your choice set and limits your ability to trade may prove very effective. It won't be as much fun, perhaps, but it will probably be more successful.

Section 3.3: Black and White Thinking

Lesson #10: Black and white thinking is a dichotomous behavior which you and I instinctively adopt under stress. This occurs when you and I see the world from an "all good" or "all bad" perspective, from one extreme to the other, with no middle ground.

We all engage in black and white thinking, especially in infancy. When we are very young, we must see the world simply. Thinking with a mental structure which employs such rigid categories is an effective management tool for children. Thus, if a toddler is burned by a stove, he or she will usually assume that all stoves are hot.

As we mature, the world becomes more nuanced. We hopefully learn to see the spectrums of judgment and behavior which are available, and black and white thinking becomes submerged.

But as psychologists will tell you, all of us retain the ability to think in black and white terms. You will easily do so if you are adequately stressed.

This explains why so many investors seem to become brainwashed during market increases or declines. What surprises most people is that black and white thinking should appear in market upturns as well as downturns. Both increasing and declining markets are psychologically two sides of the same coin, and both evoke a similar emotional trajectory.

When the market is rising precipitously, and your portfolio is growing relentlessly, it may be surprisingly stressful. Your self-image demands that you avoid losses which will result from a market correction. You also face the prospect of embarrassment and shame if you cash out prematurely.

Meanwhile, the prospect of losing recent investment gains is an ever-present potential event when you view the market rationally.

Thus, as the stock market continues to climb, the stress mounts, and you retreat from a balanced view to a black-and-white perspective. If you are normal, your emotional recourse is to retreat from situational awareness. You follow the herd and simply ordain that the market will keep rising.

When you embrace black and white thinking in such a situation, you experience an artificial sense of euphoria and control as your stress is reduced. For a time, the stock market keeps going up, which affirms your behavior.

This is why a rising "bull" market is largely characterized by rampant irrational greed. It is a form of mass hysteria, and it reaches out to us all.

"Black and white thinking" thus produces a "hot-hand fallacy": that a given investment will keep going up merely because it is going up. Statistically, we can see this as money pours into a mutual fund which is in an exciting rising sector. Here's an example in Figure 3-1.

This chart deserves a second look. What it is saying is worth the price of this book. What it is saying is that the most favored investment choice is often the least successful. Wow! So these psychological behaviors I'm writing about can actually be seen in the financial markets. Simply learning this is vastly empowering, isn't it?

At the high point of a market cycle, a normal investor is drenched in the white-washed enthusiasm of a "true-believer". As you can see in this graph, most investors actually increase buying as the market becomes more overvalued. This is clearly illogical, but it is also normal. Most people invest almost totally because the chosen investment has already gone up.

When the surging market falters, and then breaks, the most committed investors behave very similarly to people experiencing a death of a loved one. In this case it is the death of an illusion. You may first deny that the downturn is happening. You may even avoid opening your monthly statements, as if denying the loss will make it less real.

Then, if you are normal, you try bargaining with it: "If I try <u>this</u> it might work, if I try <u>that</u> it might work." You cling to bullish statements by experts, and read avidly about techniques to step sideways.

As the decline continues, the emotional pain becomes unbearable. Once again, the majority of investors deal with that pain by retreating to black and white thinking. You

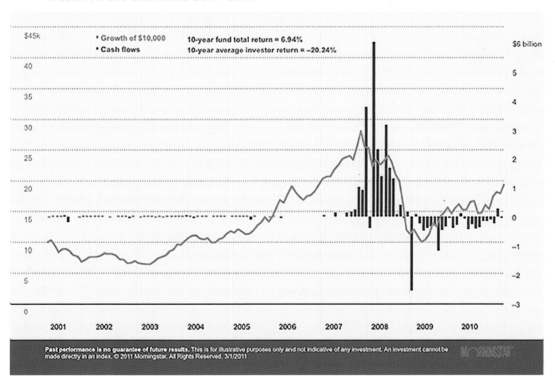

Hot-Hand Fallacy: Chasing Fund Performance
Wealth versus cash flows 2001–2010

Fig. 3-1

may decide that the market will <u>always</u> go down. Even though history is emphatic that downturns eventually recover, you may seize upon doomsday scenarios and apocalyptic visions of financial meltdown to provide competence by proxy.

Ironically, at this point, investors caught in consensus thinking will usually create an event called "market capitulation", wherein the group runs shrieking from the investment, willing to sell at any price. A drenching monochromatic wave of fear washes over the marketplace. On the preceding graph, "Hot-Hand Fallacy: Chasing Fund Performance" you can see this event in December, 2008.

As you can see on the graph, at the very point that most investors believe that the only recourse is to sell, the market is usually offering its best bargains.

The financial media knows all this. But the financial media is not in business to help you. The financial media is in business to capture an audience for their advertising. They need you to watch their channel, or read their magazine, or visit their blog.

In especially stressful times, when the herd is stampeding in one direction or the other, which will attract more viewers: a show which agrees with the herd or one which disagrees?

More people will watch a financial TV show, or read an investment article, which agrees with a point of view they already possess, because doing so will decrease their cognitive dissonance. "Cognitive dissonance" means coping with facts which are apparently at odds with each other.

As I have written, the consensus is often wrong. But in times of crisis, the media will usually feed the consensus. They will frequently kindle the fires of black and white thinking and create more extremist behavior, not less.

To make matters more challenging, humans tend to make decisions based on what they <u>last</u> sensed or experienced. Studies show that people perceive exaggerated crime rates after they watch a violent TV show. Sales of a particular consumer good will increase after it is prominently placed in a movie. Advertisements for food or restaurants make us hungry. Likewise, most people tend to invest based not on careful study of long-term investments, but based upon the investment report they saw last.

You can deal with the challenge of this herd mentality by expecting market cycles, and including them in your financial plan. You can also manage your own black and white thinking through self-aware introspection of the reasons for the financial decisions you make. And, finally, your investment plan should <u>force</u> you to buy when others are selling, and to sell when others are buying. That's what you will learn later in this book.

Section 3.4: Over-Commitment

Lesson #11: Over-commitment is when an investor becomes emotionally bonded with an investment or a course of action.

The classic example of over-commitment is a situation which investment managers encounter at least once a year: the retired client who will not diversify.

For example, let's take a hypothetical business executive who has just retired. He has $1,000,000 in stock shares from the company he once managed. He is planning to live on the income.

But this stock is more than an investment to this particular client. The client implicitly views this stock as his own history, his decades of labor and achievement, and proof of a well-lived professional career. Usually the client is intensely loyal to the company as well.

Almost always an investment manager will tell him the following:

1. $1,000,000 in one single stock is too much.
2. You need to diversify.
3. Let's sell off some of this stock gradually to manage the taxes and the re investment correctly.

In reality, you owe much more allegiance to yourself and to your family than you do to the source of your wealth. When you are already affluent, the most important goal is to STAY rich.

But quite often our hypothetical client has an emotional relationship with the investment, and is over-committed. He won't do the rational thing if it means sacrificing his relationship. Ironically, this loyalty is one of his most positive features: he is loyal to his wife, loyal to his family, and loyal to his employer. In this situation, though, his visceral sense of commitment may easily result in great financial loss.

In the 1980's I saw retired executives of utilities make this choice, and lose their nest eggs when utilities in general declined radically in the face of fears about nuclear reactor lawsuit liability.

In the 1990's, many people in nearby Silicon Valley harvested vast windfalls when the stock options of their technology companies made them millionaires, then faced financial annihilation in the 2000 tech stock crash.

In the recent financial panic, people who owned bank stocks got hammered. Often these bank stocks were inheritances from ancestors who had waxed poetic about their solidity and permanence. So the heirs didn't diversify, often for decades. They paid for that in 2008.

The crash in 2008 also hammered investors in emerging market stocks. From 2003 to 2007, investors reaped monster gains as markets all over the world rode a tide of boom-generated cash. Most of these investors allowed their holdings to swell unchecked. As you can see in this graph, they got the knife in 2008. (Fig. 3-2)

In contrast, I have a client who received a windfall of stock options for his company, which makes paper bags. He required himself to sell 20% a year, at a pre-determined date, regardless of market performance, until his stock option holding became 10% of his portfolio. When the recent turmoil washed over us all, his portfolio went down substantially, as did everyone's. But it did not drop 85%, as his company stock did. He was able to manage his over-commitment.

Section 3.5: Perfectionism

Lesson #12: Perfectionism is the belief that you can manage your portfolios without ever experiencing downturns or making flawed choices.

One reality of being human is that you artificially order your universe. You mentally

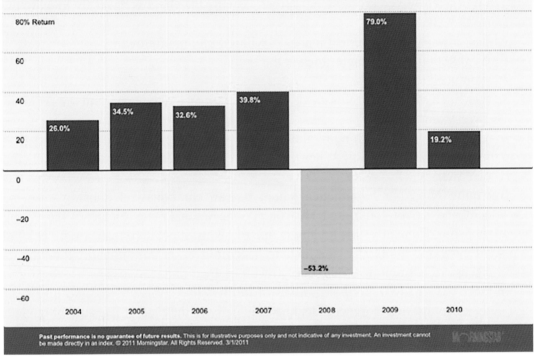

Overconfidence: False Perception
Historical performance of emerging-market stocks 2004–2010

Fig. 3-2

put things in boxes and organize things into groups. The real world is not so neat.

To hit a home run, you have to go up at bat. If you go up at bat, you might strike out. But unless you swing, you can't hit the ball.

If you become preoccupied with the losses you might make when you invest, then you might not swing at all.

Investing is by nature an exercise in uncertainty. You need to accept that to invest successfully.

The more stressed you are, the more irrational you will inevitably become.

You've seen this if you've ever watched a perfectionist friend buy a car. This person's perfectionism carries with it many genuine blessings. Her home is in order. His socks match. And your friend sets out to make his automobile purchase by gathering data from all the right places, and analyzing, and studying. Much discussion and agonizing follows. Will this car provide the carefree travel illustrated in the ads, or break and become an embarrassment? Can I afford it? Is it safe enough for my family?

And as the stress builds, he or she eventually buys a car by ignoring many of the more important criteria and selecting a vehicle simply because it is blue.

Our hypothetical friend does this because all the overwhelming variables create overwhelming stress.

In response to the stress, he or she develops tunnel vision, and makes the decision based on a spontaneously limited set of criteria. That's how many people select investments: from a position of being overwhelmed by what they do not and cannot know.

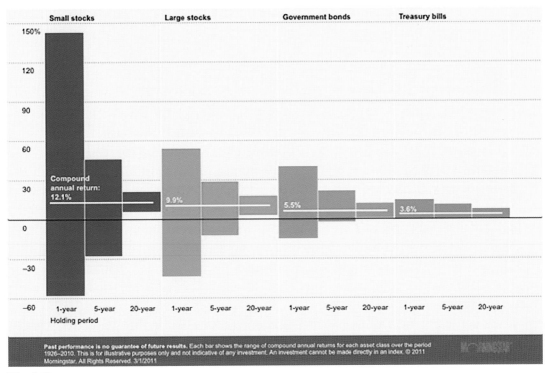

Reduction of Risk Over Time
1926–2010

Fig. 3-3

Perfectionism also plays a role in your decisions about when to sell investments. Fear of loss can be so crippling that you might delay weeding out an investment which isn't working. The reality is that the world is unpredictable, and thus occasional bad investments are inevitable, even in an investment portfolio which is successful overall.

This graph shows you what history tells us you might expect from the stock market for annual time periods, five year time periods, and twenty year time periods. (Fig. 3-3)

Please take the time to study this.

As you can see, from 1926 to 2008, annual returns for small stocks varied from about +150% to -50%. In other words, there were years that your investment might have <u>lost </u>half its value. However, the average returns to small stocks were 12.1%, so most years were resoundingly positive, with positive years taking place 72% of the time. In fact, over time, the worst 20 year performance for small stocks comes close to beating the best 20 year performance by government bonds.

So if you were in a position of losing 50% in a diversified holding of small stocks during your first year of investment, history tells you that one reasonable response is to simply hold on, wait it out, and your investment should recover.

But since we are all perfectionists to some degree, most of us feel an immense sense of loss, even shame, when one of our investments loses money. We tend to imagine that somewhere out there, somebody smarter than us didn't lose money on that investment.

Wrong. The best investors lose money too. The difference between them and everybody else is how they deal with it.

Your investment discipline should include awareness that continuing the program is a viable choice.

Or, you can allow yourself to become reactive and buy and sell based on the most short term information. As I wrote earlier, this probably worked well for our distant ancestors hunting giraffes. However, as you've seen, it doesn't work so well in the 21st Century.

And one of the most egregious forms of the irrational fantasy of control is "market timing".

At some point the most ego-extrapolated perfectionists try to "market time". That is, we extend our fallacious perception of competence out into the universe and buy and sell investments based on what we think will happen in the short run.

Timing works great, until it doesn't. Some people have managed to pull off a superb maneuver here and there, until they guess wrong and get left in the dust. Eventually timing humbles everyone, and reveals itself as a very flawed, egocentric tactic at best.

As you can see in the following graph, timing can wreak havoc on our portfolios, especially when we are trying to recover from a market crash. It is one of the main reasons why most investors tend to "buy high" and "sell low", even when the underlying financial markets show a profit. (Fig 3-4)

There are many individual investment histories revealed in this graph. As you can see, getting timing wrong can mangle your investment returns. But most people don't talk about this. Not at all.

When you meet your friends who invest, they will often talk about their winning investments. They don't talk about their losers. In fact, many people find investment losses so painful that they literally have selective memory regarding their investing choices.

The reality is that they, you, and the rest of the world will inevitably lose money occasionally when you put down your cash, at least in the short run. You can't control that. What you CAN control is what you do when you are facing a short term investment loss.

The world often takes us to unexpected places. That's life. When the mainstream financial market goes against you, your investment in that market is not the "mistake", unless you think that you ought to be precognitive. However, you might make a mistake when you respond to the inevitable volatility of that market.

The difference between you and your friends is that you know this, and you will have organized your investment style to accommodate the emotional turmoil that results from living in an uncertain world.

Looking at this holistically, the best mental discipline seems to be suggested by Olympic champion Lanny Bassham: Set your ego aside, learn from your mistakes, and then focus on what you do right.

Some very successful mutual fund managers have an error rate as high as 45% of their picks! But what they do right is to focus their time, money, and emotional energy on the long-term selections which work. That's a winning habit. We'll discuss what to do right as we go through this book. Meanwhile, the greatest investment trap of all is between your ears.

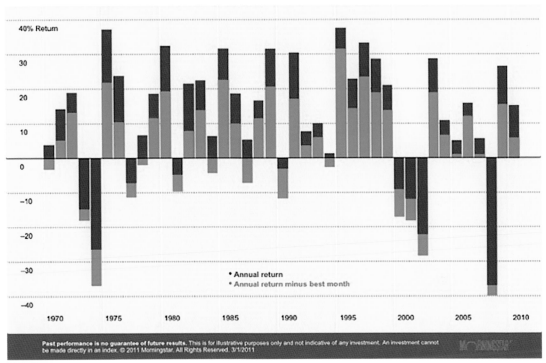

Market-Timing Risk
The effects of missing the best month of annual returns 1970–2010

Fig. 3-4

Review: The Lessons of Chapter 3

Lesson #8: Competence by proxy is a normal irrational behavior by which you diffuse your responsibility for making decisions. It leads you to perceive that risk is <u>lower</u> and your control is <u>greater</u> than they actually are.

Lesson #9: Ego extrapolation is another normal irrational behavior by which you reduce internal stress while investing. When you extrapolate your ego, you extend your competence from <u>one</u> aspect of your life to <u>all others,</u> including investing.

Lesson #10: Black and white thinking is a dichotomous behavior which you instinctively adopt under stress. This occurs when you see the world from an "all good" or "all bad" perspective, from one extreme to the other, with no middle ground.

Lesson #11: Over-commitment is when an investor becomes emotionally bonded with an investment or a course of action.

Lesson #12: Perfectionism is the belief that you can manage your portfolios without ever experiencing downturns or making flawed choices. In reality, facing financial market downturns is an inevitable part of the successful investment process.

Chapter 4

Be Cautious With Your Investments

I will not trade even a night's sleep for the chance of extra profits.
—Warren Buffet, letter to Berkshire Hathaway shareholders, 2008

Section 4.1: Use a Discount Brokerage

Lesson #13: Although there are alternatives, a nationally-established SIPC-insured discount brokerage provides the best place for your long-term investment transactions.

The whole focus of this book so far has been to establish a world view for investing. As you have read, reality is somewhat different from the way most high-cost investment salespeople portray the world. This difference is CRITICAL to your success.

The routine format for investing used by most people doesn't work, does it?

So we're looking at what does work. We're examining what have been proven by time to be the world view and investing strategy of successful investors.

Whether they use a fee-only investment advisor to help them or not, most successful investors use a discount brokerage to house their investments.

And, if they choose to employ an independent investment advisor, anyone they employ works with them in a discount brokerage framework, reaching over the clients' shoulder to make changes in the account.

Successful investors ALWAYS keep their own money under their own name.

A discount brokerage is essentially a low-cost trading venue. Think of it as an old-fashioned store with a counter. You are standing at the counter, next to the bags of flour and beans. Visualize a clerk on the other side of the counter, and she's selling you what you want with a minimal markup.

A full-service brokerage, on the other hand, is the same store with the same products, at double the markup. In return for double the markup you get extra decorations and music.

But it's the same flour and beans.

In the real world, full service brokerages are usually traditional Wall Street firms which charge expensive commissions.

Discount brokerages were created a few decades ago when Wall Street was deregulated by the Federal Government. Before then, the Wall Street houses had a monopoly: you paid a high-margin fixed rate for any transaction. Given the inevitability of kleptocracy, this led to lots of abuses. Discount brokerages sprang up in reaction to the routine mainstream client abuses which we witness on Wall Street all the time, most noticeably in 2008.

Discount brokerages are not holding companies or escrow accounts. If you have your investments at a discount brokerage, as I will discuss further later, you can ALWAYS find out where your money is, and most importantly, you can ALWAYS take it out.

If you prefer to hire an investment advisor, a good advisor is never a portal through which you must pass to get your own money.

Add the insurance of the SIPC: Securities Investor's Protection Corporation—and you are looking at the best venue for your portfolio.

The name "portfolio" comes from long ago. From about 1700 until about 1960, stocks and bonds could be had in "bearer" certificates. The piece of parchment or paper which gave legal title to the stock or bond was exchangeable, and was owned by the "bearer", whoever physically had possession of it.

This meant that a stock certificate or a bond certificate (which came complete with little payment coupons) was as good as cash…and just as vulnerable. Investors stored their stock and bond certificates in a light folding briefcase, or "portfolio", which was usually locked up in a bank vault. Now it's all done on computer, and your investments are routinely held in an online brokerage account.

Nevertheless, we still talk about our investments in terms of what is in our hypothetical "portfolio".

So why don't we use these certificates anymore? Given the kleptocracy model, you can guess. Certificates for stocks and bonds were subject to theft, fire, and any other physical catastrophe.

But what finally did them in was that they were a great way to avoid inheritance tax. The kleptocrats in governments didn't like this. The full-service brokerages of past years went along with the change because storing all your investments in an electronic account made them the gatekeeper to your money. Having them as gate keepers was not a good thing.

With the arrival of the internet, the balance has swung profoundly in favor of investors: now you can access your money anytime, anywhere. So in general, our new system is a vast improvement.

All of your investing will thus be done via computer, and you will hold your investments virtually, that is, there won't be any certificates.

You will want to save on paper or via computer backup your monthly statements and your sales confirmations to document the existence of your investments in case of computer network collapse.

However, the statements themselves are not the investments, so you don't have to secure them beyond preventing identity theft. You do NOT need to save all the prospectuses, information mailings, and proxy forms since these don't serve any documentary role whatsoever. Once you've read them, recycle them to keep your records organized. If there is an account number or other private information on the paper, shred it first.

You will also want to save the mailing you receive in spring regarding the prior tax year. These are called "1099's" and whoever does your income taxes will need these to provide you with an accurate tax return.

In other words, your annual investment file of documents from the discount brokerage should consist of monthly statements, sales confirmations, and 1099's. That's it.

Since system collapse, e-crime, and identity theft ARE issues, however, you want your holdings held in a brokerage which has SIPC insurance. SIPC insurance does not ensure against market loss, but does ensure against investment theft. In other words, if you buy an extra-aggressive mutual fund and the market plunges, you can't get your money back. But if someone at the brokerage takes your money and goes to Brazil, you can.

Compared to full-service brokerages, discount brokerages offer lower fees and access via the Internet. You will also avoid costly sales commissions and biased information.

If you decide you wish to employ a fee-only investment advisor to help you, most discount brokerages offer a limited power of attorney to give him or her trading access and ongoing observation.

As I write this, the most established discount brokerages in the United States are Charles Schwab, TD Waterhouse, Fidelity, and Vanguard. Perhaps the quality of these will change by the time you read this, so do your homework, and look for new venues as well.

We've established that aside from real estate, and especially your home, you should invest only in liquid investments which you are able to sell within a week. Aside from your short-term cash, your discount brokerage will hold all your long-term investments.

You might want your savings account, your reserve of six months or more of expenses, in a local bank to maintain physical access. But don't invest your long-term money at the bank as well. I have seen too many conflicts of interest and too many hidden fees embedded in all the bank-offered investments I have experienced in my career.

While most people should have more than one account, you also want to beware needless duplication. You don't need the option of a separate bank account connected to your long-term investment account: most non-retirement investment accounts have a check-writing option already. You don't need 42 different IRA's. You might hold both a Roth and a traditional contributory IRA, but that's about it.

You should always be able to view your discount brokerage account via computer, and you should be able to trade on-line or via phone, even if you don't wish to do so at present. The ability to view your accounts independently via computer is one more confirmation of openness and liquidity. You want computer access, even if you don't currently use it.

All representatives at your chosen brokerage should be paid salaries, not commissions for selling you things. Salary-only compensation keeps the representative working for you, instead of being preoccupied about what he'll make if he sells you something you don't need. This is important. Ask before you sign up. A commission salesperson is a person with a hidden agenda: his or her own paycheck. Avoid these people emphatically.

Section 4.2: Scams

Lesson #14: Using an established discount brokerage as your investment venue and buying only mutual funds help prevent you from being ripped off.

Earlier I discussed the Bernie Madoff scandal. It was big, it was ugly, and it nailed a bunch of people who should have known better. But mostly the victims of scams, or investments which resemble scams, are people just getting started or dealing with a transition. Simply employing an established discount brokerage as your only venue of investment does a lot to reduce the risk of abuse.

It is a reality of history that financial excess invites financial abuse. Good times attract scammers like blood attracts sharks.

During a financial bubble, when financial markets seem to do nothing but go up, scams and dishonesty proliferate as people are distracted by the potential of immense profit. But during good times, the political pressure is to deregulate. We all feel great about life, and we're all preoccupied with becoming rich or enjoying life. So our suspicions are dormant, and more people are motivated and able to carry out shady business.

When the bubble bursts, and financial markets collapse, this malfeasance is revealed, a beached and reeking carcass left by the receding financial tide.

This was the case with the bank collapses of the 1930's, the junk bond debacle of the 1980's, and the mutual fund preferential trading disgrace of the early 2000's. All these were created by investment bubbles. They were revealed when the bubbles collapsed.

When a bubble has burst and people are hurting, they get angry and want to blame someone. Lax regulation and dishonest dealers are easy targets and quickly pilloried. After all, the last person we ever want to blame is ourselves.

Thus, regulation of the financial markets increases when times are hard, when it ought to be reduced, and is relaxed when times are good….when regulation should be increasing.

When I talk to people who have been ripped off, they are usually indignant and surprised. They feel that they were pillaged without any warning. Yet in reality that's not usually the case. Scams are like rattlesnakes: they make lots of noise before they bite. The only question is whether or not we are trained to hear them. Here are some basic rules for avoiding the scams du jour and the snakes that sell them.

If it sounds too good to be true...it might be!

Every year, thousands of gullible investors find themselves caught by their own greed. Anytime you hear someone discuss an investment with an expected return of more than 10% annually, you should see a big yellow light in your brain's traffic control system. Rarely a 20% annual rate of return is real…but almost always it is not. And when any proposed annual rate of return is higher than 10%, you should keep in mind that you are playing with lots of risk. Before you invest with mega-gains in mind, you should be able to identify that risk and have a plan to manage it. Most scams I have encountered use outsized expected returns to lure you in.

In fact, most truly professional investment managers are reluctant to predict a return at all. And NEVER does a true professional PROMISE a return. Promises of a certain investment return are almost always an indication of a potential rip-off. The world simply doesn't work like that.

Fraudulent or slightly odiferous salespeople also caress you with the word "guaranteed", which of course means that if they are still solvent and you can still find them 5 years from now, they will be happy to meet their legal obligations after a lawsuit. Note the word "if".

If you are investing only in mutual funds, big returns might signal big market risk, but they aren't overtly fake. The structure of mutual funds makes faking returns almost impossible.

Bernie Madoff could not have ripped people off if he was managing a mutual fund: the oversight is too great.

Keep your investment choices *simple.*

In the past few years we've watched as Wall Street geniuses pitched a new class of mortgage-based investments to the world. Nobody could understand them, but we were assured that this was because we were less intelligent and less educated than the best and the brightest in the room. Whoops! It turned out the geniuses hadn't fully gamed out their own inventions either.

Moral: if you can't understand it, there's a decent chance they can't understand it either.

Most complex investments aren't traded publicly, and aren't part of any mutual fund. That's because they aren't real, and they can't stand the scrutiny of public markets. So, stay away from the limited partnerships, and stick to mutual funds.

Keep your investment choices *liquid.*

Almost all scams share the characteristic that once invested, your money is hard to retrieve and your investment is hard to price effectively. Scammers flock to investment types which are hard to sell, and then use that characteristic to hide their absconding with your cash. Rare coins, gold coins, oil wells, real estate, fine art, collectible firearms, antiques… the list goes on. All of these are legitimate investments, but all are hard to sell, with relatively few forums for pricing. Thus they are all high-risk environments for fraud.

In contrast, you find relatively few rip-offs involving plain old Treasury bonds and mutual funds. This is because these investments have lots of publicly available pricing information, and you can sell them in five minutes with low or non-existent fees.

Maintain a *separate portal* to your money.

Scammers make themselves the gatekeepers of your wealth. In other words, you can only get to your money by asking them for it. Scammers will also often ask you to commingle or mix your money with funds provided by other people. From the scammer's point of view, convincing you to do this obscures the financial trail and makes tracking your money that much more difficult.

To avoid this, seek an investment in your own separate account, at a third party domicile such as a discount brokerage firm. In this way you can independently access your money without anyone else's knowledge or permission.

Absolutely avoid going into <u>debt</u> as part of your investment plan.

Creating a situation where you owe money in any investment should be approached with profound suspicion. <u>Especially do not loan money to people without a written agreement, your own lawyer, and a third-party recipient such as a bank or a title company</u>.

Do I need to tell you that you should never give a financial advisor the ability to create debts in your name? Nope, didn't think so. For one thing, scammers with an authority to borrow from the investment can then borrow your own money and pay it back to you as a false dividend.

In my experience, most of the investments which involve debt are based around real estate. And most of these involve some attempt to gain tax advantages. Some even include the proposal that you borrow from your own home equity, to create the maximum tax advantages. Regard such a proposal as a suggestion that you hand over your watch and wallet as well.

In my 25 years in the investment management profession I have NEVER seen a good investment offered by any professional which required the investors to assume debt. If anyone suggests that you should include debt to either avoid taxation or increase returns, he or she is waving a giant red flag. Be warned.

Know your investment's <u>performance</u>.

If you have your own account, and you have your own access to information about the performance of that account, then you have the ability to see how the account is doing. This can be as simple as knowing if your account went up or down in value last month. Your financial advisor should be willing to provide a performance number, and then demonstrate how he or she got it.

At my company, we put our performance numbers on the front page of our quarterly reports. Obviously, they are that important. Individual mutual fund performances are all over the internet.

Bogus investments can't give you a performance number that can be validated with statistics you gather yourself.

But beware whoring after a short-term return. Most successful investors and investment managers experience entire years when they lag various indices simply because they have learned to avoid the risk of those indices. Sometimes a lower return is the mark of prudence. Before you accept it, however, you should understand why your return is what it is.

Understand the <u>expenses</u> of your investment.

It is vitally important that your financial advisor is completely honest. Especially be conscious of any self-dealing, hidden commissions, or hidden fees which accrue to any advisor. In general, I would avoid providing a limited power of attorney for trading to any advisor who is compensated by commissions. Such a document is a license to churn the account for commission-producing trades. The salesperson will get rich. You won't.

Discount brokerages and mutual funds discourage hidden fees by requiring disclosure. Also by definition, employees at discount brokerages aren't paid commissions, so they aren't so motivated to simply sell you something to garner hidden fees.

Scammers frequently use the "Gotta buy it today or it will be gone forever" sales ploy to make you put your money down.

Have you ever been to a time-share seminar? Actually the world is replete with bargains. If you miss one today, another will come along shortly.

Time, discipline, and consistency should make you rich if you are able to be patient and pay attention to the details. When a salesperson pressures you to invest NOW, don't. It's a red light. When you use a discount brokerage, you won't get sales calls from someone who offers you that bogus "once in a lifetime" opportunity.

Many scams involve "royalties" or "participation", but you don't own the actual investment.

Some examples of this include oil and gas deals where you get a cut of the action but you don't own the oil well, and movie deals where you get a cut of the gate but no ownership of the celluloid. You need to own something more than a contract. Buy the steak, not the sizzle. You get the steak by owning the common stock of the company behind any deal, and the best way to own the common stock is to....you guessed it... own a mutual fund.

Section 4.3: The Information from your Monthly Statement

Lesson #15: Understand the basic information in your monthly statement.

One of the most fascinating aspects of my investing career is the number of times I have received a phone call from a person enraged because his or her money is missing, only to discover that this investor was unable to read a monthly brokerage statement. Yet this individual will also read the *Wall Street Journal* or business magazines cover to cover, and obsess about financial markets which he or she cannot predict or control.

Learning to read the basic information of your account is worth a thirty minute lesson from your discount brokerage, on the phone or in person. Learn how to read what you get in the mail or see on the internet. You should get your lesson from your discount brokerage after you receive your first monthly statement.

The monthly statement contains key information, which <u>you need to know monthly</u>.

1. What is your portfolio worth now? Let's get basic: this is the number of dollars in your account at the end of the month. It doesn't matter as much what your individual mutual funds are doing. Since your portfolio is diversified, it is normal for some mutual funds to be moving up, some moving down, and some simply remaining the same. What counts most of all is your overall performance.

This starts with your basic value at the end of the most recent month.

2. What were the investment changes which you or your fee-only investment advisor made last month? Review the transactions section of your statement carefully and make sure that every transaction makes sense to you.

3. Were there any transfers of money which you do not remember? I have seen money moved without the client's awareness about five times in my 25 years working with investments. Moving money without the client's awareness is highly unusual. But sometimes the brokerage puts money in the wrong account or worse yet takes it out. Let me emphasize, this is so rare that most people never encounter it. But you want to catch it if it happens.

When inappropriate trades or money transfers DO happen, the brokerage will leap to correct the problem at no expense to you. They usually catch errors themselves.

Very rarely a person with a discount brokerage account will experience identity theft. If you find something on your statement which you don't understand, immediately contact the brokerage by phone or email. Perhaps you simply misunderstood…in which case the phone call is a good learning experience. On the other hand, you may catch an identity-theft in progress. Every identity theft I have witnessed or heard about evoked a tremendous response by the discount brokerage. In virtually every case, the client was made whole, with no expense incurred.

I should stress: both brokerage mistakes and identity theft are very rare.

4. What is the change from the prior month? This should be right next to the current value. Remember this number can be twisted into unreality by money you add or money you take out.

To find out a bit more about your portfolio's monthly performance, you can determine a monthly or annual performance number. Since this involves math, many investors don't like to calculate it, but you still need to know it.

The bad news is, you need to know at least the annual performance number, or a "year-to-date" number. The good news is, it isn't that hard to calculate. The formulas I provide hereafter are simple compared to the computational gyrations of any textbook in basic finance. But they work well enough to provide a general idea of your money's performance.

Another bit of good news is that if you work with a fee-only investment manager, he or she should provide a year-to-date performance number with every statement, net the fees which are charged you for advisory services.

Here's how to calculate your Simple Total Return Before Taxes (STRBT). It is a raw number and leaves out taxes and expenses. But for a rough look, it's an excellent way to assure that your investment plan is on track.

IF THE MATH I'M ABOUT TO SHOW YOU MAKES YOU UNCOMFORTABLE, OR YOU DON'T WISH TO DO IT, SIMPLY MOVE ON TO WHERE THE NUMBERS STOP. THIS IS A GOOD INDICATOR THAT YOU NEED TO HIRE A FEE-ONLY INVESTMENT ADVISOR.

STRBT = ((portfolio value at the end of the time period + money you took out – money you put in) – (portfolio value at the beginning of the time period)) / portfolio value at the beginning of the time period.

Are we having fun yet? Let's savor the joy by calculating the returns to a hypothetical portfolio for one month. For example:

You have an account worth $110,000 at the end of the most recent month.

The month before that it was worth $100,000

You took out $15,000 to buy a car.

But then you got a tax refund for $6,000.

So the formula is:

STRBT=(($110,000+$15,000-$6,000) – ($100,000))/$100,000

STRBT=($119,000-$100,000)/$100,000

STRBT=($19,000)/$100,000

STRBT=19%

This performance is for example only. If this happened in reality it would be one of the great months in history.

Also you should know that money in and money out distorts real returns. So you can calculate rough returns with this method but not exact. The more money that goes in and out, the more distortions occur. Unless you are a numbers geek like me, you don't need to know exact returns.

You can calculate returns for any period using this method.

Congratulations. That's all the math you will find in this book. You need to know this number. If you have an investment advisor, he or she should calculate it for you. But now you can always check his or her work.

Your number may not exactly correspond with the number presented by your investment advisor. Many investment advisors use short periods for valuations and compound the results. But your number should be at least roughly similar. And any decent investment advisor should readily explain how his or her number was prepared.

Section 4.4: Financial Information

Lesson #16: The best sources of financial information are your discount brokerage, *Morningstar*, the *Wall Street Journal*, and *Value Line*.

As I will discuss *ad nauseum* in later chapters, I prefer to invest in mutual funds. Mutual funds are pools of money managed by professional managers to reach investment goals.

There's a whole chapter about the basics of mutual funds later in this book. What counts now is that you will need financial information not about individual stocks and bonds, but about mutual funds themselves, which hold those stocks and bonds within their investment pools. You will need information to pick appropriate mutual funds for your portfolio.

The world is full of financial information. The vast bulk of it is unnecessary. A lot of it is advertising disguised as information.

Any media which boldly expresses a prediction of the future for either individual stocks or the greater financial markets is likely to be worthless.

So that removes about 90% of all financial drivel. All the TV shows and radio shows may be great entertainment, with the host leaping about chewing the furniture and people in suits telling us what will happen. But almost all the information you get from these shows isn't worth the time, unless you just find the financial markets entertaining.

The best primary sources of information are likely to be your discount brokerage, *Morningstar*, the *Wall Street Journal,* and *Value Line*. Most discount brokerages embed *Morningstar* information within their own mutual fund menu and label it as such, so you shouldn't have to subscribe to *Morningstar* directly.

Within your discount brokerage, you will find a mutual fund selection menu. You will be able to select from a mountain of mutual funds, and the data available will be overwhelming. Most of it can be ignored. Don't be intimidated by it. This book will show you how to sort through the information in later chapters.

You should be able to find performance information on all your mutual funds at your discount brokerage's website. They aren't going to lie about these. Because all your investments are liquid, you can move your money out in a week. Since mutual fund information is ubiquitous, they know that you can cross-check it with merely a click on a touchpad. So when performance data is displayed on a discount brokerage's website, it's reliably accurate information.

Morningstar

Within the discount brokerage menu, *Morningstar* data is especially valuable. Unlike the Wall Street brokerages which put out reams of data, they don't manage money or sell investments. Thus they have relatively small conflicts of interest. A *Morningstar* trademark is particularly reliable.

All *Morningstar* statistics are "look back" numbers, which means they are based on historical data. That's good, because they are unimpeachable. That's also bad, because statistics change when the future changes, and the past can't predict the future. I still use these statistics simply because they are the best data available. But when you interpret what you read, it is sensible to err on the side of caution. In other words, don't bet your nest egg simply on these statistics.

Morningstar produces a "star rating" which is often quoted in magazines. This is another "look back" number, but it has real merit as a screen for selecting mutual funds.

Likewise, when all is despair and the financial markets have been steamrolled, the best funds to ride back up are not necessarily the "five star" funds du jour. Any fund with five stars after a few years of pummeling is either particularly cautious or preternaturally skilled at market valuations.

For example, let us imagine that X Fund is managed by a gaggle of doomsayers. Thus their portfolio allocation is very defensive: lots of cash and other investments which preserve capital but don't make a lot of money. For years this fund lags the stock markets as they go up. The fund receives a two star rating from *Morningstar*, because it is being left in the dust.

Then the stock market goes down 35%. What will X fund do? It will probably do great, compared to everyone else. Let's say the fund goes up 5% because its gold allocation wins big.

So what does this fund get at the end of a year of great ugliness? Five stars from *Morningstar*.

But the world keeps changing, time passes, and the financial climate inevitably changes as well. Let's say that at this moment of great travail and wringing of hands, you are searching for a mutual fund.

Most but not all bear markets are followed by robust recoveries. When a market recovery begins, it usually makes mutual funds holding relatively volatile stocks soar in value. After a year of unpleasant losses, these funds usually have, as they should, *Morningstar* ratings of one, two, or three stars. In other words, their star rankings are relatively low. Yet these funds will soar in a recovery, not the X Fund.

If you then go tiptoeing through the *Morningstar* data selecting mutual funds only on their star ratings, you will select X Fund, and you will probably miss the mutual funds most likely to produce large gains in any recovery.

Rarely, a mutual fund management team will master both up and down markets. You'll pick these up by doing more research in your *Morningstar* data. And by doing more research you will also be able to determine your expectations for the future.

In the coming chapter on mutual funds, you will learn about different statistics to determine the risk and behavior of different funds. Almost all these statistics are from *Morningstar* and appear on the mutual fund's profile page on your discount brokerage's website.

The Wall Street Journal

Another place to go for key statistics is the *Wall Street Journal*. The Wall Street Journal is probably the least biased of all the financial press. It provides a second opinion, a distinctly different view from your discount brokerage. The *Wall Street Journal* may also provide you with statistics to compare with what you are reading online.

Look for Section C, simply to see what the financial markets are doing. Day-to-day is too short-term to be relevant: look at year-to-date (YTD) performance for your mutual funds. You can find these in the mutual fund section, which appears often but not always.

Compare these YTD mutual fund performance numbers to the year-to-date performance of the Vanguard Index 500 mutual fund, which mimics the S&P 500 Index in a real-world context. It does this by using computerized stock buying and selling to mimic the genuine S&P 500.

Why, you ask, do I care? And what IS the S&P 500, anyway?

You care because the Standard and Poor's 500 is a proxy, albeit imperfect, for the whole stock market. It provides one easy-to-use set of statistics for you to measure market behavior and valuation.

The Standard and Poor's 500 is an utterly theoretical creation (created by the

Standard and Poor's corporation) which averages shares of the largest 500 American stocks to create one number to show us how the overall stock markets are doing.

The Standard and Poor's takes the values and market capitalization (the size) of the largest 500 American stocks, artificially averages these stocks together, and spits out a statistic. It's just a statistic, but index mutual funds such as the Vanguard Index 500 closely replicate the index. Thus you can "own the stock market"…and you can see "the stock market's" real-world performance by watching the Vanguard Index 500.

In a similar way, you can compare your bond-oriented mutual funds' numbers to the Vanguard Total Bond Index mutual fund performance. This tells you roughly how the overall bond market is doing.

The beauty of comparing these index mutual funds to your own investment performance is that these mutual funds provide you with real-world performance statistics, with dividends included. Obviously, these numbers are dated. Use your own research to make real investment decisions.

Somewhere in Section C of the *Wall Street Journal*, you'll find an opportunity to check interest rates, especially Fed funds, which is a very short-term interest rate which banks charge each other for inter-bank loans. Then look at mortgage rates. This tells you the direction of the credit markets, and thus the direction of the economy.

When interest rates are going up, money is getting more expensive for businesses, and thus risk is increasing. Even a slight rise in interest rates is often the tipping point for an already-inflated investment bubble.

Likewise, a decline in interest rates is good news. Money becomes cheaper, and companies borrow more. You can see these declining rates in the "52 week range" graph next to the interest rate data.

Interest rates are your canaries in the coal mine: when they change, pay special attention to the financial markets. Other venues will often act like croquet balls when hit with interest rate changes and roll off to other valuations as well.

Also in Section C of the *Wall Street Journal*, you will find the current P/E's (price earnings ratios) of the S&P 500 Index. This will give you an idea of overall valuation, which you can use later to allocate your assets.

There are two kinds of P/E's: one set based on genuine past "trailing" earnings, and another calculation based on expected future "estimate" earnings. I prefer to use genuine trailing earnings, because "estimates" are simply guesses.

You will often see mutual fund company news in the *Wall Street Journal* which will alert you to what is happening internally in your mutual funds.

You might want to read the editorial page. One scan and you have an idea what people are thinking.

The online version of the Wall Street Journal has all the same data at the "Market Data Center" portion of the website.

All in all, the *Wall Street Journal* is worth the time.

Value Line

Value Line is a stock analysis corporation which has been in existence since 1931. It was created by financial visionary Arnold Bernhard after he watched his mother lose all her savings in the stock market crashes from 1929 through the 1930's. Its basic mission is to provide unbiased stock-by-stock analysis and research. The company has developed a relatively rare reputation for insight and honesty.

What separates Value Line from our other sources of information is that we're seeking it out to look at only ONE proprietary variable: the monthly Estimated Median Appreciation Potential for the next three to five years. Here at my firm, our short-hand acronym for this statistic is the "VL-MAP". That's all I look at. But it's worth the look.

Value Line employs legions of analyst's who focus their attention on the potential gains and losses of 1,700 individual stocks. They don't really do lots of the mutual fund analysis which I find useful. And since I don't invest in individual stocks, most of their work is irrelevant. But as a by-product of all their analysts churning and churning of corporate data, Value Line also produces the VL-MAP. And that one number is pure gold.

The VL-MAP has proven to be surprisingly accurate as an estimator of future stock market returns. Value Line can't see the future…nobody can…but the VL-MAP is an average of many analysts calculating the relative valuation of individual stocks. The result of all that number-crunching is one single number which is unusually accurate as a market indicator.

Several studies have indicated that when the VL-MAP is at 50% or lower, the following stock market returns for the next three to five years range from 50% to 25%. In other words, a stock market correction usually follows a VL-MAP of 50% or lower. And it tends to be one or more of the ugly portfolio-wrecking sort, such as the downturns we experienced in 2000 and 2008.

It's important to remember that stock market corrections also happen when the VL-MAP is above 50%. So far, these have not been big monster corrections which ruin us, but rather profit-taking downturns which usually last less than a year. In such cases, we just ride them out with tactics which you will read about later, such as "rebalancing" and "weeding the garden". What the VL-MAP helps us to do is identify an investment bubble.

You can almost always find a Value Line binder full of reports in your local library. The "Estimated Median Appreciation Potential" is usually on the back cover of the market analysis leaflet.

If your local library does not have Value Line and does not plan to carry it, you can always subscribe to whatever is the cheapest publication which Value Line currently produces which contains the VL-MAP statistic. That's what I do. That one number is worth the money.

Section 4.5: Selecting and Working with a Financial Advisor

Lesson #17: Working with a fee-only independent investment advisor should add genuine value to your portfolio. Select one with care, and work with one responsibly.

Out in the big wide world of finance are many people eager to help you, for a commission. "Commission" means that she or he is compensated based on what is sold to you. Because this creates a profound conflict of interest, I can't recommend paying commissions for financial advice.

Likewise, I do not recommend enlisting the advice of any financial planner who receives commissions. He or she also has a conflict of interest. It doesn't matter if the individual is loaded with prestigious initials after his or her name: CPA, CFP, CLU. If the person is selling you something via commission, the initials are simply advertising and have diminished bearing on the quality of advice you will receive.

The credentials themselves may represent genuine training and real expertise. It's just that when they are paired with commission payments, they become licenses to mislead.

Work with a fee-only advisor.

Yes, advisors may be expensive. But the results of bad choices, being caught in a bubble market or diversifying inadequately can be catastrophic. It is my opinion that an advisor is probably worth the cost if you wish to employ one.

A good investment advisor should also act as a buffer against your own irrational mind. The entire third chapter of this book is devoted to the psychology of investing. It's very important. Your advisor should be implicitly aware of the psychological snares awaiting all who venture into the world of finance.

Your investment advisor should be a skeptic at large, a bulwark against excessive optimism in good times and a guard against pessimism when times are hard. He or she should execute your long-term plan regardless of short-term market angst.

As I have said earlier, avoid commission-based advice. Even if it is good, as it often is, you are never sure that you are getting unbiased counsel. Your investment advisor should be paid either by assets under management or by the hour.

The advantage of paying by assets under management is that the investment advisor's interests are caught up with yours. He or she gets richer when your assets go up and less wealthy when your assets go down. Since there is no advantage to trade unnecessarily, you may be more confident that changes are motivated by a genuine search for investments which will thrive. Unnecessary expenses will also be avoided.

In fact, sometimes a good investment advisor will make you the most money by doing less. When the investment world is caught up in a hurricane of fear, the best possible course may be to do nothing. You simply cannot judge the quality of an advisor by the amount of trading which goes on. Some of the best advisors trade the least.

The challenge for you will be to accept this, and have the patience to invest proactively rather than reactively. One big advantage of fee-only money management is that your advisor is paid to make you money, not to make trades.

The disadvantage of paying by assets under management (AUM) is that it is expensive. The average fee is 1% per year of assets under $1 million. You should be able to obtain a discount for additional dollars under management. This means that you will pay $10,000 for a year's management of $1 million.

In genuine terms, this is less than the expenses of a normal portfolio of individual stocks under the control of a commission-based stock broker. It should also be worth it:

your investment advisor should provide ongoing monitoring and proactive management. If you receive that service, your portfolio should be better off than similar unmanaged portfolios by at least 1% a year. At the very least your manager should be able to diminish the impact of the market catastrophes which sweep over us occasionally. 1% a year is much cheaper than losing your money due to bad investing.

The other way of compensating a fee-only investment advisor is hourly. This is often much cheaper than the percentage of asset compensation plan. However, it all too often results in less effective management. The advisor is put into the position of either racking up the hours spent on your account, or ignoring your account and focusing on the billable tasks at hand, in which case you are not receiving proactive management. Your financial interests are not aligned with the manager's.

Whatever fee structure you prefer, there are some solid guidelines for selecting an investment manager.

1. He or she should be registered with either the SEC or your state. There should be a document known as an "ADV" on file and online, and a copy should be made available to you. An ADV is a bit hard to read, but it indicates at least a willingness to disclose.

REGISTRATION AND AN ADV DO NOT INSURE COMPETENCE, QUALITY OF MANAGEMENT OR EVEN HONESTY. But they do open the door for auditing and disclosure, and somewhat lessen the chances of fraud. At least they show you that the manager is aware of professional requirements.

2. Your investment advisor should always use a third party discount brokerage with SIPC insurance. You should NEVER give your investment advisor custody of your money, and he or she should NEVER be a gatekeeper who determines if you get access to your cash. He or she should not be an employee of a discount brokerage: once again, you are trying to avoid conflict of interest.

OK, here's the important part: ALWAYS give your investment advisor a LIMITED POWER OF ATTORNEY, provided by the discount brokerage, not a FULL POWER OF ATTORNEY. A limited power of attorney allows your manager to observe your account on-line, trade within it, disburse money to you only, and collect fees from your account. A full power of attorney gives your manager full access as if she owns it.

3. Your investment advisor should invest only in mutual funds or bank deposits. You should be able to sell your investments and get your cash within a week. Information about your investments should be available from places other than your investment advisor. You should be able to gather information about them on the Internet and in periodicals. This vastly reduces the potential for fraud and ensures that you have full awareness of where your money is now. Stay away from limited partnerships and hedge funds. They may sound cool but they are a financial blind man's bluff.

4. You should receive a periodic report from your advisor detailing what is in your account and what your overall portfolio's performance has been over a recent time period. Almost always this will be a "Year-To-Date" (YTD) statistic

which you might then compare to alternatives. This statistic should also be after all fees and expenses. Surprisingly few investors actually know how their investments have performed over time. You now know how to calculate your own return statistics, so you should be able to verify your fee-only investment advisor's report.

5. You should also know what you are paying your advisors. Some unscrupulous advisors will tell you that they are providing no load funds when in fact they are providing mutual funds with large 12b-1 fees. That means that you are paying your advisor a secret annual fee. If you sell out of these 12b-1 funds, you will pay an egregious back-end penalty.

However, small 12b-1 fees of about .25% are normal for mutual funds traded on a no-load basis within the structure of a discount brokerage. These should be paid to the brokerage for providing the platform, and your independent investment advisor should receive none of them. In fact these should essentially be invisible to you.

Your investment advisor should charge you one periodic clear cut fee.

6. As we have just witnessed in the past few years, it is relatively common for Wall Street to dream up a new sexy method of investing which is so complex that literally nobody really understands it. Timing and options strategies might be attractive within one or two mutual funds in your portfolio, but as techniques for managing your entire nest egg, they are historically losers' games.

If you can't understand it, it is entirely possible your manager can't understand it either. Your strategy—and that of your manager—should be simple, robust, and inexpensive. That means mutual funds that are held for reasonable periods of time, without complex rapid-fire timing strategies. Remember, nobody knows what will happen. Market timing sounds like a great idea. But it doesn't work long-term.

Review: The Lessons of Chapter 4

Lesson #13: Although there are alternatives, a nationally-established SIPC-insured discount brokerage provides the best place for your long-term investment transactions.

Lesson #14: Using an established discount brokerage as your investment venue, and buying only mutual funds, help prevent you from being ripped off.

Lesson #15: You must learn to understand the information in your monthly statement.

Lesson #16: The best sources of financial information are your discount brokerage, *Morningstar*, the *Wall Street Journal,* and *Value Line.*

Lesson #17: Working with a fee-only independent investment advisor should add genuine value to your portfolio. Select one with care, and work with one responsibly.

Chapter 5

Invest Only In Mutual Funds

Full service brokers, in this day and age of low cost mutual funds and discount brokers, are really nothing more than machines for ripping off retail investors.
—Wall Street Survival 101 by Joel Spolsky

Section 5.1: The Reality of Mutual Fund Success

WARNING: We are now entering an area containing enough detail to potentially numb you like an anaesthetized horse.

Or not. It depends on how much you want to succeed as an investor. If you really want to succeed, you need to master this material. So gulp down some chocolate and let's get started.

The good news: You don't have to know it all <u>now</u>. You can skip over this and use this chapter as a reference later. And, if you just aren't interested, this may be a legitimate indicator that a fee-only investment advisor will probably add value to your life.

An alternative choice is to read this one lesson at a time. Go slowly. Review.

Lesson #18: Your long-term liquid investments should be in mutual funds. Specifically, you should invest in no-load or transaction-fee-only mutual funds.

This is a core lesson of this book. I strongly recommend that you invest only in mutual funds. As I wrote earlier, mutual funds are pools of money managed by professionals. You may not fully understand what a mutual fund is, but you will, as you read on. Meanwhile…just let this lesson sit lightly on the tip of your brain.

Since most of Wall Street advertising is presented as genuine information, the idea that you should invest only in mutual funds is at odds with most of the "reality" which hucksters represent as the real world.

It is correct anyway.

Most of Wall Street's marketing efforts and most of the entertainment value of the financial media is related to individual issues such as stocks and bonds, not mutual funds.

In fact, if you Google them, you will find that many of Wall Street's highest paid celebrities bad-mouth mutual funds. They often imply strongly that people who invest in mutual funds are incompetent investors.

Think about why that is.

There is much more money to be gained by Wall Street from selling you individual issues and other higher priced "sophisticated" investments. Investing in individual stocks or bonds requires much more immediate information than investing in mutual funds. Investors are thus more vulnerable to the irrational thinking which we discussed before when they invest in individual issues.

Thus they are more dependent upon the competence by proxy and ego extrapolation provided by the financial media, and thus more easily manipulated by Wall Street.

Wall Street makes much more money off "sophisticated investors" and much less from mutual fund investors. Yet study after study indicates that mutual funds of equivalent risk and asset allocation do as well or better than average investors in individual stocks. Wall Street doesn't want you to stop making them rich.

That's all there is to it.

Emotionally, investing only in mutual funds is hard to do: everywhere you will hear or read of someone who is making a killing in individual stocks, third trust deeds, or private placements. They don't discuss it when these investments implode. Don't get lured by investment machismo. Keep your portfolio focused on your long-term goals via mutual funds.

To review: a mutual fund is a pool of money managed by professionals for a specific investment goal. We invest in them on-line, so basically what you are doing is buying a slice of a financial pie, in the form of shares. In that pie might be stocks, bonds, or even real estate trusts. But you are buying the pie, not the ingredients. And as always when you buy a pie, you choose based on expectations and reputation.

There are as many different kinds of mutual funds as there are different kinds of investments. Here are the categories in which I invest. We will cover these in detail later.

1. US stock mutual funds.
2. International stock mutual funds.
3. Sector mutual funds: Energy/Commodity/Health Care.
4. Global asset-allocation mutual funds (they invest globally in stocks and bonds)
5. US asset-allocation mutual funds (they invest domestically in stocks and bonds.)
6. US bond mutual funds
7. International bond mutual funds.
8. Money market mutual funds and cash accounts.

Let's look at an example, simply to illustrate how a mutual fund works:

You own 200 shares of the hypothetical "Mad Hatter Mutual Fund". It has a trading symbol of "MADHX". It is a domestic stock mutual fund. Its investment goal is to make money investing in US stocks.

Within the investment pool which comprises this mutual fund are 45 individual stocks, including Apple, Verizon, Ford, General Mills, and the fictional Magic Wombat Corporation.

What matters to you is that this mutual fund is a pool of money. You own shares of the mutual fund. You own the underlying individual stocks only because they are inside the mutual fund.

Thus you don't have to worry about what is going on with Apple, Verizon, Ford, General Mills, or Magic Wombat: that's what you pay the mutual fund manager to do. Also, you hold only a tiny bit of each company's stock, since you own the mutual fund, not the underlying stocks directly.

This makes your life much simpler.

You may hear that mutual funds are less risky than individual stocks. This is both true and not true. A mutual fund will automatically shed the specific risk of the stocks it holds simply because it doesn't own a lot of any one individual stock, as illustrated above. But a mutual fund of equivalent systemic risk to a given portfolio of individual stocks will be just as volatile as that portfolio.

Some mutual funds, such as short-term Treasury bond mutual funds, can offer extremely low risk. As you move across the spectrum of risk, you will arrive at mutual funds which are so exposed to systemic risk that they can, and have, lost or gained up to 95% in a single year. A mutual fund is simply a kind of investment vehicle. It is as risky or as profitable as what it contains within it.

But whatever a mutual fund contains, it frees you to focus on your long-term investment goals and your long-term investment techniques. That's invaluable right there.

Section 5.2: Risk

Lesson #19: Very broadly, there are two different kinds of investment risk: specific and systemic.

You *eliminate* the specific risk of individual stocks by investing in mutual funds.

You *reduce* your systemic, or non-specific risk by allocating money to different asset classes.

In the world of investing, risk is technically about the same as volatility. In other words, risk is regarded as the likelihood of your investment moving up or down.

This is measured via a statistic called standard deviation.

Risk is also measured by correlation, that is, how likely is it that two or more investments will move up and down together? Obviously this is important from the standpoint of overall portfolio safety.

This kind of risk is measured by a statistic derived from complex regression modeling, which we call "beta" risk.

But in the real world, risk is simply measured by one all-important yardstick: how likely is it that your portfolio will lose money? Even more precisely, how likely is it that your portfolio will lose money PERMANENTLY?

That's really all that matters to you as an investor.

Yes, we're going to discuss statistics. But what we're really doing is working to prevent you from permanently losing money.

So this matters.

If investing in mutual funds seems unglamorous or extreme, you might wish to talk to holders of individual stocks or bonds in recent market downturns. Some formerly safe investments simply vaporized.

A basic concept of mutual fund investing is that you can't know the future. That seems obvious, but anyone who takes a large position in an individual stock is essentially gambling that he or she can at least predict the future earnings of that corporation. Good luck with that.

For example, let's examine the fictional Magic Wombat Corporation. When you guess the future earnings of Magic Wombat, you are facing a risk which is SPECIFIC to that corporation. All entities, from planets to atoms to flatworms to people to corporations, face risks which are unique and specific. I may be hit by a meteor which completely misses you. On the other hand I may win the lottery, while your ticket, bought just 5 seconds later, may be a complete loser.

The Magic Wombat Corporation may discover that its new Purple Wombat Body Wash is a global hit, a money-making bonanza, which makes the corporation unexpectedly wealthy. It may discover shortly thereafter that the Purple Wombat Body Wash unexpectedly causes total, permanent depilation, which results in billions of dollars in lawsuits that bankrupt the company. The individual permutations are endless. We avoid these by investing in diversified mutual funds.

For example, if you own those 200 shares of the hypothetical "Mad Hatter Mutual Fund" (fictional symbol MADHX), you own small positions in 45 individual stocks which are held in the mutual fund's investment pool. These include Apple, Verizon, Ford, General Mills, and the fictional Magic Wombat Corporation. So when Magic Wombat suddenly reports the fantastic earnings of Purple Wombat Body Wash, your mutual fund shares increase in value, depending upon how many shares of Magic Wombat the mutual fund owns. On the other hand, when that news of the permanent depilatory effects of Purple Wombat Body Wash utterly destroys Magic Wombat's share value, the fund will only go down slightly.

By owning MADHX, you have successfully avoided permanently losing money in Magic Wombat. That's called diversification.

If you study the history of big corporations, you will see that while earnings can sometimes be consistent, all corporations face times of extreme uncertainty. For example, the mantra in the 1950's through the 2000's was that automobile stocks such as Ford and General Motors were utterly unsinkable, extremely safe "blue chip" stocks to buy and hold.

Yet in 2008 and 2009, they sank to levels not seen since the 1950's, or in some cases even the 1920's. The reality was that they were dreadful as "buy and hold" investments.

Nobody could predict the utter devastation which changing markets and inflexible management have brought upon them. It turns out that because a corporation is big, it does not follow that its stock is safe to own.

On the other hand, recently I met a man who invested $25,000 in Ford (symbol F) in 2009 when it was at $1. Now it is at $4, and of course he has an investment worth $100,000.

But that's not investing. That's gambling. And life is not a casino.

To reduce this kind of specific risk, we diversify within the asset class. In other words, if the asset class is US stocks, we buy a mutual fund which holds the shares of 100 or so different industrial corporations. The individual news of Ford or Magic Wombat or any other corporation will be so diluted that it is very rarely able to move the price of the mutual fund. Instead, the fund will move when the majority of the shares owned by the mutual fund go up.

When you invest in an individual stock or bond, you genuinely face the risk that the stock or bond will simply cease to exist, and that your money will literally vanish because of the SPECIFIC risk of that unique corporation. Because of diversification, mutual funds don't normally face this kind of specific risk in any meaningful way. After all, a mutual fund which holds only 3% of its pool in one stock will have only a 3% loss if that stock utterly vanishes from the planet.

As you can see, buying an assortment of individual investments quickly reduces individual risk. However, this kind of diversification within an asset class doesn't reduce systematic risk at all.

Since mutual funds are therefore diversified, individual specific risks don't affect them very much. Instead, mutual funds face SYSTEMIC risk. Some people call this risk "market" risk, or "non-systemic" risk. These different names all refer to the same kind of risk.

As you can see, there are a variety of risks which are unique to asset classes as a whole, such as US Treasury bonds, or Finnish stocks, or bonds in corporations which have lower credit ratings.

SYSTEMATIC risk is the unavoidable risk which confronts any single financial market, and thus the asset class of investments involved in that market. For example, an index fund which holds all the stocks of large US corporations, which we call "large-cap stocks", doesn't face the risks of the individual corporations. These have all been effectively diversified away. Instead, this mutual fund fully embraces the risks of the US economy. When the economy is good, this mutual fund will thrive. When the economy is weak, it will suffer.

The systematic risks to any mutual fund look like this: (Fig. 5-1)

You can't diversify these risks away with diversification <u>within</u> an asset class, because the entire asset class is exposed to the same risks. So, instead, you have to diversify <u>between</u> asset classes.

An asset class is a kind of asset which is essentially similar in economic exposure and subject at least in part to similar market risks.

For example, gold is an asset class because it behaves differently from other investments such as stocks and bonds in certain economic conditions.

Treasury bonds are also to some degree uncorrelated with either gold or large-cap stocks.

So you would provide very simple risk reduction to your portfolio by investing in a precious metals mutual fund, a Treasury bond mutual fund, and a large-cap stock portfolio. Having all three of these in your portfolio will reduce the overall impact of the systematic risks which face any single mutual fund.

Two mutual funds which both invest in one asset class CORRELATE with each other. For example, MADHX correlates to some degree with any other US stock fund because both are invested in the US stock market. Both MADHX and the other mutual fund also tend to move in market cycles in a similar manner.

But MADHX and a Treasury bond fund do not move together in any economic cycle. Treasury bonds tend to go up when the stock market is dropping and people are

Types of Risk

Fig. 5-1

scared. Of course, when the stock market is dropping, MADHX is going down to some degree as well. So the Mad Hatter Mutual Fund and a Treasury bond fund are relatively UNCORRELATED.

When you own two or more uncorrelated mutual funds, you are less likely to lose a lot of money if an unexpected economic catastrophe sweeps over us than if you have all your money in the US stock market. Welcome to the world of diversification.

But here's the big complication:

In general, <u>in the longer term</u>, investments in higher risk asset classes produce greater gains. Lower risk mutual funds produce lower gains.

In other words, there is no free lunch. Higher risk investments, and the mutual funds which hold them, historically produce higher returns OVER TIME than less risky investments inside or outside mutual funds.

But these mutual funds with higher risk and higher gains can be punishing within a year, several years, or even a decade.

It's always a balancing act.

There are several ways to cope with the risk of more volatile investments. You can choose to put the money away for a long time. As you can see in the following graph, that deeply reduces the damage of downturns.

However, you might face the most damaging downturn just at the end of your long investment period, and see much of your gains devastated. And this tactic is brutal for your nerves.

Take the time to study and understand this graph. It's important. What it is telling you is that the longer you hold a risky investment, the more likely you are to garner positive gains. But, as I wrote above, this strategy has risks as well.

The corollary to this paradigm is that you don't want to hold risky investments if your investment horizon is short. (Fig. 5-2)

As you can see, the best year's return for the "small stocks" asset class between 1926 and 2010 was a whopping gain of 142.9%. But the worst possible result for those years for small stocks was a -58% loss. That would be a very painful year, especially if it happened at the end of your 20 year investment horizon. As you can see, the asset class "small stocks" is very volatile, which is investment-speak for risky.

You would not want to have all your money in small stocks unless you are somehow stimulation-deprived.

But the *average return* for small stocks was 12.1%. That almost beat the *best ever* return to Treasury bills of 14.7%. And it certainly trounced all other average returns on this graph.

A reasonable person might conclude that the "small stocks" asset class has a place in a diversified portfolio. But how do you manage the risk?

The solution is to diversify extensively between asset classes.

This really works, but creates a short-term problem: a fully-diversified portfolio will almost always lag the best-performing market.

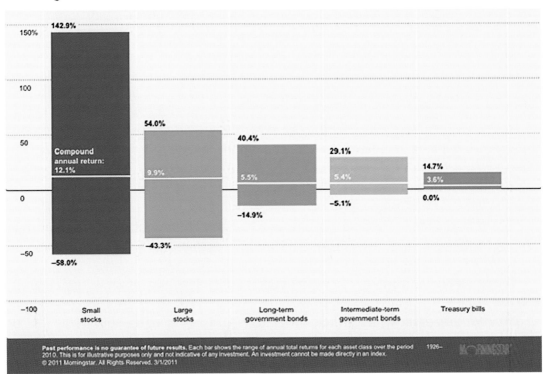

Asset-Class Returns
Highs and lows: 1926–2010

Fig. 5-2

Stocks and Bonds: Risk Versus Return
1970–2010

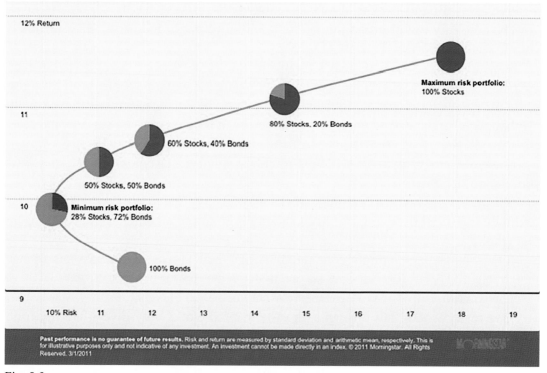

Fig. 5-3

As this graph shows, however, you can capture much of the gain and reduce your risk extensively just by blending different asset classes of mutual funds within your portfolio.

This is real, as you can see in Figure 5-3 above.

This graph covers the 40 years between 1970 and 2010. Yes, I know that the famous economist John Maynard Keynes once said, "In the long run we are all dead." But the reality is that many of us are facing a 40 year time horizon for investing. Think not? If you are younger than 50, given current life expectancy, there is a reasonable chance that you are in fact a very long term investor, and will be invested for 40 years or more. So what is on this graph is very important.

Yes, the future will be different. But basic concepts of diversification should still apply.

Risk is measured horizontally on this graph, from left to right. So the farther right you go, the more risky is that portfolio. Gains are measured vertically: the higher you go, the more you are gaining.

The perfect investment would thus be in the upper left corner: low risk, high returns. Too bad it doesn't exist in the real world.

Observe that prudent diversification DOES NOT result in an equivalent loss of potential returns. Because all asset classes, and the mutual funds which own them, face market-wide risks of some sort, diversification can actually have the effect of <u>reducing</u> overall systemic portfolio risk while <u>increasing</u> long-term gains.

Check out the "sweet spot" of investing represented by the minimum risk portfolio. That portfolio faces the least risk of any of the represented asset allocations, yet it actually contains 28% stocks. This is because the presence of those stocks diversifies the interest rate risks of the bonds to some degree.

When you consider that this graph contains the stock market debacle years of 1976, 1987, 2000 and 2008, the implications of the "sweet spot" on this graph are important to remember. In the real world, as you can see, the market-wide risks of one asset class are often quite different from the market-wide systematic risks of another asset class.

In the short run, dealing with this can be a bit challenging. Returns to your individual mutual funds within your portfolio will often be mixed. In other words, even when you are succeeding holistically, some of your individual mutual funds may be down, and so it won't seem to you that your portfolio is succeeding, when in fact it is.

For example, if you own Mad Hatter mutual fund, which is invested in US stocks, it may be soaring while your bond mutual funds linger and your energy mutual fund languishes. So your portfolio won't be beating the S&P 500 performance: it will probably be lagging. That's ok: when the S&P 500 slips on a banana peel you will probably catch up. We'll discuss how later. The important part to remember now is that:

Total portfolio return is always more important than the returns of your individual mutual fund holdings.

As I said before, it's a balancing act between objective risks and long-term goals. It's also a balancing act between your irrational mind's need for safety and gains and the realities of investment behavior. Using a bit of both tactics: investing for the long-term and diversifying between asset classes, seems to work best for almost all investors.

Thus, I have found that the best methodology to reduce portfolio risk is to adopt a blend of these different strategies:

1. **Invest only in mutual funds.**
2. **Buy several funds within each asset class.**
3. **Mix your money between asset classes.**
4. **Hold your investments for as long as possible.**

The key is to balance your expectations for your portfolio with both your time horizon and your risk tolerance.

If you are investing very long-term and have a perceived high risk tolerance, you will want a very different allocation than a person who wants to cash out the money in a few years and is insecure about investing to begin with.

The reality is that you won't fully know either your time horizon or your risk tolerance until you are investing. That's another reason for diversification: to learn about your own investment tastes as you learn about the world of investing. It's a process, it's a journey, and for most of us, it is a marathon, not a sprint.

Before we begin to explore the major asset classes of mutual funds, there are a few more features of mutual funds we need to discuss.

Section 5.3: Mutual Fund Total Return

Lesson #20: For mutual funds,

Total Return = Cash Payouts + Change in Share Value

In a more complex format, we split the cash payouts into two components:

Total Return = Cash Dividends + Paid Capital Gains + Change in Share Value

People mess this up all the time. This is a common mistake, even for some professionals.

In short, any investment makes money two ways; cash flow and capital change. Hopefully that "capital change" means that the share value increases rather than decreases.

In other words, an investment pays you money or it grows, or some combination of the two.

In reality, most investments and certainly most mutual funds provide a combination of the two.

For example, a bond is an IOU, as we will discuss later in this book. It makes most of its money by paying a coupon, a payout in cash to the holder of that bond.

But the market value of the bond also changes to reflect current interest rates and the economic climate. So the average bond's method of making you money looks like this:

Total Return = Cash Payouts + Change in Bond Value

This means there's usually a lot of cash flow but not a lot of change in bond value.

So if you own a bond mutual fund, you should expect to receive

Total Return Cash Payouts + Paid Capital Gains from Sales of Bonds + Change in Bond Value

Lots of cash flow, but not a lot of gains.

By the way, another mutual fund name for cash payout….income-taxed cash flow… is dividend.

This total return equation includes paid capital gains because a mutual fund must by law distribute net cash capital gains. Capital gains are cash profits from selling any investment which has increased in value.

Let's step away from bonds for a moment to return to our thrilling hypothetical Mad Hatter mutual fund for an example of total return.

As we saw, Mad Hatter mutual fund has positions in Apple, Verizon, Ford, General Mills, and the fictional Magic Wombat Corporation. When Magic Wombat goes up, your astute mutual fund manager sells some of the shares. So she is able to report a profit from that sale: let's say she bought Magic Wombat at $20 per share and sold at $40.

If she doesn't have any other losses to write off her profit, she must pay out the $20 per share profit to you by the end of the fiscal year. That counts as cash flow.

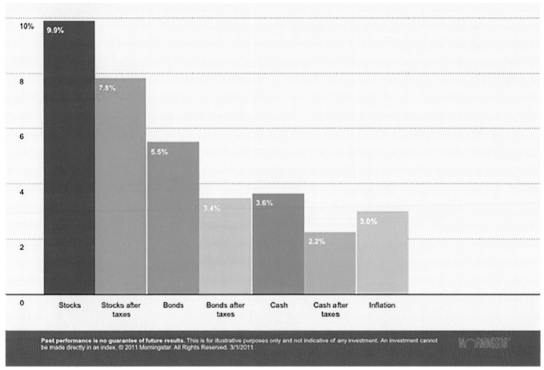

Taxes Significantly Reduce Returns
1926–2010

Fig. 5-4

If all the other stocks in the portfolio grew during that year, you will see the gain for MADHX as:

Total Return MADHX = $0 Cash Dividend + $20 Paid Capital Gains from Sales of Magic Wombat + Change in the Share Value of all the other stocks.

Got it? And now for something completely different. Let's see how this works with a bond mutual fund.

Bonds produce lots of income, but not a lot of capital change. People tend to buy bond mutual funds strictly for that cash flow.

But if you buy a poor quality bond fund which experiences a lot of individual bond defaults in its investment pool, then the benefit of the cash flow is swamped by the loss of bond value.

In other words, the three components of total return are always implicitly present even when they may not be visible.

One or more of the triad of total return components may simply be too small to matter.

Whenever you invest, you MUST consider all three components of total return, even if they don't seem important at the time.

In the case of a bond mutual fund, the cash dividend is so great a component of total return that the fund itself often won't increase in value at all unless you ___reinvest___ **your cash dividends.**

This is another advantage of mutual funds. Many individual investments do not have a provision to reinvest any cash payouts.

But YOU in your wisdom can set your purchasing parameters at your discount brokerage to reinvest your cash payouts. This will provide you with the benefits of diversification while maximizing long-term total return.

For all mutual funds:

Total Return = Cash Payouts + Change in Share Value

In greater detail:

Total Return = Cash Dividends + Paid Capital Gains + Change in Share Value

To maximize mutual fund returns, reinvest dividends and capital gains payouts.

Section 5.4: Mutual Funds and Taxes

Lesson #21: Mutual funds create taxes.

As you saw above, all mutual funds in a taxable account create taxable events when they pay out dividends or capital gains. Some mutual funds pay more dividends or capital gains than others. This tends to be roughly but not entirely predictable.

In general, bond funds pay out more current income in the form of dividends. Stock-oriented funds tend to pay out more capital gains. These payouts are simply due to the nature of the underlying investments within the funds.

How much taxes affect the performance of a given mutual fund is very dependent upon the kind of fund and its management. As you can see in this graph, stock-based, equity-oriented mutual funds are impacted but not catastrophically so: (Fig. 5-5)

This is because most of these funds emphasize growth and capital gains. Capital gains are traditionally but not always taxed at lower rates than income.

Tax codes change, so at least hire a tax professional who can stay aware of this for you. My experience has been that most professional tax preparers more than return their fees in savings. And, more importantly, they can help you avoid tax catastrophes which you might miss on your own.

Proportionally, bond-based mutual funds lose much more to taxes. This can be offset by using tax-free municipal bond funds (more on that later). Obviously, most taxable bonds pay out a coupon, which creates an income-taxed dividend for the mutual funds which hold them.

As you can see, holding cash in a taxable savings account or money market fund is a long-term disaster. Returns are run flat by taxes and inflation.

That's worth reading again. The graph above shows you that holding cash long term in a tax-exposed account has actually produced a NEGATIVE REAL RETURN after taxes and inflation. So holding cash long term is a good thing for your emergency account, but for your long term investments such a choice leaves a lot to be desired.

You can pick funds to suit your tax needs.

As I review different mutual fund types for you in the coming chapters, keep in mind that within each category are individual mutual funds which are more tax-efficient than others. These can be identified by the "tax efficiency" ratings provided by

Benefits of Deferring Taxes

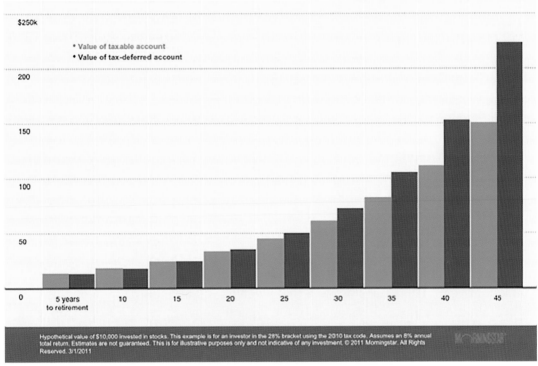

Fig. 5-5

Morningstar for each mutual fund. This "tax efficiency" statistic isn't utterly reliable. For one thing, it is hostage to the choices made by the fund managers, who may or may not elect to make portfolio changes which have taxable consequences. In very basic terms, however, the statistics provided by *Morningstar* can be used for generic planning.

Some investors pay too much attention to taxes.

The primary goal is long-term after-tax total return. It is very possible to pay lots of taxes while holding excellent mutual funds and deliver excellent returns anyway. Don't let fear of taxes drive you towards avoiding rebalancing or a warped asset allocation. Make money first. Pay taxes later.

Lesson #22: Whenever possible, select more tax-exposed funds for tax-deferred accounts such as IRA's or retirement plans. In practical terms, put your bonds and asset allocation funds in your retirement plans and your higher-risk stock funds in your tax-exposed brokerage accounts.

As you can see in this *Morningstar* graph, not paying taxes annually on your investments allows money to accrue and compound at an accelerated rate.

This has genuine benefits, especially for that portion of your asset allocation which is highly taxed. I generally seek to put my clients' very taxable <u>bond and cash</u>

allocations into tax-deferred retirement plans such as IRA's and 401(k)'s. By doing this, these low risk mutual funds can thrive without the penalties which normally hinder the performance of such cash flow-rich funds.

If possible, I then place the less-highly taxed <u>stock-oriented mutual funds</u> in a taxable venue such as a brokerage account or trust. These funds produce less taxes year to year.

Also, except for the case of the Roth IRA, all monies removed from a retirement plan are currently taxed as ordinary income. This is no great penalty for bond funds and other highly taxed vehicles, since the money placed into these accounts was pretax anyway.

But having an additional taxable account allows you to cash in equity-based mutual funds and pay only lower capital gains taxes.

Many of us simply don't have enough money to contribute to both. If that's the case, pack your retirement plan and manage your entire portfolio in a tax-deferred account. The tax deduction up front is enough to make this worth doing.

One golden exception to keep in mind: the Roth IRA. This little gem allows you to invest post-tax dollars in a tax-deferred vehicle with no taxes for money removed. Are you kidding me? This is as close to a free lunch as you are going to see on this mortal earth. Talk to your tax professional: If you are able, contribute to a Roth. Since there is no taxable event when you remove money, consider allocating a part of your equity position here.

Lesson #23: Take advantage of taxable losses via fund swaps.

The following is a bit sophisticated but I add it to this chapter because it's a nice little technique to make lemonade out of lemons. Do this only after you discuss it in detail with your tax pro.

If you are considering investing in a relatively risky mutual fund, do so in a taxable venue if possible. As I mentioned above, if this mutual fund grows, taxable events are likely to be some sort of low-taxed capital gains event.

However, if the mutual fund drops like a rock, you then have another option which is not available within a tax-deferred account: you can declare a tax loss. You do this by selling the demolished fund and immediately investing the proceeds in an almost identical fund managed by a different company.

You shouldn't sell a fund and then buy back its twin from the same management team. This may trigger a "wash sale" which renders the tax loss invalid.

Likewise, be sure you invest in essentially the same mutual fund immediately after the sale of the losing fund. Otherwise you risk locking in a genuine loss at the bottom of the market cycle and being unable to recover later.

The goal here is to change horses, and not take yourself out of the race. You want to sell your original high-risk mutual fund on which you have lost money and IMMEDIATELY buy a different-but-equal high-risk mutual fund to capture the market's eventual recovery.

While you wait for the stock market recovery, your taxable loss by selling your high-risk mutual fund should add measurably to your after-tax total return.

Since this works only on a case-by-case basis, let me stress once again: discuss each and every tax-motivated sale with your tax professional to make sure that you have done your calculations accurately. The details to a tax swap are critical and ephemeral.

Review: The Lessons of Chapter 5

Lesson #18: Your long-term liquid investments should be in no-load or transaction-fee-only mutual funds.

Lesson #19: You eliminate the SPECIFIC risk of <u>individual</u> stocks by investing in mutual funds. You reduce your SYSTEMIC (non-specific) risk by allocating money to different asset classes.

Lesson #20: For mutual funds:

Total Return = Cash Dividends + Paid Capital Gains + Change in Share Value

Lesson #21: Some mutual funds create more taxes than others. You can pick funds to suit your tax needs.

Lesson #22: Whenever possible, select more tax-exposed funds for tax-deferred accounts such as IRA's or retirement plans.

Lesson #23 Take advantage of taxable losses via fund swaps. Always work with your tax professional when you do this.

Chapter 6

Keeping It Safe...Money Market Funds and Conservative Bond Mutual Funds

I've been rich and I've been poor. Believe me, honey, rich is better.
—Sophie Tucker

Section 6.1: A Place for Safety

Lesson #24: Money market funds and bond mutual funds keep you rich by not crashing when financial markets become volatile. They seldom <u>make</u> you rich, because they don't grow. These mutual funds are VERY valuable, because they diversify you against unforeseen catastrophe.

In Chapter 5, I wrote that we allocate to eight different asset classes, in eight different kinds of mutual funds:
1. US stock mutual funds.
2. International stock mutual funds.
3. Sector mutual funds: Energy/Commodity/Health Care.
4. Global asset-allocation mutual funds (they invest globally in stocks and bonds)
5. US asset-allocation mutual funds (they invest domestically in stocks and bonds.)
6. International bond mutual funds.
7. US bond mutual funds
8. Money market mutual funds and cash accounts.

We're now going to explore these from the safest to the riskiest, starting with the bottom three on the list. The reason we are starting at the bottom is that safety is paramount, and you should have bank accounts or money market funds in place before you do anything else.

By the way, in the investment world, "cash" means bank accounts, checking accounts, and money market funds, not simply the green bills you carry around in your pocket. So when I talk about "cash", I'm not just referring to your Jacksons.

The word "cash" is itself fascinating: ancient China had coins known as "cash", the French have a Provencal word, "caisse" meaning "money box", and the Malayans apparently call currency "cash" as well. For whatever reason, the word "cash" seems to indicate money the world over. All these words stand for something which is wonderful, portable, and usually low risk.

The problem with low-risk investments is that they don't usually make a lot of money for you over the longer term.

The fundamental reason you don't make a lot of money with bank deposits or money market funds is that you are loaning money instead of owning something.

In most cases, the intrinsic safety you derive from loaning money is that you generally have some sort of collateral. "Collateral" is what people must surrender to you if they can't pay your loan back. If you look at this cynically, that makes everyone who loans money a glorified pawn broker. On the other hand, the real effect is that when you loan money properly, you should experience less risk to your investments than if you are an owner.

Bank accounts are loans to the bank: you bring money to them, they borrow it to lend to others, and for this they pay you interest. Their "collateral" is the full faith and credit of the bank. Actually, prior to the 1930's, that was often regarded with extreme suspicion, and banks failed routinely, deposits and all. To protect the financial system, the US government instituted an insurance program, so that now your bank deposits are insured against loss. On the other hand, you don't make much in bank accounts, for the most part.

One very common form of debt is the short-term "IOU," accrued by loaning money to corporations or governments. These are packaged and managed professionally as money market funds, which look almost exactly like bank accounts. The key differences are that you are generally investing in a mutual fund, not a bank. The management of that money market mutual fund will hold very low risk…at least they are SUPPOSED to be low risk…very short-term debt. So in concept, money market funds are more diversified. We'll look at these more later.

What matters now is…bank accounts are a form of debt. And money market funds are not the same as bank accounts.

When you want more income and are willing to accept a bit more risk than money market funds, you may choose to look at mutual funds containing bonds. Bonds are simply longer term loans which have been securitized: that is, they have been cut up into bits and are bought and sold in secondary markets.

Even with bonds, however, there is a key theme concerning high-quality loans, otherwise known as debt instruments: they don't make a lot of money historically. You can see this over the very long-term: (Fig. 6-1)

This graph is worth pondering. You can see that $1 invested in 1926 in small stocks became $16,055 while $1 invested in cash-proxies such as Treasury bills became $21. Setting aside the ridiculously long term of the investment, that's a mind-blowing difference, isn't it? Why then would anyone invest in cash, money market funds, or conservative bond funds?

Answer: safety. These investments are <u>crucial</u> for a properly diversified portfolio. They provide a patchwork parachute for times of economic hardship.

The key to employ these investments correctly is to use debt for diversification, not growth, and emphasize ownership of assets in the form of stock mutual funds for long-term investing.

Now let's take a look at the debt-oriented mutual funds you will include in your portfolio.

Section 6.2: Money Market Mutual Funds

Lesson #25: A money market mutual fund is a relatively very low-risk mutual fund which invests in very short-term debt instruments. These funds are usually very

Ibbotson® SBBI®
Stocks, Bonds, Bills, and Inflation 1926–2010

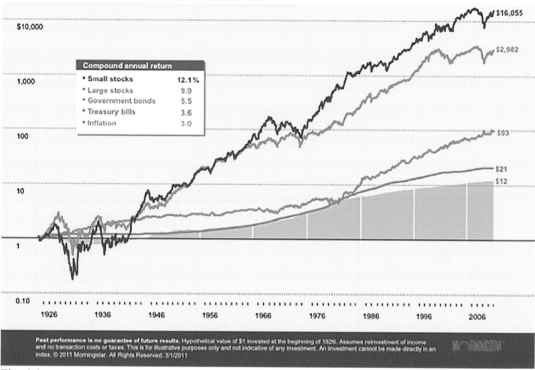

Compound annual return	
• Small stocks	12.1%
• Large stocks	9.9
• Government bonds	5.5
• Treasury bills	3.6
• Inflation	3.0

Past performance is no guarantee of future results. Hypothetical value of $1 invested at the beginning of 1926. Assumes reinvestment of income and no transaction costs or taxes. This is for illustrative purposes only and not indicative of any investment. An investment cannot be made directly in an index. © 2011 Morningstar. All Rights Reserved. 3/1/2011

Fig. 6-1

safe. They also usually produce lower returns, especially after taxes and inflation.

People don't normally consider money market funds to be mutual funds, but in fact they are. They are pools of money managed by professionals to obtain specified investment goals. Essentially, they should behave and yield just like bank accounts.

Money market fund managers take the money you send them and go out and buy very short-term debt instruments. Think of <u>very</u> short-term IOU's, sometimes as short as a few hours, which pay interest for the right to borrow. The corporation or the municipality or the government borrows money from investors and pays it back quickly with interest.

The rate of return for these money market funds is almost always <u>annualized</u>. That means that even if the debt instruments inside it have an average maturity of 3 days, the rate of return is expressed as what those investments would yield if reinvested for an entire year. Obviously, the interest rate will change in the coming year. So when you read that a money market fund is yielding 3%, that's what it is producing on an annualized basis now. The probability of actually getting 3% in that money market fund if you hold it for a year is actually low. Interest rates may go higher or lower, and since the investments within the money market fund will roll over many times in one year, the rate will change. Meanwhile, if you invest in a money market fund for one week, you won't get that 3%. You will get 7/365 of about 3%.

Normally money market funds have almost no risk. But in the panic of 2008, that wasn't the case. Esoteric artificial short-term investments within money market funds sometimes collapsed. The US government stepped forward to insure these funds and to keep the capacity to loan and to borrow on a short-term basis alive. But we can't be sure that this sort of crisis will or will not happen again.

Therefore, I would recommend that you use only Treasury money market funds when investing in a retirement plan such as an IRA or in an account where taxes aren't an issue. Presently these are yielding 0%. But that's the price of safety. Treasury money funds use only very short-term Treasury bills issued directly from the US government.

In 2011 the safety of Treasury bills became an issue in the media, and Treasury debt in general received a ratings downgrade. This is all relatively meaningless when you are considering investing in very short term Treasury debt, because the capacity of the US government to meet its obligations in the short term in a genuine sense is absolute. So even after the downgrades of 2011, I still use Treasury money market funds.

"Government" money market funds might issue agency debt as well, so I prefer not to use them. Vanilla-grade corporate money market funds tend to buy a lot of private sector commercial paper from small and large businesses, most of which is simply very short-term borrowing by corporations. I avoid these money market funds because of their capacity to drift into the far and distant country of iffy corporate debt.

This means that I DON'T simply pick out the money market fund which has the highest yield. The highest-yielding of anything is often the most risky. Instead, I simply look for a competent Treasury fund. The difference in annual gain between an uncertain money market fund and a sure thing Treasury fund may be as high as 2%. You can get that in the stock market in one week. In other words, the risk of a high-yielding money market fund unexpectedly failing isn't worth it. Face your risks out in the open, not in your money market fund.

When I am investing in a tax-exposed account for a client in a very high federal tax bracket, I DO invest some money in state-specific municipal money market funds. Because the short-term debt in these is issued by states and municipalities, returns are often tax-free. Obviously this kind of money market fund is for use in a taxable account only. But keep in mind that there are obvious risks, and don't bet your whole nest egg.

Cash keeps you rich, but it won't make you rich. The graph above shows you approximate money market fund yields in the form of the "Treasury bill" line. As you can see, money market funds deliver very calm results. But add in inflation and taxes, and the after-tax total return approaches zero. Clearly, money market funds play an essential role in your portfolio. But you need more ownership to have your portfolio grow over time. To get a somewhat higher long-term return, you will need to take more risk.

Section 6.3: Bond Mutual Funds

Lesson #26: Bonds are longer-term IOU's than the very short-term notes which make up money market funds. They pay income, and their market values in secondary markets change when interest rates change. But they don't grow. Their risk levels vary tremendously depending upon the kind of bond. Bond mutual

funds can vary tremendously in terms of potential risks and returns.

Bonds are longer-term IOU's. Let's say the government, or a corporation, wants to borrow money from you. They tell you in a written offer, "You loan me $10,000 and I will pay it all back to you in 5 years, exactly. In the meantime I will pay you 5% a year, divided into two payments, one every six months."

So you loan them the money.

And every six months you get $250. That doesn't change. It comes in like clockwork, unless the corporation can't make the payment, in which case the company is said to **default** on its debt.

But let's assume that the corporation keeps making the payments. And at the end of 5 years, exactly, you get a final check for $250 and another check for $10,000.

This is called "**getting your principal back.**" It is a good thing.

But let's say you get tired of the bond before it matures. You want to buy a condo near Mount St. Helens instead. So you sell your bond on the secondary market.

A "secondary market" simply means you sell your bond through a brokerage.

The price of that bond will have accrued interest built in. When you sell the bond, you will get the purchase price plus pro-rated interest for the time since the last payment when you have owned the bond.

But interest rates don't stay fixed, do they? Interest rates are always changing due to market demand, bond supply, and the actions of central banks.

If your bond pays 5%, and, when the bond has 2 years left to maturity, the current interest rate is 10%, your bond will **decline** in value on the secondary market! After all, it is now possible to buy a shiny new bond which will deliver a 10% yield. So to be priced attractively, the bond must come down in price until the coupon of the bond…. that twice a year $250 or $500 total…is at an expected rate of about 10%.

Existing bonds go down when interest rates go up. The longer their maturities, the more they go down!

Thus longer-term bonds are exposed to interest rate risk more than short-term bonds! In fact, the magic point in history seems to be about the ten year maturity. After that, there's not much value in investing longer term.

Of course, the opposite is also true.

Bonds go UP when interest rates go DOWN. And the big money in capital gains…the value of the bond itself, rather than the interest…is made on the longer end, when that happens.

As you can see, interest rate risk is an occupational hazard in the bond market. *You can reduce interest rate risk by selecting short-term bond mutual funds instead of longer term choices.* (Fig. 6-2)

Having said all that, it's important to keep in mind that for most high-quality bonds, the interest rate risk is less than the overall risks to the stock markets.

The graph Figure 6-3 measures the returns to ownership in the form of stock mutual funds, and debt in the form of bond mutual funds and money market funds. Treasury bills are simply very short-term debt issued by the US Treasury. As such they have only interest rate risk. As you can see, by themselves most bond mutual funds offer you less

Relationship Between Bond Prices and Yields
When yields increase, bond prices decrease

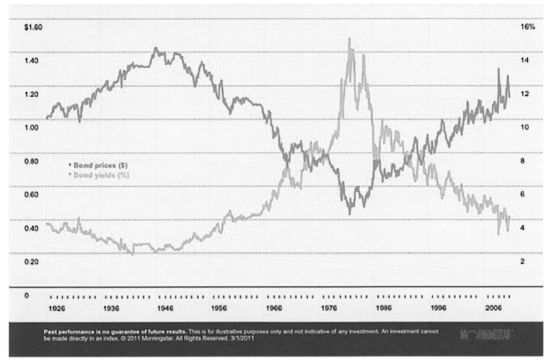

Fig. 6-2

risk and less return than holdings in the stock market.

But here's where things get interesting. As you can see in the following graph, bond mutual funds can add a lot when combined with stock mutual funds. They can diversify your portfolio so that you aren't betting your nest egg in one market. They provide more income. The result of adding a dab of bond mutual funds to your portfolio can be downright synergistic. (Fig. 6-4)

Although most of us invest for the long run, the reality is that the longest term most of us can think is in 12 month holding periods. As you can see in this graph, the best return for a 12 month holding period was a fantastic 162.9%. Wow, that would make you feel rich, wouldn't it? But the worst 12 month holding period was also in a portfolio holding 100% stocks: -67.6%. That would be so painful that many investors would make the worst possible choice: they would abandon their long term investing plans and sell out at the bottom, and lock in a horrendous loss.

In other words, to invest in a portfolio of 100% stock is to invite abuse. You CAN see a market crash coming, in a rather opaque way, but market catastrophes take years to shape up, and we usually aren't that patient. So timing…buying and selling in and out of the stock market…doesn't work. You shouldn't rely on portfolio changes to save your bacon.

In contrast, a 50%/50% mix of stocks and bonds provided investors with a maximum gain of 77.8% and a maximum loss of -40.7%. That was much more tolerable. And more importantly, an investor had choices when markets fell.

As we will discuss later, having bonds when the stock markets fall gives you the

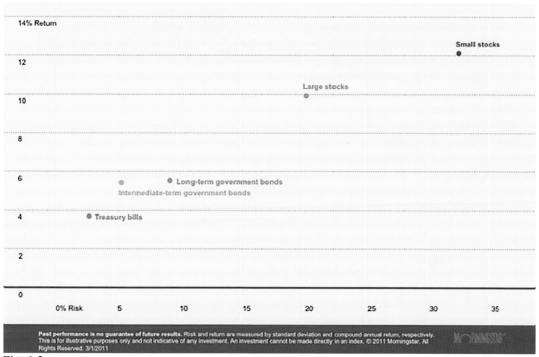

Risk Versus Return
Stocks, bonds, and bills 1926–2010

Fig. 6-3

Here's another way to look at it, expressed in a commonly used graphic technique. Risk is on the bottom. The farther right on the page you go, the higher the risk. Return is along the left side. The higher you go, the higher the return. So a wonderful investment is in the upper left quadrant: the farther left and up you go, the better. Mostly this is undoable. The worst investment is lower right: more right is higher risk, and lower is less return.

ability to buy stock market bargains, rather than simply endure. Holding some of your money in bonds also gives you the emotional stability to stay on your long term plan.

Diversification pays.

Another value of bonds is that they tend to produce income when the economy is relatively flat. Setting aside stock market gains, income can be a genuine game-changer when overall market returns are single-digit. Bonds may thrive when the stock market is lackluster. (Fig. 6-5)

Putting all this together, bond mutual funds are a genuine core holding for your portfolio, even though generally they don't make as much in the long term as stock market mutual funds. In future chapters we'll discuss using these very important bond mutual funds to change the game a bit: we'll discuss TAKING ADVANTAGE of stock market declines to buy stock market mutual funds, using the money you've sheltered in your bond funds.

As you can see in the following graph, you can construct a portfolio with roughly equivalent returns with less overall risk. By smoothing out stock market volatility, bond mutual funds add a lot more value than their returns alone would suggest. (Fig. 6-6)

Let's take a look at what bond funds should be on your mutual fund menu. In the process, we want to take a look at the bond market in general, to understand why we choose what we choose.

Portfolio Summary Statistics
Rolling periods 1926–2010

		12-month holding period			60-month			120-month		
	Average return	Highest return	Lowest return	Negative periods	Highest return	Lowest return	Negative periods	Highest return	Lowest return	Negative periods
100%	9.9%	162.9%	–67.6%	26.7%	36.1%	–17.4%	13.1%	21.4%	–4.9%	5.9%
25% 75%	9.1%	118.7%	–55.7%	24.2%	29.0%	–11.5%	7.9%	17.7%	–1.3%	1.0%
50% 50%	8.1%	77.8%	–40.7%	19.5%	22.2%	–6.1%	5.0%	16.2%	1.5%	0.0%
75% 25%	6.8%	40.9%	–22.0%	11.7%	20.0%	–1.2%	0.3%	14.9%	3.3%	0.0%
100%	5.4%	32.7%	–5.6%	8.4%	19.5%	0.7%	0.0%	13.7%	1.2%	0.0%

• Stocks
• Bonds

Past performance is no guarantee of future results. This is for illustrative purposes only and not indicative of any investment. An investment cannot be made directly in an index. © 2011 Morningstar. All Rights Reserved. 3/1/2011

Fig. 6-4

The bond market is gigantic, bigger even than the stock market. It is populated by a Star War's cantina of traders and investors who sometimes perform so strangely that they resemble alien life forms. There are arbitragers and scalpers, who make mere cents on bond trades but do such massive quantities that they might make themselves rich. There are insurance companies and other fixed-income investors simply intending to buy and hold.

However, that's not what we do, is it? We might effectively subdivide the bond markets into several asset sub-classes which may add diversification to your portfolio. The rest we'll simply ignore.

Lesson #27: Treasury bond mutual funds can be a key component of your portfolio. They have very low default risk. They DO have interest rate risk, depending upon the maturity. Use them as a parachute, not to get rich.

Short-term Treasury mutual funds buy bills and notes with up to three year's maturity issued by the US Government. They are very safe since they are both short maturity and top credit quality. Invest in these funds for safety. They generally don't deliver big returns. If you are using these funds correctly, you are investing to add safety and diversification.

You can see here one of the biggest reasons to hold short-term Treasury mutual funds. This is what happened in 2008-2009. Even corporate bonds got hurt in the Financial Panic of 2008. As you know, returns to short-term Treasury funds are, in the

Bonds Produced Greater Income
Percentage of total return 1970–2010

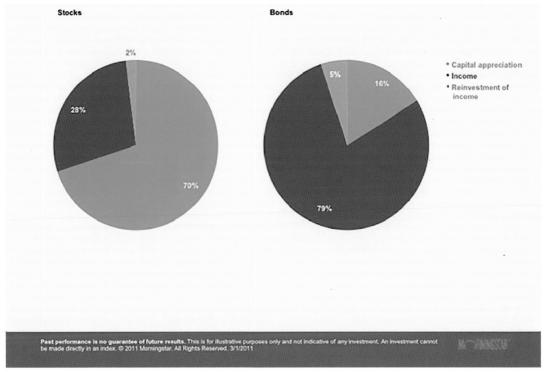

Fig. 6-5

Adding a Bond Allocation to Diversify
1970–2010

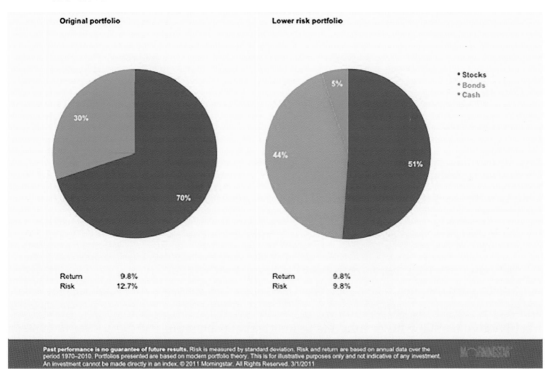

Fig. 6-6

long-term, paltry. But about every 10 years or less the stock markets decline and the money you have stashed in short-term Treasury mutual funds makes excellent seed corn to re-grow your wealth. (Fig. 6-7)

Mid and Long-term Treasury mutual funds buy the same US government bonds, but with longer maturities. These are decent buys for a small portion of your money when interest rates are higher, over 5%, since these mutual funds will soar from capital gains when interest rates decline.

If you are investing for a very long-term, and you are buying monthly ("dollar cost averaging"), buying this type of fund when interest rates are rising with a little of your

Investment Growth

Item(s) from 1-1-2008 to 12-31-2009

	Cumulative Return %	Annualized Return %	Max Front Load %	Max Back Load %	Gross Exp Ratio %	Amount at End of Period $
■ Vanguard 500 Index Investor	-20.34	-10.75	NA	NA	0.17	7965.97
■ Vanguard Short-Term Investment-Grade Inv	8.62	4.22	NA	NA	0.22	10861.71

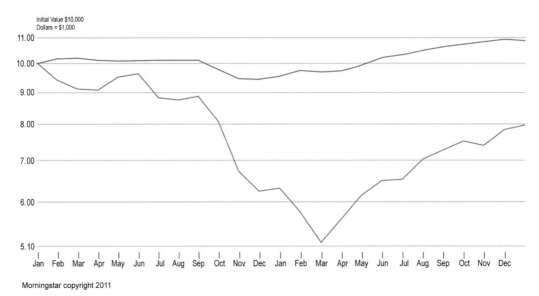

Initial Value $10,000
Dollars = $1,000

Morningstar copyright 2011

Fig. 6-7

money is a good strategy. You'll reap a harvest when rates go down again.

Lesson #28: Corporate bond mutual funds invest in the debt of private corporations. They can have low or high risk depending upon default risk and interest rate risk. They also usually pay a bit more interest than Treasuries.

Investment grade corporate bond mutual funds hold IOU's issued by agencies or private corporations. They face the same interest rate risks as Treasuries. In other words, the longer the term of the bond, the higher interest rate risk and the greater the likelihood of capital gain or loss due to interest rates changing.

Corporate bonds also face another source of risk: credit quality. Credit quality measures the risk of default. As I mentioned above, that is the likelihood that the corporation won't be able to pay you back interest, or worse yet, your principal upon maturity. Rating agencies like Moody's and Standard and Poor's make millions of dollars each year rating the probability of a given bond defaulting, and they assign grades. AAA is the best, and it goes down from there.

The challenge for us all is that once again, these ratings change. And you guessed it, they often change after the bad news and the price decline is on the table. It's a classic case of shutting the barn door after the horse has escaped. If you own an individual bond, this kind of sudden change can be a disaster since you can't react in time. If you own a corporate bond mutual fund, you may see the fund decline a bit, but you won't lose your money.

In 2008 we witnessed one allegedly "safe" corporate bond fund, with no history of investment mistakes and great risk statistics, plummet 30% in a few days. The reason was that the managers were deeply invested in bank bonds, and the financial crisis exposed that the banks were financially hollow shells. The managers had allowed their faith in these bonds to draw them into an un-diversified portfolio. Since the average return to "investment grade" bond funds is fairly mediocre, it will probably take years for investors to recover their losses. Investors who held more than one fund, and better yet as many as five bond funds, lost much less and recovered much faster. Lesson: if you are investing in an "investment grade" corporate bond fund, diversify by holding several different funds.

One investment grade bond mutual fund to add to your holdings should be the Vanguard Total Bond Index fund. You want to own a small amount of this to capture the full movement of the bond market, and to enable you to track the performance of the larger bond market within your own portfolio.

Lesson #29: Municipal bond mutual funds offer you a chance to buy bonds issued by states, counties, and other municipalities. As a result, these are usually federally tax-exempt. These have a spectrum of risks and rewards depending upon the issuers, average credit quality, and average maturity. These should never be held in a retirement plan because the tax benefits are thereby wasted.

A truly tax-exempt investment is a very rare entity. You can invest in a Roth IRA, but your contributions are limited. Other retirement plans offer a tax-deduction for the contribution and tax-deferred growth, but then you pay ordinary income rates when you take the money out. Other schemes spring up annually like weeds. Usually these are scams or else quickly disallowed by the IRS.

Muni bonds are an unusual chance to minimize taxes.

Think this through. Assuming that we live in a reasonably efficient world, how will these bonds be priced? Answer: these bonds are usually priced to produce a yield which almost exactly equals the taxable rate of a bond with approximately the same risks, less the highest tax bracket.

Whenever that relationship is strained, and municipal bond funds are genuinely yielding more or less after tax than bonds of equivalent risk, there's a reason. Usually you will discover a simmering political issue having to do with state's possibility of default (almost always overstated) or possible changes to the tax code. Otherwise, Wall Street arbitragers rush in and return the relationship back to its normal stasis.

In other words, municipal bond funds aren't usually a bargain. Everybody in the highest tax bracket wants them.

However, there are times when muni's make a lot of sense. If you are in a very high tax bracket, and you need a bond investment in a taxable account, investing in several investment-grade short-term municipal bond funds makes a lot of sense. Diversification is still key: there are millions of government entities out there, and they default as often as anyone else. Obviously, "high yield" muni funds have higher risk, as do longer-term funds. Some municipal funds offer "insured" bonds, but as we saw in the past few years, when large defaults occur, the insurance companies can't handle the liability. So I don't trust any bond insurance.

Given the tax-exempt status of these bonds and their lower coupons, these belong only in tax exposed accounts. Their tax-exempt benefits are utterly wasted in retirement accounts.

You will probably also want state-specific funds. By holding a fund which contains the bonds of your state of residence, you will make your income from that fund state and federal tax free.

When selecting municipal bond funds, be particularly aware of average maturity. That statistic is usually readily available. Since these bonds usually pay such low coupons, rising interest rates can damage them deeply. Shorter average maturities are better.

When interest rates were surging in the early 1980's, we called long-term municipal bonds "trust busters" because their capital losses were staggering. Likewise, as interest rates were declining, these funds often produced taxable capital gains, to the consternation of many smug shareholders. **To avoid this turbulence, short-term investment grade single state municipal bond funds are safest.**

Lesson #30: There are many different types of bond mutual funds. Some bond mutual funds you don't need.

For simplicity's sake, and simply because many bond mutual fund categories aren't necessary, keep the majority of your bond picks conservative, high quality, and short-term.

High-yield corporate bond mutual funds tend to pay very high yields but are deeply exposed to default risk.

Remember the toadfish? It is one ugly cuss, the pug-ugly of the fish world. It looks like a pop-eyed obese hippie after an eight day drunk. And it tastes GREAT!

Fish marketers had a challenge after some courageous soul finally sampled this fish: how do you market a fish that looks this ugly? Answer: a new name. Now it is "white Chilean sea bass" or something like that and it sells wonderfully.

Essentially marketers of corporate junk bonds are in the same boat. A "junk bond" is an IOU from someone who probably won't be able to pay back the money. So the bond's rating is bad.

Question: Who would buy a toadfish like that?

Answer: People who buy these funds aren't paying attention and are simply seeking yield. Clever marketers have renamed these putrid gems "high yield bonds" so that people will focus on the higher coupons instead of the high risk.

As my father used to say, you can't polish horse manure.

Make no mistake: these funds can be as risky as any equity fund. As a result, I recommend you own "high yield bonds" (Oh, the STENCH!) only via more nimble asset allocation funds.

International bond funds are investors in the bonds of corporations or governments outside the US.

Periodically the dollar declines against other currencies and these funds garner giant capital gains, become rock stars, and attract vast inflows of investor's dollars. A little holding in these might be acceptable to diversify against currency upheaval.

I assume that most investors are especially clueless about foreign debt. We can't even predict our own interest rates! Therefore I suggest that you choose to invest in these through international "world allocation" funds.

World allocation mutual funds search the planet to invest in stocks, bonds, and anything else which seems appropriate. By choosing these funds for your international bond allocation you provide the manager an assortment of escape hatches to exit international bonds should the markets reverse. You have also removed your own potentially irrational role as asset allocator from this especially unpredictable asset class.

Convertible bonds are another asset class which is best held in asset allocation funds. These unusual bonds sometimes morph into stocks under the right conditions. Usually a company issues these bonds because it can't qualify for investment grade IOU's. In other words, these bonds are often "iffy" credit risks.

Since credit quality and specific risk play a large role in these, I invest via domestic asset allocators, which are sometimes known as "hybrid funds" or "balanced funds". I will write about them in an upcoming chapter. Given their unique charters, these funds sometimes go into smaller venues where most others lack the specific expertise. Convertible bonds are in a methane-breathing world of their own. A little goes a long way.

Most other unique bond mutual funds simply aren't worth the effort. Whenever you see a bond fund which offers "income plus" or any complicated strategies, watch out. Usually that kind of investment philosophy results in uneven gains and unpredictable risk. Bonds keep you rich. If you want more risk and more potential returns, look to stocks. (Fig. 6-8)

Review: The Lessons of Chapter 6

Lesson #24: Money market funds and bond mutual funds keep you rich by not crashing when financial markets become volatile. They seldom make you rich, because they don't grow. These mutual funds are VERY valuable, because they diversify you against unforeseen catastrophe.

Bond Market Performance
1926–2010

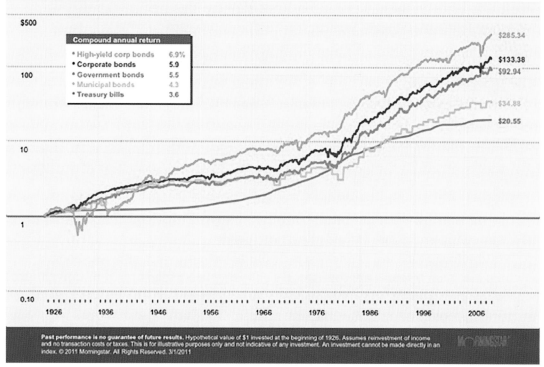

Fig. 6-8

Choosing a spectrum of bond types in the past provided a rainbow of risk/return profiles, as well as genuine diversification. Corporate bonds provided marginally more returns than government bonds. Municipal bonds produced returns which were largely tax free, and thus lower in absolute terms. And, as we've discussed, Treasury bills were very safe but their minimal returns barely beat inflation.

Lesson #25: A money market fund is a relatively very low-risk mutual fund which invests in very short-term debt instruments. These funds are usually very safe. They also usually produce lower returns, especially after taxes and inflation.

Lesson #26: Bonds are longer-term IOU's than the very short-term notes which make up money market funds. They pay income and their market values change when interest rates change. But they don't grow. Their risk levels vary tremendously depending upon the kind of bond. Bond mutual funds can vary tremendously in terms of potential risks and returns.

Lesson #27: Treasury bond mutual funds can be a key component of your portfolio. They have very low default risk. They DO have interest rate risk, depending upon the maturity. Use them as a parachute, not to get rich.

Lesson #28: Corporate bond mutual funds invest in the debt of private corporations. They can have low or high risk depending upon default risk and interest rate risk. But they also usually pay a bit more interest than Treasuries.

Lesson #29: Municipal bond mutual funds offer you a chance to buy bonds issued by states, counties, and other municipalities. As a result, these are usually tax-exempt. These have a spectrum of risks and rewards depending upon the issuers, average credit quality, and average maturity. These should never be held in a retirement plan because the tax benefits are thereby wasted.

Lesson #30: There are many different types of bond mutual funds. Some bond mutual funds you don't usually need. These include junk-bond funds, international bond funds, convertible bond funds, and mutual funds with gimmicks to increase income.

Diversified Asset Allocation Mutual Funds

I've found that when the market's going down and you buy funds wisely,
at some point in the future you will be happy. You won't get there
by reading 'Now is the time to buy.'
— Peter Lynch

Lesson #31: Asset allocation mutual funds provide a unique venue to minimize risk, maximize returns, and reduce subjective decision-making.

In the last chapter, I mentioned several kinds of bonds which you don't want to own in separate mutual funds. These bonds are simply too arcane or complex to warrant an entire mutual fund of their own and their markets can be hot or cold.

We want to let genuine specialists invest in these for us. Also we want to provide escape hatches for managers to completely shun any small sector of the bond market if that makes sense at any given time.

Asset allocation mutual funds provide you with access to these bond types, since the managers are able to combine both stocks and bonds to seek maximum gains. Asset allocation funds are also called "hybrid" mutual funds, or "balanced" mutual funds. Managers of these funds are able to access both bond and stock markets.

The best of these funds sometimes occupy the slender no-man's land of bond-like stocks or stock-like bonds. Good asset allocation fund managers construct portfolios which are something approximately like the minimum risk portfolio on this next graph, which you saw earlier in Chapter 5. (Stocks and Bonds: Risk Versus Return) Asset allocation mutual funds choose allocations of investments which are not 100% stock. They work surprisingly well. (Fig. 7-1)

For example, here's the long-term performance of Vanguard Wellesley Income fund, with a 60% bond/40% stock mix. Note that the results somewhat lag the performance of the S&P 500 Index of large corporate stocks, realistically represented by the Vanguard S&P 500 Index fund. But here's the important lesson: asset allocation funds like Vanguard Wellesley Income fund blow the doors off any comparative bond-only mutual fund. A little equity position goes a very long way, without a lot of risk.

I've left this graph intentionally dated, with an ending date of 2/28/2010. You will note that in bear market conditions, asset allocation funds often outperform stock-based mutual funds. When the equity markets are humming, asset allocation funds often get left behind. But it's surprising how often the performances of these mixed marvels actually equal or exceed the performances of most equity funds. (Fig. 7-2)

Choosing asset allocation funds provides you with an opportunity to minimize decisions. As you have read earlier in this book, we want to reduce the number of potentially irrational decisions we make in our portfolio. Selecting an asset allocation fund in lieu of bonds provides a layer of diversification to the portfolio of a relatively aggressive investor. Selecting such a fund also provides a lower risk investor with a

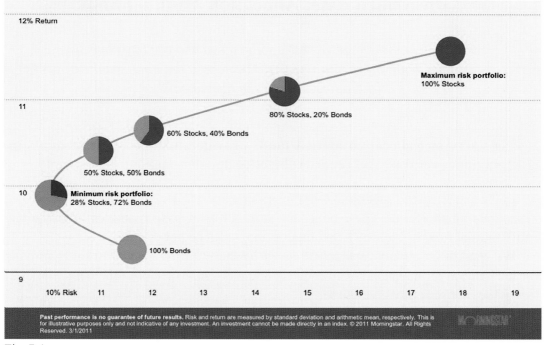

Stocks and Bonds: Risk Versus Return
1970–2010

Fig. 7-1

dab of equities without exposing the portfolio to undo risk. Indeed, for many investors, asset allocation funds occupy a veritable "sweet spot" in the risk-reward continuum.

So how do we select "good" asset allocation funds?

Lesson #32: Use *Morningstar* data pages to select your mutual funds.

Here's a normal *Morningstar* page for an asset allocation fund. This is NOT A RECOMMENDATION FOR THIS FUND! You can use these selection guidelines for any mutual fund you care to study. So this is practice not only for selecting an asset allocation fund, but also for selecting a bond fund, a stock fund, etc. (Fig. 7-3)

You can see the *Morningstar* Category in the upper right of the page, in detail #1, which indicates that this is a "moderate allocation" fund. There are also "conservative allocation" funds, as well as a "global allocation' category.

You can see several indicators of excellence for this fund. First, in detail #2, you can see the five stars. That's great, but it's also a look-back indicator and not necessarily indicative of the best fund for the next five years. Still, any fund with less than three stars, even in the worst possible environment, is probably too inflexible for you. You need a mutual fund with a management who knows when to get out of the way.

Also, in detail #2 you can also see the "historical box" profile in the center top of the page. "High Return" and "Average" risk is a great indicator.

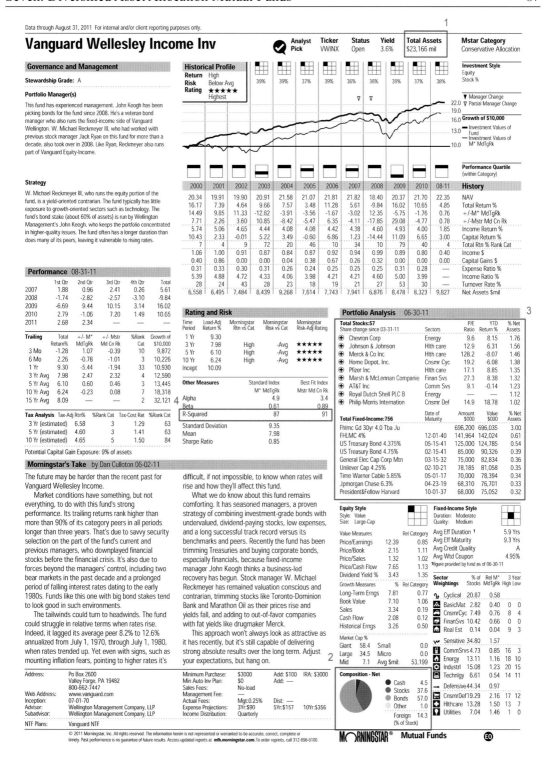

Fig. 7-2

(Inclusion in this book does not constitute an endorsement of Vanguard Wellesley Income fund. There may be other asset allocation funds which are equally successful.)

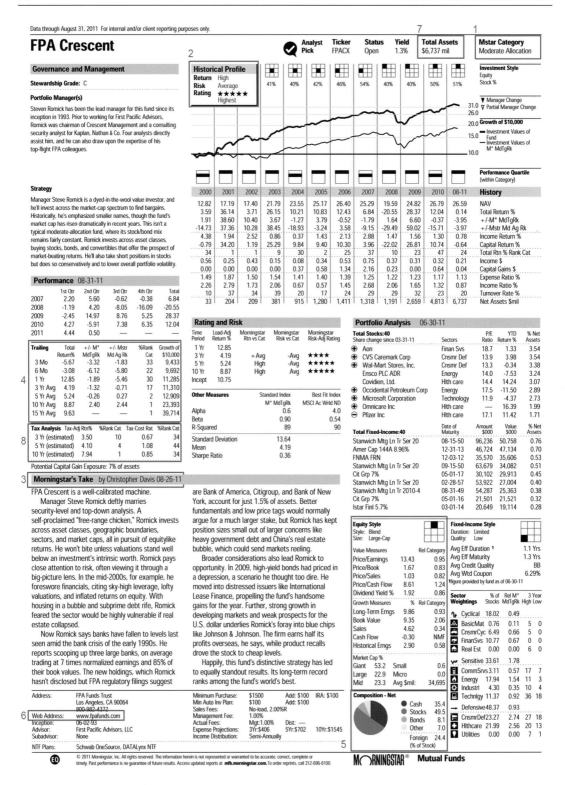

Fig. 7-3

(Inclusion in this book does not constitute an endorsement of Vanguard Wellesley Income fund. There may be other asset allocation funds which are equally successful.)

The "Morningstar's Take" section in Detail #3 provides a written analysis which lets you know what is happening with the management. Check the date of this analysis: mutual funds change portfolios, so the date of this study becomes important. The older the data, the less valid it becomes. Still, mutual funds tend to follow a behavioral pattern in general, so even a dated *Morningstar* page is better than nothing.

You can see trailing returns on the left side of the page, above the analysis, in detail #4. These tell you how the fund has behaved over the long-term relative to its peers. I like to look at these with an eye for consistency. How did it perform when markets were hard? Is its rating due to former glory days which seem to be passing? This can be especially important when the mutual fund is growing rapidly. The fund managers may be quite adept at managing a small mutual fund, yet they may be unable to corral a multi-billion dollar investment pool.

To the right of the analysis, in detail #5 is a small checkerboard-chart with data underneath. Below that is big information: you can see in the pie chart that this fund has (when this review was written) a bit more than 35% in cash, 49% in stocks, and 8% in bonds. You can also see that about 24% of the stocks are foreign. There's your sweet spot. This fund is clearly successful in venues which are too arcane for many investors.

In detail #6, you can see a website address which provides a direct link to the fund. This is important. Visit the site and look around. What you see should make sense to you, and it should be clearly presented. The fund's investment techniques should avoid any whiff of mystery or unnecessary complexity. You don't want to have all your fund managers agree with you, because you, like the rest of us, will often be wrong. If the manager can create value consistently over time, that's more important than what she thinks about today's stock markets.

High up on the page, on the right side, you can see detail #7. That's the amount of money in the mutual fund at the time of the report, and it's important: in general, smaller funds are more nimble and tend to provide more independence relative to the financial indices. They may or may not outperform larger brethren, but they tend to exhibit lower correlation. As you will read later, that's important. Of course, size is relative. In some market sectors, such as in S&P 500 index funds, size is irrelevant. In others, such as small stocks, size is more important. For you, in general, smaller is better.

Lesson #33: Use data from your discount brokerage to confirm your mutual fund selections and to ensure you can purchase them at your discount brokerage.

Whether or not you begin your mutual fund search at Morningstar or at your discount brokerage, you should view both portals of information to select mutual funds. And both these venues should provide you with approximately the same information about any fund you study. The reason data about any one fund is likely to be approximate is that different information-gatherers are likely to choose different dates to collect the data. That means that the numbers which you see in different information portals should differ slightly. But big differences in what you are reading about any one fund should signal that further study is needed.

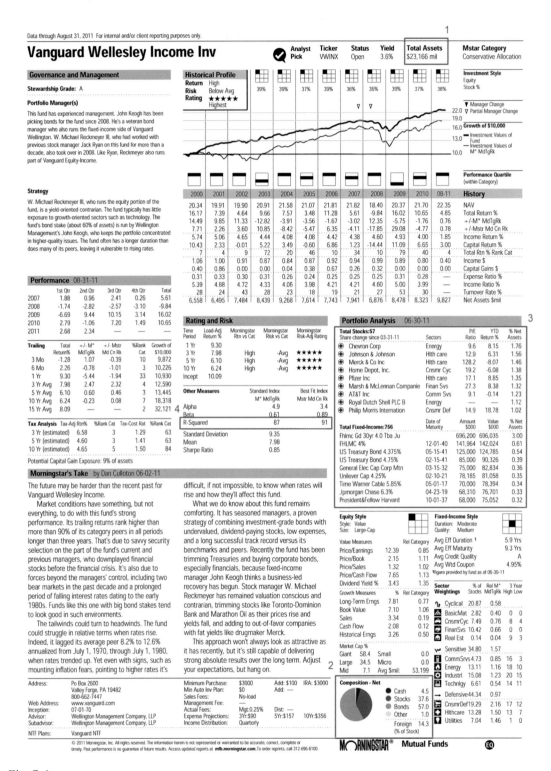

Fig. 7-4

(Inclusion in this book does not constitute an endorsement of Vanguard Wellesley Income fund. There may be other asset allocation funds which are equally successful.)

From the very beginning, something should leap out at you. Obviously the funds you seek should outperform their category. You don't want average, do you? With your asset allocation funds you are seeking "all weather" funds. That means you shouldn't see numbers for 2008 which indicate the fund managers were willing to take big losses. Big losses belong in more risky mutual fund categories, if at all. Select asset allocation funds which have better 2008 performances than the S&P 500 in 2008.

Next, check to see if this fund is available at your discount brokerage. There's no sense researching this fund if you can't buy it.

Lesson #34: Seek out asset allocation funds which add synergy and diversification. Look for something different.

I find that the best buys in the "asset allocation" category have a distinctive, uncorrelated style. Mutual funds which simply hold a percentage of blue chip stocks and a matching percentage of investment grade corporate bonds don't add as much diversification and value. So search for the unusual with a proven track record of success. As an example of the "plain vanilla" asset allocation fund, here's Vanguard Wellesley's page. (Fig. 7-4)

When I use the term "plain vanilla" or "vanilla grade" I am referring to mutual funds which essentially mimic index funds for one reason or another. Within the limitations of diversification, these funds are quite valuable, because they give you access to the mainstream markets. As you can see in a comparison of Vanguard Wellesley vs. FPA Crescent, when you invest in VWINX you are investing in a very large fund in terms of assets under management (detail #1). The net composition (detail #2) shows you that you are investing in a fund with 37.6% in stocks and 57.0% in bonds. The portfolio analysis (detail #3) shows you that the holdings are all very large and mainstream, and the R-squared (detail #4) of 87 says to you that this fund is relatively highly correlated with the larger financial markets.

Does that make this fund less valuable in any way? Not at all. This kind of fund has a definite place in your holdings. For an investor who wants more zip than what you can get from plain bond funds, any of these asset allocation funds serve as "bond funds on steroids" to add a dollop of growth to what would otherwise be a simple income investment. Vanguard Wellesley and others of its ilk do this very well, as you can see.

As with all mutual funds, you want a selection of these funds from different fund families whenever possible. The reason for this is that you want to find managers with successful track records who generally disagree with each other. In larger fund families, which may contain hundreds of mutual funds, managers win their spurs in smaller funds, and then play musical chairs to the bigger, more famous holdings.

One management result of large fund families with rotating management teams is "group think". The family's managers tend to talk between themselves and hold a similar outlook on investing. In many cases similar funds within one fund family will actually hold many of the same stocks and bonds. The result, for you, is lack of diversification and a stifling of independence of management. You don't want that.

So when you invest in any mutual fund, including asset allocation mutual funds, select them from different management companies or fund families whenever possible. **The ability to do this is one major reason why I recommend investing via a discount brokerage.**

The best possible choice is a manager who is also an owner in the fund's management company. That way, your manager has some skin in the game. Studies indicate that fund managers who are eating the same dish they are cooking for you tend to pay attention, to your benefit.

If you look back to the *Morningstar* page for FPA Crescent, check out detail #6. You can find ownership information on the fund's website. See if the fund manager is an owner before you invest.

As I have written, in the world of mutual funds, a smaller investment pool is often better, at least in my experience. There are certainly efficiencies in size, but except for index mutual funds, as I will point out later, mutual fund pools of money can become so big that they become cumbersome.

Check out the mutual fund's portfolio size listed as detail #7 on the FPA Crescent page. Compare that to the same statistic for Vanguard Wellesley. As you can see on the *Morningstar* page, Vanguard Wellesley Income has a portfolio size at the time of this study of a bit more than $23 billion dollars. FPA Crescent has a portfolio size of about $6.7 billion.

It is much harder for an asset allocation fund to buy a meaningful position in a small issue of convertible bonds when the pool of money is $23 billion than when it is $1 billion. In asset allocation funds, as in all actively managed funds, smaller portfolios often behave very differently from large portfolios. In a perfect world, you own a bit of both.

The downside of selecting a smaller mutual fund is that smaller portfolios are often managed by beginning portfolio managers. The difficulty is that managers with limited experience tend to be one-trick ponies. They fit into the current market climate perfectly, and they become rock stars of finance. They make millions of dollars before they are 30 years old. Then the market paradigm changes for an unexpected reason, and these relative beginners are lost. Their funds sink into oblivion. These battered fund managers---veterans at age 35---either learn, and go on to become all-weather professionals or take their earnings and sneak off to drink mojitos in Miami for the rest of their days. That is, if they have any earnings left.

I have several asset allocation funds that I regard as long-term holdings. But all asset allocation funds can change from house cats to panthers as they change investments over time. So, in addition to your "vanilla grade" asset allocation funds, seek creative thinking and something genuinely different to provide diversification.

Lesson #35: Whenever possible, invest in asset allocation funds in a tax-deferred account, to ameliorate their tax inefficiency.

Data bit #8 on the *Morningstar* page for FPA Crescent fund is tax analysis. This information is located just above the analysis section on the left. As you can see, asset allocation funds are relatively tax <u>inefficient.</u> That is, you may pay a relatively large amount of taxes annually on your gains since so much of those gains are distributions from bonds.

As you can see, the 10 year performance number of 8.87% for FPA Crescent becomes 7.94% after taxes, a 10% haircut from the untaxed gains. Vanguard Wellesley sees a 10 year performance of 6.24% reduced to 4.65%, a loss of 25% of pre-tax gains. Clearly Vanguard Wellesley relies on fully-taxed bond income for a great deal of its results.

If you were choosing to own both these investments, you might find it more efficient to keep either both or at least Vanguard Wellesley in a tax deferred account such as a 401(k) or an IRA. By doing this you will minimize your taxes and maximize the long-term benefits of these very useful funds.

Lesson #36: International or world allocation funds add a great deal to your portfolio as well.

As Cat Stevens once sang, "Oh baby, it's a wild world. It's hard to get by just upon a smile." International investing is fraught with unexpected hazards. World asset allocation funds can help reduce your exposure to these. They are especially useful to enter markets which can be hazardous in an all-equity format.

Here's a Morningstar page of First Eagle Overseas fund, which is available without load at many discount brokerages. As you can see in detail #1, Regional Exposure and Country Exposure, this fund invests world-wide. (Fig. 7-5)

If you look at the center of the Morningstar page at detail #2, you will see the standard deviation statistic. That's a measurement of raw risk: bigger is riskier. You'll see these for all mutual funds.

The standard deviation statistic of First Eagle Overseas fund (SGOVX) is 15.65. The standard deviation for the Vanguard Index 500 fund (VFINX), aka the US stock market, is 21.50. During the last 15 years, the Vanguard Index 500 fund produced an average total return of 6.05%. First Eagle Overseas produced an average return of 11.90%. $10,000 invested in First Eagle Overseas became $54,007 during those 15 years, compared to the $24,136 result from $10,000 invested in the Vanguard Index 500 fund.

I AM NOT ADVISING YOU TO OWN SGOVX AND AVOID VFINX! Market performances over the next 15 years are likely to differ substantially from what we experienced in the past 15 years.

What I <u>AM</u> saying is that diversifying via asset allocation funds, including world allocation funds, can sometimes produce both lower risk and higher returns, and thus is a worthy strategy.

So, when you find yourself contemplating an investment in a highly volatile segment of the investment world, ALWAYS look for a less-risky alternative. Be sure to look for the asset allocation diamond hidden among the rocks. Discovering such a fund can add lots of diversification and value to your investment portfolio.

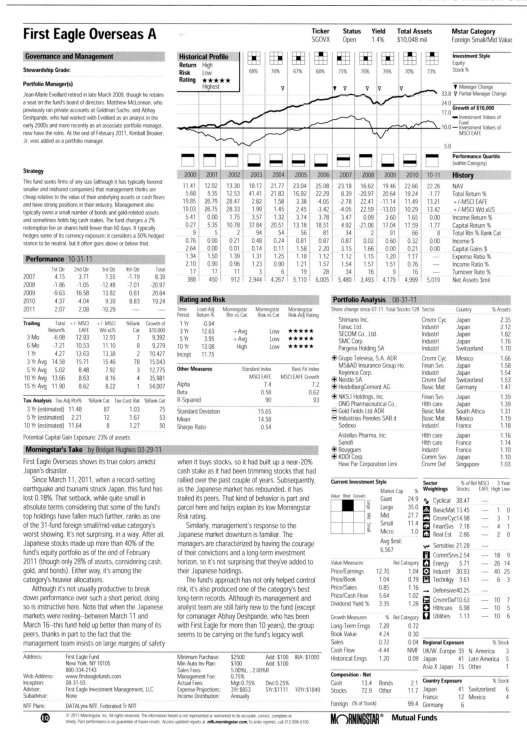

Fig. 7-5

(Inclusion in this book does not constitute an endorsement of Vanguard Wellesley Income fund. There may be other asset allocation funds which are equally successful.)

- In general, asset allocation funds have a use for almost every investor.
- Low-risk investors find that conservative asset allocation funds provide a relatively low risk portal to stock markets.
- Moderately risky investors find that asset allocation funds provide an energetic bond alternative to diversify without giving up a great deal of potential returns.
- Market risk investors who can tolerate a lot of volatility find that asset allocation funds provide relatively controllable risk when compared to alternatives in high-risk venues.
- International asset allocation funds allow you additional diversification and they allow you a superb relatively low-risk entry into a high-risk market.

Review: The Lessons of Chapter 7

Lesson #31: Asset allocation mutual funds provide a unique venue to minimize risk, maximize returns, and reduce subjective decision-making.

Lesson #32 Use *Morningstar* data pages to select your mutual funds.

Lesson #33: Use data from your discount brokerage to confirm your mutual fund selections and to ensure you can purchase them at your discount brokerage.

Lesson #34: Seek out asset allocation funds which add synergy and diversification. Look for something different.

Lesson #35: Whenever possible, invest in asset allocation funds in a tax-deferred account, to ameliorate their tax inefficiency.

Lesson #36: International or world allocation funds may add a great deal to your portfolio.

Chapter 8

Stock Market Focused Mutual Funds

I am not against (bull fighting). Every nation has their own affairs and
own sports. Some nations like to see blood, and some like to see
their victims suffer from speculation. It's all in your point of view.
They kill the bull very quick. Wall Street lets you live and suffer.
—*Will Rogers, Nov. 1, 1931*

Section 8.1: Stocks and Risk

Lesson #37: Stocks represent ownership in corporations. A bond is an IOU, a glorified loan. A stock is a piece of the action, a slice of the pie, a percentage of the profits or losses. Stocks, also called "equities", are OWNERSHIP. Stock mutual funds are a key part of your portfolio.

Let's start this section off with a bang: why do you want mutual funds containing stocks in your portfolio? Because stocks in general, in their most highly diversified forms, outperform almost all other asset classes. They can be very risky, but as you can see on the following graph, they are usually also very rewarding to long-term investors.

Stocks give your portfolio the liquidity to avoid ugly markets and the oomph to outperform inflation. Unless you are very risk phobic, they are must-haves in your portfolio, to some degree. (Fig. 8-1)

So what kind of risk are we talking about when we discuss stock market risk? Remember, the REAL risk is that you will lose money. Here's a graph of the last ten years. Mostly, this has been a decade of pain. If you include the year 2000, the recent past years have certainly the worst in the modern era, perhaps the worst in at least a century. A simple ten year look-back includes both 9/11 and the 2008 financial panic. Both of these miseries were very unpleasant and reduced thousands of undiversified investors to at least temporary poverty. (Fig. 8-2)

But the graph shows us that as ugly as these ten years have been, stocks did not utterly collapse. In fact, small stocks outperformed bonds. Small stocks were genuinely a good investment. So if you are a very long-term investor, the real risk to your portfolio is that you aren't really diversified enough. After all these years of underperformance by large cap stocks, there is a real chance that your portfolio doesn't contain ENOUGH stock mutual funds. Of course we don't really know what will happen, but history tells us that stocks are unlikely to be permanently obliterated. In fact, in the long-term, stocks are likely to thrive because they represent ownership.

Why are stocks so risky, and why can they also gain so much? Unlike bonds, stocks are designed to go up and down in value. As a result, stocks have an intrinsic risk that investment grade bonds theoretically don't have: they can individually vanish. Of course, we know that in the real world, bonds can vanish too. But in the real world, individual stocks exist on a very wide spectrum of risk, from the vanilla pudding level

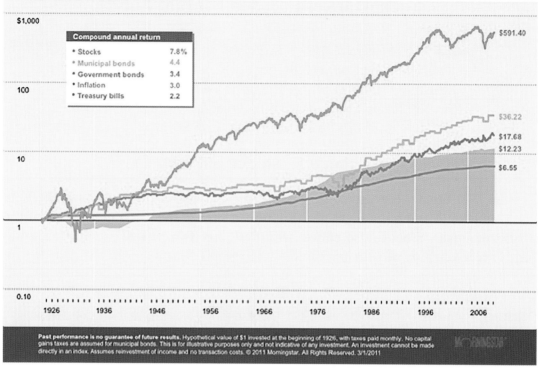

Ibbotson® SBBI® After Taxes
1926–2010

Compound annual return	
• Stocks	7.8%
• Municipal bonds	4.4
• Government bonds	3.4
• Inflation	3.0
• Treasury bills	2.2

$591.40
$36.22
$17.68
$12.23
$6.55

Fig. 8-1

to the running-down-the-street-with-your-hair-on-fire kind of risk. Managing this risk is an important part of your investment management.

Section 8.2: Index Mutual Funds

Lesson #38 Index mutual funds are a famous money management choice. They DO have a role to play in your portfolio, but not as much as you may think. Performance is episodic: sometimes better and sometimes worse than alternatives. They tend to do better in up markets and less well in sideways or down markets.

In distant decades past, the "John Bogle" school of investing held that indexing was all you needed, ever. That concept has been disproven by the realities of financial history, but you still sometimes hear this myth in dive bars and other gathering places of people who prefer mythology.

Here's the secret about index mutual funds: while we often use an index to represent a given financial market, it is not the underlying market itself. For example, the Standard and Poor's 500 is an index of 500 of the largest companies in the US. But it isn't really an index of the biggest 500 corporations in the US. That task is performed by the Fortune 500 Index. Instead, the S&P 500 is a selection of 500 large companies which a committee of Standard and Poor's employees consider representative of the United

The Past 10 Years
2001–2010

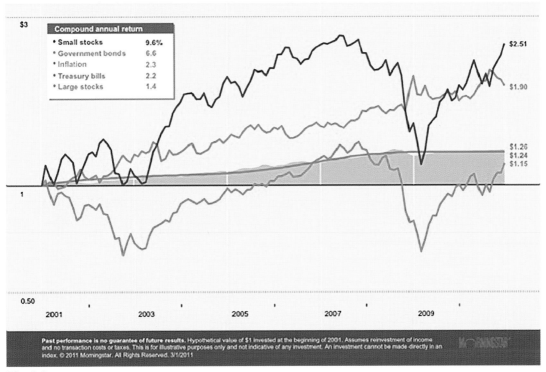

Fig. 8-2

States economy. Since the committee attempts to keep the index current, less timely stocks are often replaced by the stocks of companies now in vogue. For example, there were over 200 stock changes in the S&P 500 in the 1990's as the committee sought to make the index more representative of the Internet era.

To make the S&P 500 Index even more successful, it is market-cap weighted. This means that the larger the corporation's size, the larger percentage of the index it receives. Thus, while the index as a whole represents about 70% of the total stock market, the top ten stocks make up a bit more than 20% of the index. The largest stocks profoundly control the performance of the S&P 500.

As a result of these biases, the S&P 500 tends to follow trends rather aggressively. It tends to emphasize overvalued stocks and under-represent stocks that are temporarily unloved. When managers do this actively, it is called "momentum investing." Inside the S&P 500 Index, it is accomplished simply by adding to what is going up and by reducing in percentage terms what is in decline.

Why would anyone put together such an index? Because it paints a rosier picture of the financial markets than actually exists. When you can automatically flush out your losers and grow your winners, you've got a great mechanism for accenting the positive. Unweighted indices such as the Value Line Index reveal a stock market wherein average performance is much slimmer than indicated by the S&P 500. That's the real world where active mutual fund managers really live.

The S&P 500 may be a flawed index, but it makes a wonderful trend-following growth fund. Because of its ability to emphasize winners at low cost, an S&P 500 index fund makes an almost unbeatable selection when the broader stock market is booming irrationally. When the stock markets are stalled by uncertainty, value-oriented mutual funds tend to outperform. But when blind greed is running the game, the index funds will rule, until the bubble breaks.

It is fair to extend this rule to other artificially created indices. Since index mutual funds became popular in the '90's, many other indices have been created to enable "index investing" in most if not all market sectors. Most of these other indices are biased in the same way that the S&P 500 is biased. As a result, they suffer from the same inaccuracies.

For example, in 1989, the Morgan Stanley EAFE International Index was 68% invested in Japan since that country was in its tenth year of a gigantic stock market bubble. In 1998, after a devastating decline in the Japanese stock market, the index contained only 21% in Japan.

As is true of the S&P 500, these other indices offer very attractive investment opportunities when their underlying markets are roaring upwards. In sideways or undervalued markets, they usually get left in the dust.

However, not only is an S&P 500 index fund a reasonable diversification, but owning a position also gives you an ongoing indicator to the behavior of the larger stock markets. As a result, I advocate holding a small position--5%--in Vanguard Index 500 fund, symbol VFINX, or something identical. If your discount brokerage charges a transaction fee for this fund and your account size is small, you may benefit from finding another low-fee S&P 500 index fund.

Whatever you decide, one S&P 500 index fund is a must-have for your portfolio. That way you are always tied to the stock market, which in history tends to do well. In the process, your own irrational investment biases are removed from the table. But you don't want to own more than 5%, because that would reduce portfolio diversification.

Section 8.3: Pure Stock Mutual Funds

Now we enter the much-larger world of pure-stock mutual funds. These funds usually own nothing but stocks and thus are fully exposed to the market actions of one or more stock market venues.

Most data bases and information sources distribute stock market mutual funds on a grid. As you can see on the next page, one criterion is the size of the average stock held within the mutual fund: small, mid-cap, and large. The other criterion is the kind of management used by the managers: Value, Blend, here described as "core", and Growth.

Thus at any one time, a mutual fund might be classed as holding the stocks of large corporations using a "value" selection process. Or it might be classified as holding small stocks, based on a "growth' management methodology.

As you can see, mutual funds in different boxes on the grid tend to behave differently by themselves and in relation to each other from year to year. So you need to hold mutual funds which hold different-sized stocks, and which have managers with divergent views to obtain true diversification. (Fig. 8-3)

Here's an even more challenging aspect of categorizing mutual funds: mutual funds change both management styles and the average size of the corporations of which they own stock. This is called "drift". Unless you are dealing with an asset allocation fund which has a mandate to leap around, a tremendous change in the category of any one mutual fund is unlikely. But they DO drift, simply because their underlying holdings change. So "drift' is inevitable, and in fact even somewhat desirable in an active manager. (Fig. 8-4)

As you can see, you don't buy a fund based on its current portfolio. The portfolio will inevitably change. Instead, you invest, or "rent" the services of the mutual fund's management team, to obtain long-term returns.

You will meet people who invest in mutual funds due to the portfolio, and who track portfolio changes with religious intensity. Aside from the sense of enjoyment which these investors derive from such behavior, they are simply displaying irrational investing behavior. This kind of activity doesn't enhance investment returns. It's probably healthier to take up bicycling.

Also because we don't know the future, we don't know what the near-term stock markets will do. It is entirely possible that Growth Fund A may do great this year, and lag next year, while Growth Fund B lags this year and surges next year. What counts

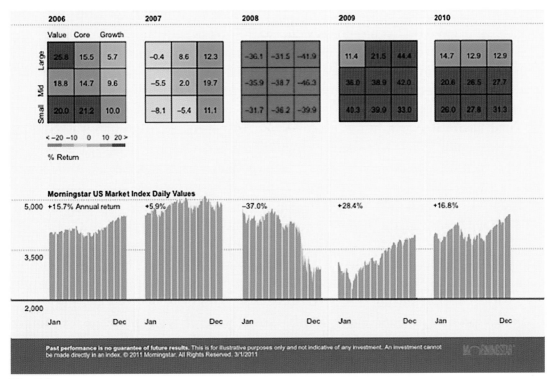

Fig. 8-3

Fund Style May Shift Over Time
Two types of style analysis for one fund 2001–2010

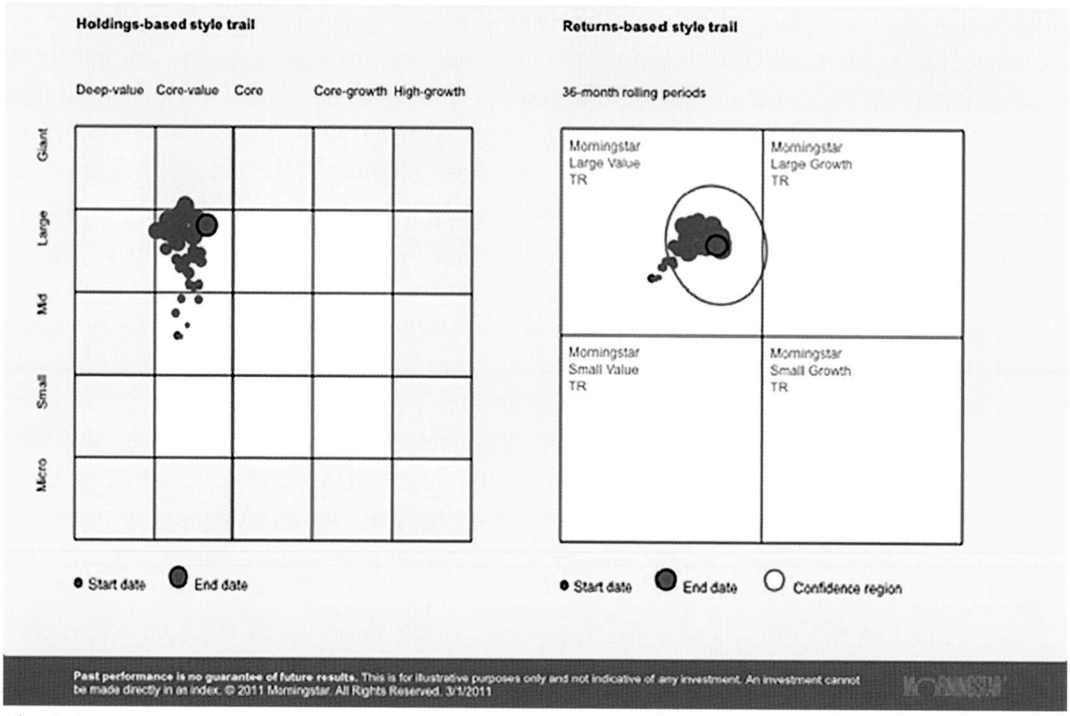

Holdings-based style trail   Returns-based style trail

Deep-value Core-value Core   Core-growth High-growth   36-month rolling periods

(chart, left: Giant / Large / Mid / Small / Micro axis)

Morningstar Large Value TR | Morningstar Large Growth TR

Morningstar Small Value TR | Morningstar Small Growth TR

● Start date ● End date   ● Start date ● End date ○ Confidence region

Fig. 8-4

is long-term return. If you have invested in both Growth Fund A and Growth Fund B, you are more likely to capture the gains produced by both management teams. So diversification pays on the upside, as well as the downside. (Fig. 8-5)

Lesson #39: Over the long-term, stocks of smaller corporations have historically outperformed larger stocks, albeit with more risk. Therefore, mutual funds which invest in small stocks may offer you an opportunity for greater participation in growing economies. (Fig. 8-6)

Small stocks tend to be less well known, so active managers have more opportunities to discover unloved gems. In such an environment, indexing is a bit of a joke.

However, it's also possible to overrate the potential gains in small stocks. For one thing, successful small stocks become mid-cap stocks, and then large-cap stocks. Thus, by charter, small stock mutual funds tend to sell individual issues in mid-growth. Also, good mutual funds rapidly become swamped by investors adding cash.

Obviously, a smaller pool of money is more nimble in the small stock arena. The manager of a smaller fund can take a meaningful position in a small corporation without creating "bootstrapping": mechanical price rises which happen simply because people are trying to buy the stock.

When you buy small stock funds, select several with fewer assets under management.

Here's the *Morningstar* page for a classic small stock mutual fund. You can see that this fund is in the small stock arena by the listing "Small Value" under "Mstar Category"

Understanding Fund Behavior
Some funds do not behave as advertised

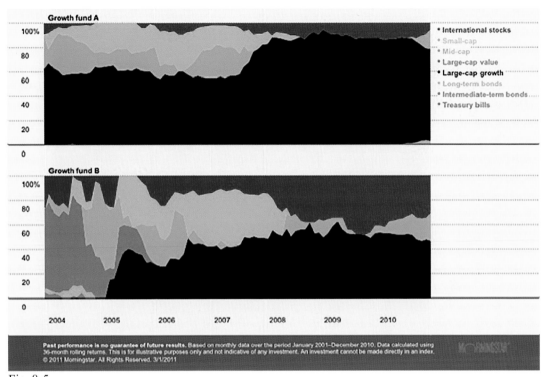

Fig. 8-5

Ibbotson® SBBI®
Stocks, Bonds, Bills, and Inflation 1926–2010

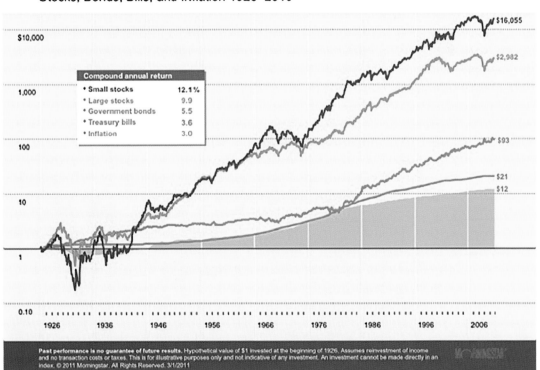

Fig. 8-6

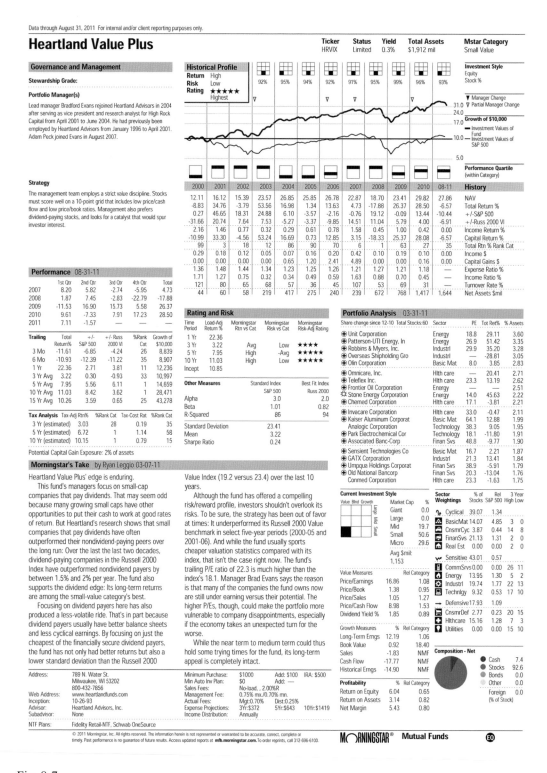

Fig. 8-7

(Inclusion in this book does not constitute an endorsement of Heartland Value Plus fund. There may be other small cap funds which are more appropriate for your portfolio.)

in the upper right corner of the page. You can also see its orientation described under "Strategy" in the mid-upper left side of the page. As shown in the upper right of the page under "Total Assets", these managers are investing about $1,912 million. (Fig. 8-7)

Because of the concentrated holdings of these smaller pools, a manager's correct actions can be magnified. But so can mistakes. For that reason, you need more than one fund, and perhaps as many as five.

One way of getting some of the benefits of a small stock fund without locking the manager into a pre-set course is simply to buy basic value or growth funds with smaller asset pools, which buy attractive stocks of any size. We call these "multi-cap" funds, and they have a definite role in your investment plans.

All successful fund management teams have management styles. Whether they are managing the stocks of smaller corporations, larger corporations, or simply any size company they find attractive, they are likely to approach these stocks by evaluating them with a "value" methodology or a "growth" methodology, or aspects of both.

Section 8.4: Value Mutual Funds

Lesson #40: Value mutual funds are run by managers who are seeking to buy "undervalued" stocks through research, bean-counting, and leg work. These managers tend to buy stocks which have been damaged, but which have prospects of recovering.

Usually these funds are listed as "value" funds in the checkerboard chart on their *Morningstar* pages. As you can see, *Morningstar* may list a value fund as "large cap", "mid cap", or "small cap". This merely refers to the average capitalization size of the corporations which issued the stocks in the portfolio. Unless expressly defined, cap size is subject to change at the whim of the managers. From your perspective, if the mutual fund is successful, cap size is largely irrelevant.

The extreme side of value investing is "vulture" investing, in which the managers buy bankrupt companies and work actively to create turnaround opportunities. These managers are almost business consultants, because many of them actually take a hands-on approach to salvaging the company.

A portfolio full of reeking carrion will sometimes result in an historical performance with surprisingly low systematic risk, because these stocks are already as dead as they are probably going to get. But obviously the raw risk…the risks for the individual stocks…can be quite high. A little of this in your portfolio goes a long way.

Such manager behavior lets you avoid the compulsion to buy the individual stock of a large corporation when it is badly injured and you think it will recover. You can pass on gambling on an individual issue, confident that your value managers are circling the kill.

For example, as I write this, banks and auto manufacturers are financially devastated. You know that in the future we will live in a world full of banks and cars. So you can expect that some of these stocks will recover magnificently. But you don't really know which ones. Some will thrive, and others will unexpectedly wither. Since you are a dispassionate mutual fund investor, you can pass this entire question over to your value funds and get on with your life.

Sometimes value funds outperform growth funds, and sometimes growth funds outrun value. It depends on what part of the economic cycle we are in and what the valuations of the stock markets are. It's important to own both. (Fig. 8-8)

When markets are booming, value funds tend to lag, sometimes quite badly. At that time these funds are actually bargains as money pours into the bubble market elsewhere and value stocks are utterly shunned. As I will discuss fully in a later chapter, a gradual rebalance from your booming growth and index funds into your value funds can be a helpful risk reducer.

When stock markets crash, these funds can sometimes float high and dry as they did in the 2000-2003 tech crash. Many committed value fund managers produced positive performances when the larger market indices were suffering dreadfully. That downturn produced many a feast for these bottom-feeders, so when the market turned in 2003, these managers were admirably positioned.

However, value fund managers have one psychological flaw in their paradigm. When a routine market crash becomes a gigantic market route, the managers of these funds tend to exhibit Pavlovian behavior: they can't resist rushing like koi to the fish pellets dropped into a pond. So they will tend to buy what is down, only to watch these stocks drop further. It's reflexive: this is the value managers' Achilles Heel. Value funds can lose lots of money, so they need rebalancing as well.

Here's a classic value fund. Check out in particular the "Value-Large cap" designation in the checkerboard. In the long-term, value funds are a core holding which you need in your portfolio. (Fig. 8-9)

Section 8.5: Growth Mutual Funds

Lesson #41: Growth mutual funds are the mutual funds with snap and sizzle. They hold the "story" stocks that all your friends are discussing. The managers of these funds tend to invest in stocks with expected increasing earnings.

This means that these managers are essentially doing educated guessing since nobody can truly tell the future. This also means that they tend to buy expensive popular stocks which other investors have already bid up. As a result, growth fund managers tend to have a higher turnover ratio than value fund managers since they buy many stocks which don't turn out well. One advantage of these funds is that you don't have to buy the individual hot stocks du jour because your growth funds have already smelled their aroma.

Turnover ratio deserves a bit of discussion. That's the percentage of the portfolio which is turned over every year.

As you can see on this *Morningstar* page for Brandywine Blue, in the history section for 2008, the turnover rate %, aka the turnover ratio, was 267%. That means

Three-Year Growth and Value Cycles
1970–2010

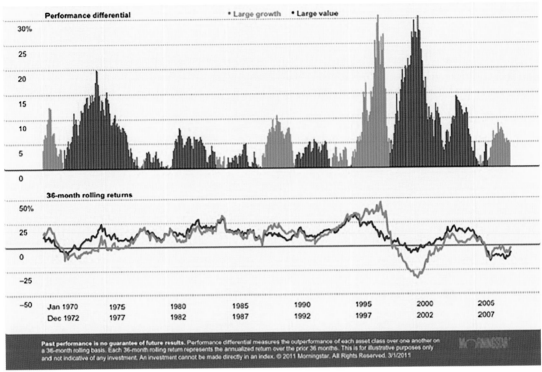

Fig. 8-8

that the mutual fund's portfolio turned over 267% in one year. These are clearly not buy-and-hold managers. (Fig. 8-10)

Such a high turnover costs a lot in terms of the commissions and fees which the managers pay on behalf of the mutual fund to buy and sell. It also creates a lot of tax inefficiencies. In reality, though, you don't care. What you care about is total after-tax performance. If the mutual fund is succeeding despite the impediments of a high turnover rate, it should not concern you.

As you can see on the *Morningstar* page for Amana Trust Growth, this fund has a very low turnover rate—7% in 2008. This technique seems to be working for them. (Fig. 8-11)

When the bull market is stampeding, and the bubble is growing, and investors are gradually going ballistic with euphoria, these are the funds which will take advantage of the insanity. They tend to have higher risk statistics than value funds, and higher correlations because they tend to go with the momentum of the market. But unlike index funds, they can rapidly reshuffle their portfolios to emphasize what is bubbling. For this reason, growth funds are another major core holding.

One aspect of a "good fund" is risk. As I've said, risk is both variable and hard to estimate in the future. I have also written that one statistic for past risk is standard deviation. Another valuable risk statistic is in the middle of the page: "Beta" measures risk relative to a comparative index. It is useful for stock funds because it largely relates

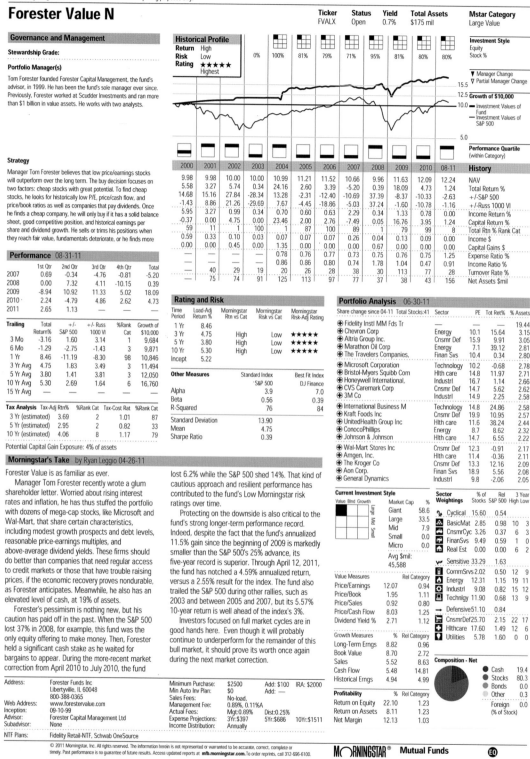

Forester Value N

	Ticker	Status	Yield	Total Assets	Mstar Category
	FVALX	Open	0.7%	$175 mil	Large Value

Governance and Management

Stewardship Grade:

Portfolio Manager(s)

Tom Forester founded Forester Capital Management, the fund's advisor, in 1999. He has been the fund's sole manager ever since. Previously, Forester worked at Scudder Investments and ran more than $1 billion in value assets. He works with two analysts.

Strategy

Manager Tom Forester believes that low price/earnings stocks will outperform over the long term. The buy decision focuses on two factors: cheap stocks with great potential. To find cheap stocks, he looks for historically low P/E, price/cash flow, and price/book ratios as well as companies that pay dividends. Once he finds a cheap company, he will only buy it if it has a solid balance sheet, good competitive position, and historical earnings per share and dividend growth. He sells or trims his positions when they reach fair value, fundamentals deteriorate, or he finds more

Performance 08-31-11

	1st Qtr	2nd Qtr	3rd Qtr	4th Qtr	Total
2007	0.69	-0.34	-4.76	-1.79	-5.20
2008	0.00	7.32	4.11	-10.15	0.39
2009	-8.94	10.92	11.33	5.02	18.09
2010	2.24	-4.79	4.86	2.62	4.73
2011	2.65	1.13	—	—	

Trailing	Total Return%	+/- S&P 500	+/- Russ 1000 Vl	%Rank Cat	Growth of $10,000
3 Mo	-3.16	1.60	3.14	1	9,684
6 Mo	-1.29	-2.75	-1.43	3	9,871
1 Yr	8.46	-11.19	-8.30	98	10,846
3 Yr Avg	4.75	1.83	3.49	3	11,494
5 Yr Avg	3.80	1.41	3.81	3	12,050
10 Yr Avg	5.30	2.69	1.64	6	16,760
15 Yr Avg	—	—	—		

Tax Analysis	Tax-Adj Rtn%	%Rank Cat	Tax-Cost Rat	%Rank Cat
3 Yr (estimated)	3.69	2	1.01	87
5 Yr (estimated)	2.95	2	0.82	33
10 Yr (estimated)	4.06	8	1.17	79

Potential Capital Gain Exposure: 4% of assets

Historical Profile

Return	High
Risk	Low
Rating	★★★★★ Highest

0%	100%	81%	79%	71%	95%	81%	80%	80%

	2000	2001	2002	2003	2004	2005	2006	2007	2008	2009	2010	08-11	History
	9.98	9.98	10.00	10.00	10.99	11.21	11.52	10.66	9.96	11.63	12.09	12.24	NAV
	5.58	3.27	5.74	0.34	24.16	2.60	3.39	-5.20	0.39	18.09	4.73	1.24	Total Return %
	14.68	15.16	27.84	-28.34	13.28	-2.31	-12.40	-10.69	37.39	-8.37	-10.33	-2.63	+/-S&P 500
	-1.43	8.86	21.26	-29.69	7.67	-4.45	-18.86	-5.03	37.24	-10.78	-1.16	+/-Russ 1000 Vl
	5.95	3.27	0.99	0.34	0.70	0.60	0.63	2.29	0.34	1.33	0.78	0.00	Income Return %
	-0.37	0.00	4.75	0.00	23.46	2.00	2.76	-7.49	0.05	16.76	3.95	1.24	Capital Return %
	59	11	1	100	1	87	100	89	1	79	99	8	Total Rtn % Rank Cat
	0.59	0.33	0.10	0.03	0.07	0.07	0.07	0.26	0.04	0.13	0.09	0.00	Income $
	0.00	0.00	0.45	0.00	1.35	0.00	0.00	0.00	0.67	0.00	0.00	0.00	Capital Gains $
	—	—	—	—	0.78	0.76	0.77	0.73	0.75	0.76	0.75	1.25	Expense Ratio %
	—	—	—	—	0.86	0.86	0.80	0.74	1.78	1.04	0.47	0.91	Income Ratio %
	—	40	29	19	20	26	28	38	30	113	77	28	Turnover Rate %
	—	75	74	91	125	113	97	77	37	38	43	156	Net Assets $mil

Investment Style
Equity
Stock %

▼ Manager Change
▽ Partial Manager Change

15.5
12.5 **Growth of $10,000**
10.0 — Investment Values of Fund
— Investment Values of S&P 500
5.0

Performance Quartile
(within Category)

Rating and Risk

Time Period	Load-Adj Return %	Morningstar Rtn vs Cat	Morningstar Risk vs Cat	Morningstar Risk-Adj Rating
1 Yr	8.46			
3 Yr	4.75	High	Low	★★★★★
5 Yr	3.80	High	Low	★★★★★
10 Yr	5.30	High	Low	★★★★★
Incept	5.22			

Other Measures	Standard Index	Best Fit Index
	S&P 500	DJ Finance
Alpha	3.9	7.0
Beta	0.56	0.39
R-Squared	76	84
Standard Deviation	13.90	
Mean	4.75	
Sharpe Ratio	0.39	

Portfolio Analysis 06-30-11

Share change since 04-11 Total Stocks:41	Sector	PE	Tot Ret%	% Assets
⊕ Fidelity Instl MM Fds Tr	—	—	—	19.44
⊕ Chevron Corp	Energy	10.1	15.64	3.15
⊕ Altria Group Inc.	Cnsmr Def	15.9	9.91	3.05
⊕ Marathon Oil Corp	Energy	7.1	39.12	2.81
⊕ The Travelers Companies,	Finan Svs	10.4	0.34	2.80
⊕ Microsoft Corporation	Technology	10.2	-0.68	2.78
⊕ Bristol-Myers Squibb Com	Hlth care	14.8	11.97	2.71
⊕ Honeywell International,	Industrl	16.7	1.14	2.66
⊕ CVS Caremark Corp	Cnsmr Def	14.7	5.62	2.62
⊕ 3M Co	Industrl	14.9	2.25	2.58
⊕ International Business M	Technology	14.8	24.86	2.58
⊕ Kraft Foods Inc	Cnsmr Def	19.9	10.95	2.57
⊕ UnitedHealth Group Inc	Hlth care	11.6	38.24	2.44
⊕ ConocoPhillips	Energy	8.7	8.62	2.32
⊕ Johnson & Johnson	Hlth care	14.7	6.55	2.22
⊕ Wal-Mart Stores Inc	Cnsmr Def	12.3	-0.91	2.17
⊕ Amgen, Inc.	Hlth care	11.4	-0.36	2.11
⊕ The Kroger Co	Cnsmr Def	13.3	12.16	2.09
⊕ Aon Corp.	Finan Svs	18.9	5.56	2.08
⊕ General Dynamics	Industrl	9.8	-2.06	2.05

Current Investment Style

Value Blnd Growth		Market Cap	%
	Large	Giant	58.6
	Mid	Large	33.5
	Small	Mid	7.9
		Small	0.0
		Micro	0.0

	Avg $mil:
	45,588

Value Measures		Rel Category
Price/Earnings	12.07	0.94
Price/Book	1.95	1.11
Price/Sales	0.92	0.80
Price/Cash Flow	8.03	1.25
Dividend Yield %	2.71	1.12

Growth Measures	%	Rel Category
Long-Term Erngs	8.82	0.96
Book Value	8.70	2.72
Sales	5.52	8.63
Cash Flow	5.48	14.81
Historical Erngs	4.94	4.99

Profitability	%	Rel Category
Return on Equity	22.10	1.23
Return on Assets	8.11	1.23
Net Margin	12.13	1.03

Sector Weightings	% of Stocks	Rel S&P 500	3 Year High Low
↻ Cyclical	15.60	0.54	
⚒ BasicMat	2.85	0.98	10 3
⚙ CnsmrCyc	3.26	0.37	6 3
💰 FinanSvs	9.49	0.59	1 0
⌂ Real Est	0.00	0.00	6 2
∿ Sensitive	33.29	1.63	
📡 CommSrvs	2.02	0.50	12 9
⚡ Energy	12.31	1.15	19 11
⚙ Industrl	9.08	0.82	15 12
💻 Technlgy	11.90	0.68	13 9
→ Defensive	51.10	0.84	
🛒 CnsmrDef	25.70	2.15	22 17
✚ Hlthcare	17.60	1.49	12 6
🔌 Utilities	5.78	1.60	0 0

Composition - Net

		%
● Cash		19.4
● Stocks		80.3
● Bonds		0.0
● Other		0.3
	Foreign	0.0
	(% of Stock)	

Morningstar's Take by Ryan Leggio 04-26-11

Forester Value is as familiar as ever.

Manager Tom Forester recently wrote a glum shareholder letter. Worried about rising interest rates and inflation, he has thus stuffed the portfolio with dozens of mega-cap stocks, like Microsoft and Wal-Mart, that share certain characteristics, including modest growth prospects and debt levels, reasonable price-earnings multiples, and above-average dividend yields. These firms should do better than companies that need regular access to credit markets or those that have trouble raising prices, if the economic recovery proves nondurable, as Forester anticipates. Meanwhile, he also has an elevated level of cash, at 19% of assets.

Forester's pessimism is nothing new, but his caution has paid off in the past. When the S&P 500 lost 37% in 2008, for example, this fund was the only equity offering to make money. Then, Forester held a significant cash stake as he waited for bargains to appear. During the more-recent market correction from April 2010 to July 2010, the fund

lost 6.2% while the S&P 500 shed 14%. That kind of cautious approach and resilient performance has contributed to the fund's Low Morningstar risk ratings over time.

Protecting on the downside is also critical to the fund's strong longer-term performance record. Indeed, despite the fact that the fund's annualized 11.5% gain since the beginning of 2009 is markedly smaller than the S&P 500's 25% advance, its five-year record is superior. Through April 12, 2011, the fund has notched a 4.59% annualized return, versus a 2.55% result for the index. The fund also trailed the S&P 500 during other rallies, such as 2003 and between 2005 and 2007, but its 5.57% 10-year return is well ahead of the index's 3%.

Investors focused on full market cycles are in good hands here. Even though it will probably continue to underperform for the remainder of this bull market, it should prove its worth once again during the next market correction.

Address:	Forester Funds Inc	Minimum Purchase:	$2500	Add: $100	IRA: $2000
	Libertyville, IL 60048	Min Auto Inv Plan:	$0	Add: —	
	800-388-0365	Sales Fees:	No-load,		
Web Address:	www.forestervalue.com	Management Fee:	0.89%, 0.11%A		
Inception:	09-10-99	Actual Fees:	Mgt:0.89%	Dist:0.25%	
Advisor:	Forester Capital Management Ltd	Expense Projections:	3Yr:$397	5Yr:$686	10Yr:$1511
Subadvisor:	None	Income Distribution:	Annually		
NTF Plans:	Fidelity Retail-NTF, Schwab OneSource				

MORNINGSTAR® Mutual Funds

Fig. 8-9

(Inclusion in this book does not constitute an endorsement of Heartland Value Plus fund. There may be other small cap funds which are more appropriate for your portfolio.)

Fig. 8-10

(Inclusion in this book does not constitute an endorsement of Heartland Value Plus fund. There may be other small cap funds which are more appropriate for your portfolio.)

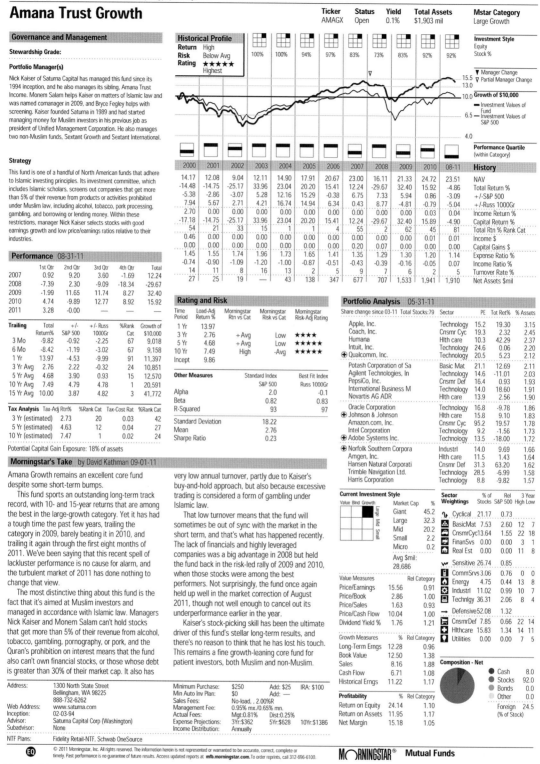

Data through August 31, 2011 For internal and/or client reporting purposes only.

Amana Trust Growth

	Ticker	Status	Yield	Total Assets	Mstar Category
	AMAGX	Open	0.1%	$1,903 mil	Large Growth

Governance and Management

Stewardship Grade:

Portfolio Manager(s)

Nick Kaiser of Saturna Capital has managed this fund since its 1994 inception, and he also manages its sibling, Amana Trust Income. Monem Salam helps Kaiser on matters of Islamic law and was named comanager in 2009, and Bryce Fegley helps with screening. Kaiser founded Saturna in 1989 and had started managing money for Muslim investors in his previous job as president of Unified Management Corporation. He also manages two non-Muslim funds, Sextant Growth and Sextant International.

Strategy

This fund is one of a handful of North American funds that adhere to Islamic investing principles. Its investment committee, which includes Islamic scholars, screens out companies that get more than 5% of their revenue from products or activities prohibited under Muslim law, including alcohol, tobacco, pork processing, gambling, and borrowing or lending money. Within these restrictions, manager Nick Kaiser selects stocks with good earnings growth and low price/earnings ratios relative to their industries.

Performance 08-31-11

	1st Qtr	2nd Qtr	3rd Qtr	4th Qtr	Total
2007	0.92	9.20	3.60	-1.69	12.24
2008	-7.39	2.30	-9.09	-18.34	-29.67
2009	-1.99	11.65	11.74	8.27	32.40
2010	4.74	-9.89	12.77	8.92	15.92
2011	3.28	-0.00	—	—	

Trailing	Total Return%	+/- S&P 500	+/- Russ 1000Gr	%Rank Cat	Growth of $10,000
3 Mo	-9.82	-0.92	-2.25	67	9,018
6 Mo	-8.42	-1.19	-3.02	67	9,158
1 Yr	13.97	-4.53	-9.99	91	11,397
3 Yr Avg	2.76	2.22	-0.32	24	10,851
5 Yr Avg	4.68	3.90	0.93	15	12,570
10 Yr Avg	7.49	4.79	4.78	1	20,591
15 Yr Avg	10.00	3.87	4.82	3	41,772

Tax Analysis	Tax-Adj Rtn%	%Rank Cat	Tax-Cost Rat	%Rank Cat
3 Yr (estimated)	2.73	20	0.03	42
5 Yr (estimated)	4.63	12	0.04	27
10 Yr (estimated)	7.47	1	0.02	24

Potential Capital Gain Exposure: 18% of assets

Morningstar's Take by David Kathman 09-01-11

Amana Growth remains an excellent core fund despite some short-term bumps.

This fund sports an outstanding long-term track record, with 10- and 15-year returns that are among the best in the large-growth category. Yet it has had a tough time the past few years, trailing the category in 2009, barely beating it in 2010, and trailing it again through the first eight months of 2011. We've been saying that this recent spell of lackluster performance is no cause for alarm, and the turbulent market of 2011 has done nothing to change that view.

The most distinctive thing about this fund is the fact that it's aimed at Muslim investors and managed in accordance with Islamic law. Managers Nick Kaiser and Monem Salam can't hold stocks that get more than 5% of their revenue from alcohol, tobacco, gambling, pornography, or pork, and the Quran's prohibition on interest means that the fund also can't own financial stocks, or those whose debt is greater than 30% of their market cap. It also has

very low annual turnover, partly due to Kaiser's buy-and-hold approach, but also because excessive trading is considered a form of gambling under Islamic law.

That low turnover means that the fund will sometimes be out of sync with the market in the short term, and that's what has happened recently. The lack of financials and highly leveraged companies was a big advantage in 2008 but held the fund back in the risk-led rally of 2009 and 2010, when those stocks were among the best performers. Not surprisingly, the fund once again held up well in the market correction of August 2011, though not well enough to cancel out its underperformance earlier in the year.

Kaiser's stock-picking skill has been the ultimate driver of this fund's stellar long-term results, and there's no reason to think that he has lost his touch. This remains a fine growth-leaning core fund for patient investors, both Muslim and non-Muslim.

Address:	1300 North State Street Bellingham, WA 98225 888-732-6262	Minimum Purchase:	$250	Add: $25	IRA: $100
		Min Auto Inv Plan:	$0	Add: —	
		Sales Fees:	No-load, .2.00%R		
Web Address:	www.saturna.com	Management Fee:	0.95% mx./0.65% mn.		
Inception:	02-03-94	Actual Fees:	Mgt:0.81%	Dist:0.25%	
Advisor:	Saturna Capital Corp (Washington)	Expense Projections:	3Yr:$362	5Yr:$628	10Yr:$1386
Subadvisor:	None	Income Distribution:	Annually		
NTF Plans:	Fidelity Retail-NTF, Schwab OneSource				

Historical Profile

Return	High
Risk	Below Avg
Rating	★★★★★ Highest

100% 100% 94% 97% 83% 73% 83% 92% 92%

Investment Style
Equity
Stock %

▼ Manager Change
▽ Partial Manager Change

Growth of $10,000
— Investment Values of Fund
— Investment Values of S&P 500

15.5
13.0
10.0
6.5
4.0

Performance Quartile
(within Category)

	2000	2001	2002	2003	2004	2005	2006	2007	2008	2009	2010	08-11	History
	14.17	12.08	9.04	12.11	14.90	17.91	20.67	23.00	16.11	21.33	24.72	23.51	NAV
	-14.48	-14.75	-25.17	33.96	23.04	20.20	15.41	12.24	-29.67	32.40	15.92	-4.86	Total Return %
	-5.38	-2.86	-3.07	5.28	12.16	15.29	-0.38	6.75	7.33	5.94	0.86	-3.09	+/-S&P 500
	7.94	5.67	2.71	4.21	16.74	14.94	6.34	0.43	8.77	-4.81	-0.79	-5.04	+/-Russ 1000Gr
	2.70	0.00	0.00	0.00	0.00	0.00	0.00	0.00	0.00	0.00	0.03	0.04	Income Return %
	-17.18	-14.75	-25.17	33.96	23.04	20.20	15.41	12.24	-29.67	32.40	15.89	-4.90	Capital Return %
	54	21	33	15	1	1	4	55	2	62	45	81	Total Rtn % Rank Cat
	0.46	0.00	0.00	0.00	0.00	0.00	0.00	0.00	0.00	0.00	0.01	0.01	Income $
	0.00	0.00	0.00	0.00	0.00	0.00	0.00	0.20	0.07	0.00	0.00	0.00	Capital Gains $
	1.45	1.55	1.74	1.96	1.73	1.65	1.41	1.35	1.29	1.30	1.20	1.14	Expense Ratio %
	-0.74	-0.90	-1.09	-1.20	-1.00	-0.87	-0.51	-0.43	-0.39	-0.16	-0.05	0.07	Income Ratio %
	14	11	8	16	13	2	5	9	7	6	2	5	Turnover Rate %
	27	25	19	—	43	138	347	677	707	1,533	1,941	1,910	Net Assets $mil

Rating and Risk

Time Period	Load-Adj Return %	Morningstar Rtn vs Cat	Morningstar Risk vs Cat	Morningstar Risk-Adj Rating
1 Yr	13.97			
3 Yr	2.76	+Avg	Low	★★★★
5 Yr	4.68	+Avg	Low	★★★★★
10 Yr	7.49	High	-Avg	★★★★★
Incept	9.86			

Other Measures	Standard Index S&P 500	Best Fit Index Russ 1000Gr
Alpha	2.0	-0.1
Beta	0.82	0.83
R-Squared	93	97
Standard Deviation	18.22	
Mean	2.76	
Sharpe Ratio	0.23	

Portfolio Analysis 05-31-11

Share change since 03-11 Total Stocks:79	Sector	PE	Tot Ret%	% Assets
Apple, Inc.	Technology	15.2	19.30	3.15
Coach, Inc.	Cnsmr Cyc	19.3	2.32	2.45
Humana	Hlth care	10.3	42.29	2.37
Intuit, Inc.	Technology	24.6	0.06	2.20
⊕ Qualcomm, Inc.	Technology	20.5	5.23	2.12
Potash Corporation of Sa	Basic Mat	21.1	12.69	2.11
Agilent Technologies, In	Technology	14.6	-11.01	2.03
PepsiCo, Inc.	Cnsmr Def	16.4	0.93	1.93
International Business M	Technology	14.0	18.60	1.91
Novartis AG ADR	Hlth care	13.9	2.56	1.90
Oracle Corporation	Technology	16.8	-9.78	1.86
⊕ Johnson & Johnson	Hlth care	15.8	9.10	1.83
Amazon.com, Inc.	Cnsmr Cyc	95.2	19.57	1.78
Intel Corporation	Technology	9.2	-1.56	1.73
⊕ Adobe Systems Inc.	Technology	13.5	-18.00	1.72
⊕ Norfolk Southern Corpora	Industrl	14.0	9.69	1.66
Amgen, Inc.	Hlth care	11.5	1.43	1.64
Hansen Natural Corporati	Cnsmr Def	31.3	63.20	1.62
Trimble Navigation Ltd.	Technology	28.5	-6.99	1.58
Harris Corporation	Technology	8.8	-9.82	1.57

Current Investment Style

Value Blnd Growth

Market Cap	%
Giant	45.2
Large	32.3
Mid	20.2
Small	2.2
Micro	0.2

Avg $mil: 28,686

Value Measures		Rel Category
Price/Earnings	15.56	0.91
Price/Book	2.86	1.00
Price/Sales	1.63	0.93
Price/Cash Flow	10.04	1.00
Dividend Yield %	1.76	1.21

Growth Measures	%	Rel Category
Long-Term Erngs	12.28	0.96
Book Value	12.50	1.38
Sales	8.16	1.88
Cash Flow	6.71	1.08
Historical Erngs	11.22	1.17

Profitability	%	Rel Category
Return on Equity	24.14	1.10
Return on Assets	11.95	1.17
Net Margin	15.18	1.05

Sector Weightings	% of Stocks	Rel S&P 500	3 Year High Low
↻ Cyclical	21.17	0.73	
⊞ BasicMat	7.53	2.60	12 7
⊞ CnsmrCyc	13.64	1.55	22 18
⊞ FinanSvs	0.00	0.00	3 1
⊞ Real Est	0.00	0.00	11 8
↝ Sensitive	26.74	0.85	
⊞ CommSrvs	3.06	0.76	0 0
⊞ Energy	4.75	0.44	13 8
⊞ Industrl	11.02	0.99	10 7
⊞ Technlgy	36.31	2.06	8 4
→ Defensive	52.08	1.32	
⊞ CnsmrDef	7.85	0.66	22 14
⊞ Hlthcare	15.83	1.34	14 11
⊞ Utilities	0.00	0.00	7 5

Composition - Net

	%
● Cash	8.0
● Stocks	92.0
● Bonds	0.0
● Other	0.0
Foreign (% of Stock)	24.5

M⊙RNINGSTAR® Mutual Funds

Fig. 8-11

(Inclusion in this book does not constitute an endorsement of Heartland Value Plus fund. There may be other small cap funds which are more appropriate for your portfolio.)

to the S&P 500 Index. So you can compare any fund's market-related volatility, as well as its raw risk.

If a fund has a beta of 1, it theoretically goes up or down $1 whenever the stock market goes up or down $1. It (theoretically) correlates utterly with the stock market. As you can see by turning back to the *Morningstar* page for Forester Value N, that fund has a beta of .56. In theory, if the overall stock market goes down $1, this fund goes down $.56. Of course the same is true in the opposite direction.

Another example can be seen on the *Morningstar* page for Amana Trust Growth. With a beta of .82, it has, theoretically, about 82% of the correlated risk of the larger stock market.

What does all this mean to you? Beta provides you with yet another tool for diversification. Unless you like skydiving and bungee jumping you'll want to diversify your stock mutual funds with an assortment of choices with both higher and lower betas.

Growth funds can go way up spectacularly for years. Bull markets may take years to unfold. If you try to guess the top of an investment bubble, you may simply be left standing there watching your pretty balloon float away as your portfolio lags the markets for years. Instead, by gradually rebalancing, you can maximize gain and minimize loss. That means that even at a market top you will still have a little in growth funds, because you don't really know what's going to happen.

The psychological blind spot of growth managers is that they can't see a bubble and step sideways. They tend to ride the tsunami all the way to the top, and then smash into the shore with the rest of the market. Investing too much in an aggressive growth fund can hurt you badly.

Since growth fund managers are such trend followers, they tend to boom during roaring economies and recover slowly from recessions. As you can see, they lag in recoveries. Booming growth stock mutual funds often indicate a mature economy and mature stock markets. They indicate that increased caution is appropriate. (Fig. 8-12)

Review: The Lessons of Chapter 8

Lesson #37: Stocks represent ownership in corporations. A bond is an IOU, a glorified loan. A stock is a piece of the action, a slice of the pie, a percentage of the profits or losses. Stocks, also called "equities", are OWNERSHIP. Stock mutual funds are a key part of your portfolio.

Lesson #38 Index mutual funds are a famous money management choice. They DO have a role to play in your portfolio, but not as much as you may think. Performance is episodic: sometimes better and sometimes worse than alternatives. They tend to do better in up markets and less well in sideways or down markets.

Lesson #39: Over the long-term, stocks of smaller corporations have historically outperformed larger stocks, albeit with more risk. Therefore, mutual funds which

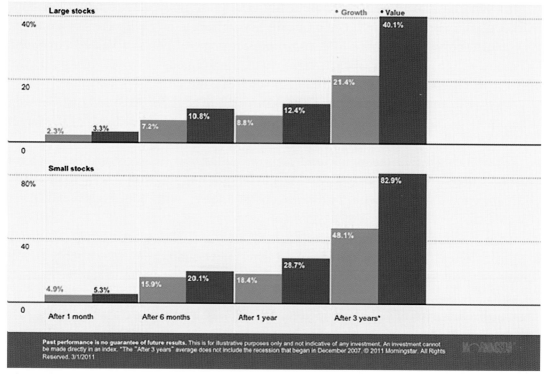

Growth and Value Performance After Recessions
1970–2010

Fig. 8-12

invest in small stocks may offer you an opportunity for greater participation in growing economies.

Lesson #40: Value mutual funds are run by managers who are seeking to buy "undervalued" stocks through research, bean-counting, and leg work. These managers tend to buy stocks which have been damaged, but which have prospects of recovering.

Lesson #41: Growth mutual funds are the mutual funds with snap and sizzle. They hold the "story" stocks that all your friends are discussing. The managers of these funds tend to invest in stocks with expected increasing earnings.

Chapter 9

Create a 21ˢᵗ Century Portfolio with International Mutual Funds

The knock on diversified (international) funds is that they're index-huggers, which given the geographic breadth of where we invest, is not at all the case for us. I know the argument that you should only own your best 30 or 40 ideas, but I've never proven over time that I actually know in advance what those are.
—Jean-Marie Eveillard, formerly the manager of the First Eagle Global Fund.

Section 9.1: International and Global Mutual Funds

Lesson #42: Mutual funds which exclude stocks or bonds of the US but invest in the rest of the world are known as international funds. These can operate in any part of the financial markets. As you explore, you will find international value funds, international growth funds, and international sector funds. All of these funds have all of their holdings outside the US.

Funds which include stocks or bonds of the United States, but only as a minority of their holdings, are called global mutual funds. Only SOME of their holdings are outside the United States.

These funds can be used interchangeably to diversify your portfolio. They should play a major role.

With the onset of the global economy, the line between domestic and international funds has blurred. Managers are often going wherever the bargains might be found.

At the same time, correlations between domestic and international investments are increasing. Thirty years ago it was normal to invest overseas in self-contained systems such as the Japanese stock market, which at the time had very little correlation to the US markets. Now, the correlation has increased dramatically, and thus the diversification benefits of investing internationally have diminished. However, they are still present.

While perhaps they are shifting, the benefits are very real. (Fig. 9-1)

With that in mind, international investing still makes sense. You may or may not lower the overall risk of your portfolio by investing globally. But you will certainly obtain the benefits of investing in rapidly growing international corporations around the globe. In today's economy, that reality cannot be ignored.

You can see on this graph that the global economy is growing more rapidly abroad, outside the U.S. There are a variety of reasons for this, some sustainable and some not. But given that this growth is happening, you should have some of your money in those venues. It is quite possible to invest successfully if the US falls behind economically in the 21ˢᵗ Century. You will simply need money invested internationally in the form of mutual funds.

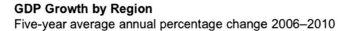

GDP Growth by Region
Five-year average annual percentage change 2006–2010

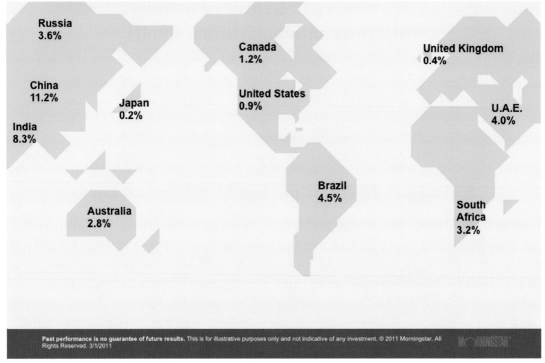

Fig. 9-1

Another feature is that the rise of the global mega-corporation has made international investing necessary simply to fully participate in the US economy! As your eyes scan these names, you will see many you recognize simply from shopping locally! (Fig. 9-2)

The result of all this growth and globalization is that in the recent decades, even if we include the recent meltdown in Europe, international investments have performed as well as US investments. We don't really know if this will continue. But given what we know, can you afford to NOT invest internationally? (Fig. 9-3)

Part of this relatively good performance by international investments is due to the currency changes between the dollar and other currency. When the dollar declines in value compared with other currencies, as it has in recent years, investments that are denominated in other currencies are worth more in dollars. In other words, they retain their value when the dollar declines. But this isn't always what happens.

International investments have some advantages compared with domestic investments. They also have some unique risks. The dollar may also RISE against other currencies, thus making international investments worth LESS. In addition, there is always political risk when you are investing in exciting venues such as Russia, China, or anywhere else with political instability or a nascent financial structure. This includes the chance that the government might change the rules of investing so you get mauled while a local crony wins big. The risks are higher in some geographical locations than in others. And the risks can change rapidly. (Fig. 9-4)

Global Household Names

Fig. 9-2

Global Investing
1970–2010

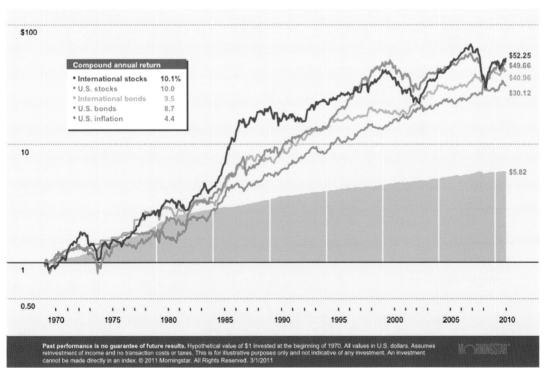

Fig. 9-3

Risk Level by Region
Annual standard deviation 2001–2010

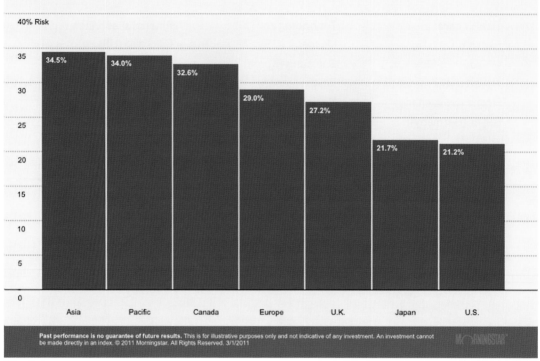

Fig. 9-4

The fact remains, though, that since a lot of this risk can be diversified away, holding international mutual funds in moderation can REDUCE the overall risk of your portfolio by diminishing the impact of domestic risks. As you can see, this works quite effectively.

Thus international and global funds should play a large role in your portfolio. A vast menu of very low risk to very high risk mutual funds are available, depending on what you wish to own. (Fig.9-5)

As I discussed in an earlier chapter, world allocation mutual funds provide essentially the same benefits as asset allocation funds, but across the globe. These can add both diversification and unique venues for unexpected gains. As a result, they are a "sweet spot" for your portfolio to gain diversification and moderate returns without adding great amounts of international risk.

Here's a *Morningstar* page for the perennial favorite global asset allocator First Eagle Global fund. By now you should be relatively skilled at reading these pages. I've left the page a bit dated, because it's a case study, not a current mutual fund report. Let's run through this:

    o   The category is World Allocation Fund.

    o   Total assets are around $29.3 billion. This is a giant fund! If you invest in it, you'll also want to hold some other World Allocation funds with smaller asset sizes to create some nimbleness in your portfolio. Making changes in

Domestic Versus Global
1970–2010

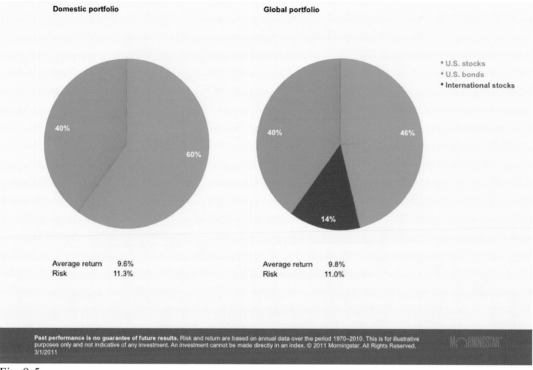

Fig. 9-5

a $29.3 billion portfolio is likely to be as cumbersome as turning an aircraft carrier.

o   The *Morningstar* Rating is 5 stars, and return is high while risk is average. That's attractive!

o   The Standard Deviation is relatively moderate, but the beta is relatively high. That means this fund correlates a lot with its index.

o   Looking at the checkerboard, you can see that this is partially value, partially growth, and in large stocks.

o   In the lower right corner, you can see that this fund, as of the time of this review, was 42% in the US, 25% in Japan, 8% in France, 4% in Mexico, and 4% in Switzerland. This is a global fund, instead of an international fund. In other words, it includes the US in its holdings.

o   Looking at the center bottom of the page, you see that this fund sells for a 5% commission, which is a gigantic no! But when you research this on your discount brokerage site, you will find that this fund sells there as a no-load, without the sales fee. ***Sometimes great mutual funds with commissions are available no-load on discount brokerages! You need to check to find bargains.*** (Fig.9-6)

Data through September 30, 2011 For internal and/or client reporting purposes only.

First Eagle Global A

	Ticker	Status	Yield	Total Assets	Mstar Category
	SGENX	Open	1.5%	$29,274 mil	World Allocation

Governance and Management

Stewardship Grade:

Portfolio Manager(s)

In early September 2008, Matt McLennan joined the firm as the head of First Eagle's global-value team and as a comanager on this fund. He joined Jean-Marie Eveillard, who retired (again) in March 2009 but remains on the fund's board of directors. Abhay Deshpande, who worked with Eveillard in the early 2000s, as well as during his second stint here, serves as comanager. Kimball Brooker, Jr. was promoted to associate portfolio manager at the end of February 2011. He joined First Eagle in January 2009 and is now also a comanager on Overseas and U.S. Value.

Strategy

This fund uses a value-oriented approach. Management errs on the side of caution, favoring securities whose assets and cash flows appear undervalued by the market. Broad diversification (individual positions are kept small) also helps reduce risk. The fund invests more in stocks and less in bonds than most world-allocation funds. It favors smaller and midsize stocks but often buys big companies, too. Turnover is low. Management engages in currency hedging; it considers a 50% hedged position against a particular currency to be neutral but often veers far

Performance 09-30-11

	1st Qtr	2nd Qtr	3rd Qtr	4th Qtr	Total
2007	2.38	4.48	1.37	1.36	9.90
2008	-1.60	4.48	-8.72	-10.66	-21.06
2009	-8.28	14.47	14.58	2.16	22.91
2010	4.23	-5.42	9.29	9.14	17.58
2011	3.37	1.77	-9.94		

Trailing	Total Return%	+/- M* MdTgRk	+/- MSCI World	%Rank Cat	Growth of $10,000
3 Mo	-9.94	-0.82	6.67	42	9,006
6 Mo	-8.35	0.04	7.87	35	9,165
1 Yr	3.40	2.37	7.75	5	10,340
3 Yr Avg	6.95	2.14	7.02	13	12,233
5 Yr Avg	5.02	2.02	7.25	12	12,775
10 Yr Avg	12.55	6.25	8.84	2	32,618
15 Yr Avg	11.00	—	7.00	1	47,846

Tax Analysis	Tax-Adj Rtn%	%Rank Cat	Tax-Cost Rat	%Rank Cat
3 Yr (estimated)	4.40	17	0.70	22
5 Yr (estimated)	2.65	17	1.25	40
10 Yr (estimated)	10.69	3	1.15	62

Potential Capital Gain Exposure: 12% of assets

Morningstar's Take by Bridget Hughes 03-23-11

There's more to First Eagle Global than its Japan stake.

At nearly one fourth of its stock portfolio as of the end of January 2011, this fund's commitment to Japanese stocks is the largest among world-allocation funds. Fund managers Matthew McLennan, Abhay Deshpande, and Kimball Brooker (who was recently promoted) have long been attracted to the country's low valuations, which they think afford them a large margin of safety. They own a variety of companies, but the emphasis here is on industrial firms with global dominance, such as top holdings SMC and Fanuc.

To be sure, the fund's Japanese stake has stung in the aftermath of Japan's recent record-setting earthquake and tsunami. Since March 11, 2011, the fund is roughly flat, landing in the category's worst quartile. While some of its Japanese holdings have seen limited setbacks, top-five holding SECOM is down more than 10% in local-currency terms. The fund's investments in two non-life insurers, MS&AD

and NKSJ, which together account for about 2% of assets, have fallen even further. McLennan says, though, that the selling that has taken place is largely indiscriminate and based on fear. Given that the fund's managers are characterized by having the courage of their convictions and a long investment horizon, it's not surprising that they've been adding to their holdings despite uncertainty.

Japan is certainly front of mind for investors, and many others, today. But the influence (for good or ill) of its Japanese holdings is modest because this is among the industry's widest-ranging funds. Stocks and bonds have largely rallied in the past couple of years, so management has maintained a higher cash position as it's trimmed investments and found it harder to find stocks or bonds priced at bargain levels. About 10% of the portfolio remains in gold and gold companies.

The time-tested approach has produced great long-term results, even including bouts of turmoil.

Historical Profile

Return	High
Risk	Average
Rating	★★★★★ Highest

	2000	2001	2002	2003	2004	2005	2006	2007	2008	2009	2010	09-11	History
	22.29	23.82	25.35	33.32	38.81	42.06	45.80	44.90	32.99	39.98	46.36	43.92	NAV
	9.72	10.21	10.23	37.64	18.37	14.91	20.50	9.90	-21.06	22.91	17.58	-5.26	Total Return %
	8.04	12.67	16.92	15.16	6.89	7.87	7.55	1.27	1.13	1.14	5.17	-0.36	+/-M* MdTgRk
	22.90	27.03	30.12	4.53	3.65	5.42	0.43	0.86	-7.08	5.82	6.94	+/-MSCI World
	5.64	2.83	2.06	2.66	1.29	2.18	2.91	2.33	0.32	1.74	1.60	0.00	Income Return %
	4.08	7.38	8.17	34.98	17.08	12.73	17.59	7.57	-21.38	21.17	15.98	-5.26	Capital Return %
	11	6	9	4	6	4	32	42	19	56	2	36	Total Rtn % Rank Cat
	1.39	0.63	0.49	0.68	0.43	0.85	1.23	1.07	0.14	0.57	0.64	0.00	Income $
	3.19	0.09	0.40	0.85	0.18	1.68	3.63	4.39	2.31	0.00	0.00	0.00	Capital Gains $
	1.32	1.40	1.34	1.32	1.24	1.20	1.13	1.12	1.14	1.19	1.16	—	Expense Ratio %
	2.68	2.20	2.14	1.91	1.46	1.21	1.31	1.40	1.48	1.14	1.36	—	Income Ratio %
	12	29	20	7	5	12	29	38	30	13	17	—	Turnover Rate %
	1,651	1,611	1,976	3,738	7,171	10,038	12,373	13,041	9,612	11,071	13,251	13,384	Net Assets $mil

Rating and Risk

Time Period	Load-Adj Return %	Morningstar Rtn vs Cat	Morningstar Risk vs Cat	Morningstar Risk-Adj Rating
1 Yr	-1.77			
3 Yr	5.13	+Avg	Avg	★★★★
5 Yr	3.94	+Avg	Avg	★★★★
10 Yr	11.98	High	Avg	★★★★★
Incept	11.91			

Other Measures	Standard Index M* MdTgRk	Best Fit Index M* MdTgRk
Alpha	1.6	1.6
Beta	1.12	1.12
R-Squared	97	97
Standard Deviation	16.06	
Mean	6.95	
Sharpe Ratio	0.49	

Portfolio Analysis 07-31-11

Total Stocks:140 Share change since 06-30-11	Sectors	P/E Ratio	YTD Return %	% Net Assets
SECOM Co., Ltd.	Industrl	—	—	1.85
⊖ Fanuc Ltd.	Industrl	—	—	1.84
SMC Corp.	Industrl	—	—	1.57
⊕ Cisco Systems Inc	Technology	14.8	-16.76	1.50
Keyence Corp.	Industrl	—	—	1.42
Cintas Corporation	Industrl	19.1	0.86	1.36
Microsoft Corporation	Technology	11.9	-4.23	1.31
Sysco Corporation	Cnsmr Def	15.2	-8.78	1.29
FirstEnergy Corp	Utilities	14.4	24.10	1.29

Total Fixed-Income:19	Date of Maturity	Amount $000	Value $000	% Net Assets
Hong Kong Government	12-17-12	732,250	97,160	0.31
Hong Kong Government	09-17-12	586,700	78,732	0.25
Taiwan Govt Reconstruct	01-16-13	1,826,000	64,803	0.21
Hk Govt Bond Programme	09-03-12	371,900	47,862	0.15
Japan Govt Cpi Linked	06-10-18	2,185,452	29,045	0.09
Yankee Acquisition 9.75%	02-15-17	22,554	24,076	0.08
Catalyst Paper 11%	12-15-16	28,460	22,555	0.07
Emin Leydier Bond	07-31-16	15,000	21,566	0.07

Current Investment Style

		Market Cap	%
Value Blnd Growth	Giant	33.7
	Large	39.1
	Mid	19.9
	Small	6.8
	Micro	0.5
	Avg $mil:	15,324

Value Measures		Rel Category
Price/Earnings	8.87	0.65
Price/Book	1.40	0.73
Price/Sales	0.98	0.81
Price/Cash Flow	5.72	0.87
Dividend Yield %	2.81	1.00

Growth Measures	%	Rel Category
Long-Term Erngs	8.90	0.80
Book Value	3.95	0.31
Sales	-0.97	NMF
Cash Flow	-2.95	NMF
Historical Erngs	2.33	0.30

Composition - Net			
Cash	15.3	Bonds	1.5
Stocks	75.7	Other	7.5
Foreign	(% of Stock)		58.3

Sector Weightings	% of Stocks	Rel M* MdTgRk	3 Year High Low
℩ Cyclical	36.60	1.02	
BasicMat	10.80	1.51	2 2
CnsmrCyc	9.21	0.93	5 3
FinanSvs	13.99	0.91	5 1
Real Est	2.60	0.74	4 0
Sensitive	21.43	0.77	
CommSrvs	3.00	0.63	19 11
Energy	6.06	0.54	19 9
Industrl	27.14	1.28	35 20
Technlgy	8.77	0.71	7 4
Defensive	41.97	1.16	
CnsmrDef	8.58	0.93	11 6
Hlthcare	6.18	0.68	11 6
Utilities	3.67	0.76	10 8

Regional Exposure	% Stock
UK/W. Europe 22	N. America 43
Japan 25	Latn America 4
Asia X Japan 5	Other 1

Country Exposure	% Stock
United States 42	Mexico 4
Japan 25	Switzerland 4
France 8	

Address:	First Eagle Fund New York, NY 10105 800-334-2143
Web Address:	www.firsteaglefunds.com
Inception:	04-28-70
Advisor:	First Eagle Investment Management, LLC
Subadvisor:	None
NTF Plans:	DATALynx NTF, Federated Tr NTF

Minimum Purchase:	$2500	Add: $100	IRA: $1000
Min Auto Inv Plan:	$100	Add: $100	
Sales Fees:	5.00%L, , 2.00%R		
Management Fee:	0.75%		
Actual Fees:	Mgt:0.75%	Dist:0.25%	
Expense Projections:	3Yr:$850	5Yr:$1106	10Yr:$1839
Income Distribution:	Annually		

MORNINGSTAR® **Mutual Funds**   ⊞

Fig. 9-6

(Inclusion in this book does not constitute an endorsement of First Eagle Global fund. Please do your own research.)

So how do you find mutual funds with smaller asset bases? The problem is that you are really hiring managers, not buying mutual funds. The solution is to get on the web and use a search engine such as Google, Yahoo! or Bing. Look for information about your mutual fund by searching for information about the managers, by name.

Here's what we found: a hatchling mutual fund run by former managers of the very successful First Eagle Global mutual fund. We tracked this fund by following the internet trail of breadcrumbs left by the managers. The result: a great small fund to provide diversification and the possibility of great management. Great management usually equals great returns. Doing your research pays off! (Fig.9-7)

When doing your mutual fund searches, don't get discouraged by funds that are closed (not open to new purchases), too big, or require a commission. Move on. There are MANY mutual funds, and a genuine assortment of great managers from whom to choose.

International mutual funds tend to organize themselves like conventional equity mutual funds. There are "World Stock" and "International Stock" mutual funds, but these also tend to divide further by "value" and "growth" genres. For diversification's sake, you want some of all. Apply standard equity mutual fund procedures here, and do your homework.

Section 9.2: Emerging Markets

Emerging Market mutual funds invest in developing markets outside the United States. Some of these are relatively easy-going, and some are absolutely crazed. If you like to watch old World War II movies, and savor Hellcat fighter gun camera images of Japanese Zeros blazing out the sky at the Battle of Marianas, then you might enjoy one or two of these. Remember to keep your allocations very small, 5% maximum, and don't try to guess which country will thrive, because you can't. On the other hand, these markets represent the economies with the greatest boom potential out there in the 21ˢᵗ Century global economy. Risk-tolerant investors will have a place for these funds in their portfolios. People who don't enjoy roller coasters will probably want to avoid these entirely.

Here's a *Morningstar* page for Harding Loevner Emerging Markets fund. Note the monster standard deviation: truly world-class volatility. Note also, in the annualized "History" section, the hysterical roller coaster ride. Up 56.34% in 2003. Down 52.33% in 2008. Hold on to your socks. A small investment in this kind of fund will add the potential of big risks and big returns. (Fig.9-8)

As I mentioned, most International and Global mutual funds follow the structures of domestic funds: small cap, large cap, value, blended style, and growth. Simply do your research and remember to diversify. We'll discuss that in the next chapter.

Data through August 31, 2011 For internal and/or client reporting purposes only.

IVA Worldwide A

	Ticker	Status	Yield	Total Assets	Mstar Category
	IVWAX	Closed	0.4%	$9,731 mil	World Allocation

Governance and Management

Stewardship Grade:

Portfolio Manager(s)

Charles de Lardemelle and Charles de Vaulx are comanagers here. They are now partners in a new investment advisor, International Value Advisors, after leaving Arnhold and S. Bleichroeder, advisor to four First Eagle funds, in 2007. De Lardemelle was an analyst and portfolio manager with First Eagle, starting there in 1996. De Vaulx worked alongside Jean-Marie Eveillard for many years, then ran several First Eagle funds on his own when Eveillard retired in 2005. IVA currently has six other analysts (four also from First Eagle) and two traders, one of whom joined from First Eagle.

Strategy

The managers here are concerned with a good long-term result, but they also emphasize capital preservation. As a result, cash is typically part of the portfolio, as is gold. The fund uses a value-oriented approach and invests from the bottom up. Unlike other world-allocation funds, its fixed-income stake is usually for bottom-up reasons and consists mainly of corporate bonds. Its bond stake will thus vary and tends to be smaller. The portfolio consists of stocks of all sizes.

Historical Profile
Return
Risk
Rating Not Rated

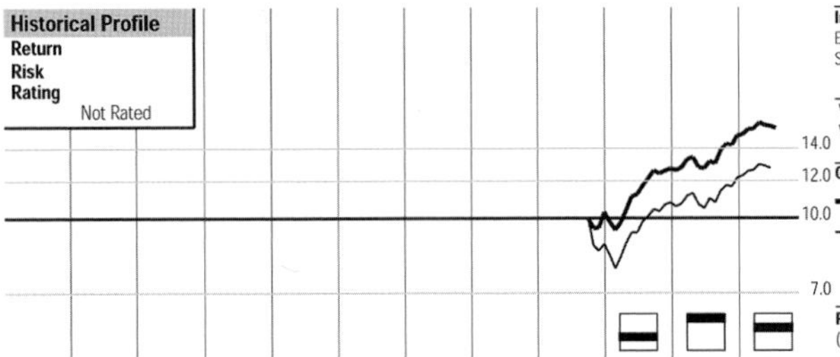

Growth of $10,000
— Investment Values of Fund
— Investment Values of M* MdTgRk

Investment Style
Equity
Stock %

▼ Manager Change
▽ Partial Manager Change

Performance Quartile (within Category)

	2000	2001	2002	2003	2004	2005	2006	2007	2008	2009	2010	08-11	History
	—	—	—	—	—	—	—	—	12.30	14.68	16.72	16.70	NAV
	—	—	—	—	—	—	—	—	—	23.03	17.22	-0.12	Total Return %
	—	—	—	—	—	—	—	—	—	1.26	4.81	-4.21	+/-M* MdTgRk
	—	—	—	—	—	—	—	—	—	-6.96	5.46	-3.50	+/-MSCI World
	—	—	—	—	—	—	—	—	—	0.84	0.44	0.00	Income Return %
	—	—	—	—	—	—	—	—	—	22.19	16.78	-0.12	Capital Return %
	—	—	—	—	—	—	—	—	—	56	3	47	Total Rtn % Rank Cat
	—	—	—	—	—	—	—	—	0.04	0.10	0.06	0.00	Income $
	—	—	—	—	—	—	—	—	0.00	0.35	0.42	0.00	Capital Gains $
	—	—	—	—	—	—	—	—	—	1.36	1.31	—	Expense Ratio %
	—	—	—	—	—	—	—	—	—	2.51	1.41	—	Income Ratio %
	—	—	—	—	—	—	—	—	—	55	29	—	Turnover Rate %
	—	—	—	—	—	—	—	—	79	1,016	2,390	2,916	Net Assets $mil

Performance 08-31-11

	1st Qtr	2nd Qtr	3rd Qtr	4th Qtr	Total
2007	—	—	—	—	—
2008	—	—	—	2.82	—*
2009	-4.88	14.53	11.94	0.89	23.03
2010	4.50	-4.24	9.12	7.35	17.22
2011	3.35	1.22	—	—	—

Trailing	Total Return%	+/-M* MdTgRk	+/-MSCI World	%Rank Cat	Growth of $10,000
3 Mo	-5.01	-2.66	0.36	40	9,499
6 Mo	-3.08	-6.12	-4.18	47	9,692
1 Yr	14.35	-0.39	-4.19	22	11,435
3 Yr Avg	—	—	—	—	—
5 Yr Avg	—	—	—	—	—
10 Yr Avg	—	—	—	—	—
15 Yr Avg	—	—	—	—	—

Tax Analysis	Tax-Adj Rtn%	%Rank Cat	Tax-Cost Rat	%Rank Cat
3 Yr (estimated)	—	—	—	—
5 Yr (estimated)	—	—	—	—
10 Yr (estimated)	—	—	—	—

Potential Capital Gain Exposure: 9% of assets

Rating and Risk

Time Period	Load-Adj Return %	Morningstar Rtn vs Cat	Morningstar Risk vs Cat	Morningstar Risk-Adj Rating
1 Yr	8.63			
3 Yr	—			
5 Yr	—			
10 Yr	—			
Incept	12.42			

Other Measures	Standard Index M* MdTgRk	Best Fit Index
Alpha	—	—
Beta	—	—
R-Squared	—	—
Standard Deviation	—	
Mean	—	
Sharpe Ratio	—	

Morningstar's Take by Bridget Hughes 12-27-10

IVA Worldwide is ahead of the pack during a volatile but prosperous year.

Comanagers Charles de Vaulx and Chuck de Lardemelle exercise an opportunistic, yet price-conscious approach to investing--which has led to good downside protection as a hallmark of their strategy. They have also said, though, that they consider themselves equity investors first and foremost. So, while this portfolio, like others in the world-allocation category, owns stocks and bonds as well as cash, the roles each investment plays here can mean different things. Consider as an example the fund's allocation to bonds: Instead of the expectation of ballast (which they can provide at times), de Vaulx and de Lardemelle are often instead looking for "equitylike" returns from them. That's the reason why the fund's bond stake is generally composed of high-yield corporate bonds.

Even the fund's cash stake can play different parts. Mostly, it's merely residual of their value approach, and investors should thus expect it to increase as market valuations are rising. (The managers say that cash has increased over the past several months to just less than 17% here, as they've continued to trim some of their bonds.) But consider the shorter-term Singaporean, Hong Kong, and Taiwanese bonds in the portfolio, or what de Vaulx calls "quasi-cash." De Lardemelle says that these represent a way for the fund to "park money in what they consider sound paper currencies," but both managers also say they expect equitylike returns primarily from currency gains. So far over the fund's holding period, the Singapore dollar has gained 6% versus the U.S. dollar.

With this uncommon approach in mind, it's perhaps not surprising to see the fund up roughly 17% for the year to date through Dec. 23, 2010, and ahead of the vast majority of the category. On the other hand, it's important to note that helping its showing this year was a particularly resilient summer--investors should be happy to see that this characteristic still seems intact.

Address:	645 Madison Avenue New York, NY 10022 866-941-4482
Web Address:	www.ivafunds.com
Inception:	09-30-08
Advisor:	International Value Advisers, LLC
Subadvisor:	None
NTF Plans:	Fidelity Instl-NTF, Schwab Instl NTF

Minimum Purchase:	Closed	Add: —	IRA: —
Min Auto Inv Plan:	Closed	Add: —	
Sales Fees:	5.00%L, , 2.00%R		
Management Fee:	0.90%, 0.04%A		
Actual Fees:	Mgt:0.90%	Dist:0.25%	
Expense Projections:	3Yr:$894	5Yr:$1182	10Yr:$2000
Income Distribution:	Annually		

Portfolio Analysis 06-30-11

Total Stocks:107 Share change since 03-31-11	Sectors	P/E Ratio	YTD Return %	% Net Assets
Astellas Pharma, Inc.	Hlth care	—	—	2.86
⊕ Microsoft Corporation	Technology	11.9	-4.37	2.73
⊕ MasterCard Incorporated A	Finan Svs	15.9	47.48	2.70
⊕ Nestle SA	Cnsmr Def	—	—	2.65
⊕ Total SA ADR	Energy	8.5	-8.94	2.57
⊕ Hewlett-Packard Company	Technology	11.4	-38.55	2.49
⊖ SECOM Co., Ltd.	Industrl	—	—	2.46
⊕ Genting Malaysia Bhd	—	—	—	2.36
⊕ Dell, Inc.	Technology	13.0	8.49	2.28

Total Fixed-Income:26	Date of Maturity	Amount $000	Value $000	% Net Assets
Singapore(Govt Of) 2.25%	07-01-13	593,799	506,077	5.00
Wendel 4.375%	08-09-17	116,950	157,143	1.55
Norway(Kingdom Of) 6.5%	05-15-13	495,043	99,120	0.98
Hong Kong(Govt Of) 2.66%	12-17-12	735,050	97,944	0.97
Wendel 6.75% 20-Apr-2018		61,000	89,288	0.88
Wendel 4.875%	05-26-16	56,800	77,718	0.77
Sirius Xm Radio 144A 8.75	04-01-15	61,574	69,540	0.69
Mohawk Inds 6.875%	01-15-16	37,016	41,613	0.41

Current Investment Style

Value Blnd Growth			Market Cap	%
		Large	Giant	30.9
		Mid	Large	41.8
		Small	Mid	20.5
			Small	5.5
			Micro	1.3
			Avg $mil: 16,078	

Value Measures		Rel Category
Price/Earnings	13.41	0.99
Price/Book	1.61	0.84
Price/Sales	0.88	0.73
Price/Cash Flow	7.69	1.17
Dividend Yield %	3.10	1.11

Growth Measures	%	Rel Category
Long-Term Erngs	7.91	0.71
Book Value	2.20	0.17
Sales	-3.39	NMF
Cash Flow	-6.46	NMF
Historical Erngs	3.06	0.40

Composition - Net

Cash	6.7	Bonds	13.5
Stocks	69.0	Other	10.8
Foreign (% of Stock)			59.0

Sector Weightings	% of Stocks	Rel M* MdTgRk	3 Year High Low
⤴ Cyclical	23.37	0.64	
⬛ BasicMat	0.87	0.12	— —
⬛ CnsmrCyc	14.11	1.43	— —
⬛ FinanSvs	7.74	0.48	— —
⬛ Real Est	0.65	0.19	— —
⤳ Sensitive	44.92	1.17	
⬛ CommSrvs	4.69	0.86	— —
⬛ Energy	7.01	0.60	— —
⬛ Industrl	18.28	1.49	— —
⬛ Technlgy	19.63	1.59	— —
→ Defensive	31.72	1.24	
⬛ CnsmrDef	19.63	2.31	— —
⬛ Hlthcare	4.87	0.57	— —
⬛ Utilities	2.53	0.55	— —

Regional Exposure % Stock

UK/W. Europe	25	N. America	42
Japan	20	Latn America	0
Asia X Japan	11	Other	2

Country Exposure % Stock

United States	42	South Korea	7
Japan	20	Switzerland	5
France	16		

© 2011 Morningstar, Inc. All rights reserved. The information herein is not represented or warranted to be accurate, correct, complete or timely. Past performance is no guarantee of future results. Access updated reports at **mfb.morningstar.com**. To order reprints, call 312-696-6100.

MORNINGSTAR® Mutual Funds ⓔⓞ

Fig. 9-7

(Inclusion in this book does not constitute an endorsement of IVA Worldwide fund.)

Data through September 30, 2011 For internal and/or client reporting purposes only.

Harding Loevner Emerging Markets

	Ticker	Status	Yield	Total Assets	Mstar Category
	HLEMX	Open	0.5%	$1,549 mil	Diversified Emerging Mkt

Governance and Management

Stewardship Grade:

Portfolio Manager(s)

Co-lead manager Rusty Johnson has been at the helm since the fund opened in late 1998, and he spent nearly 10 years working on Asia equities before joining Harding Loevner in 1994. Co-lead Craig Shaw has been part of the team since 2006, and he had a decade of investment and operational experience in the developing world when he joined Harding Loevner in 2001. Comanager Simon Hallett, who also serves as the firm's CIO, focuses his attention on portfolio construction and risk control. He ran the firm's foreign large-growth fund for 17 years and did a

Strategy

This fund's management team focuses on companies with strong revenue, earnings, and dividend growth that boast good free cash flows and sound balance sheets. It looks for proven and shareholder-friendly company managers that have sound business plans and ongoing competitive advantages. The team considers opportunities in smaller emerging markets, as well as large ones, makes full use of the sector spectrum, and pays attention to risk control. The fund levies a 2% redemption fee on shares held fewer than 90 days and makes extensive use of fair value pricing.

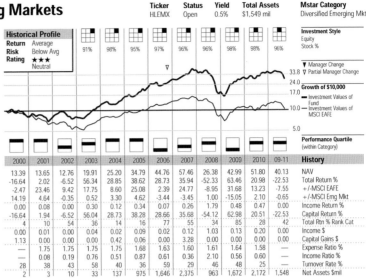

Historical Profile
Return Average
Risk Below Avg
Rating ★★★ Neutral

91% 98% 95% 97% 96% 96% 98% 98% 96%

Investment Style
Equity
Stock %

▼ Manager Change
▽ Partial Manager Change

33.8

24.0

Growth of $10,000
17.0 — Investment Values of Fund
10.0 — Investment Values of MSCI EAFE

5.0

Performance Quartile (within Category)

	2000	2001	2002	2003	2004	2005	2006	2007	2008	2009	2010	09-11	History
	13.39	13.65	12.76	19.91	25.20	34.79	44.76	57.46	26.38	42.99	51.80	40.13	NAV
	-16.64	2.02	-6.52	56.34	28.85	38.62	28.73	35.94	-52.33	63.46	20.98	-22.53	Total Return %
	-2.47	23.46	9.42	17.75	8.60	25.08	2.39	24.77	-8.95	31.68	13.23	-7.55	+/-MSCI EAFE
	14.19	4.64	-0.35	0.52	3.30	4.62	-3.44	-3.45	1.00	-15.05	2.10	-0.65	+/-MSCI Emg Mkt
	0.00	0.08	0.00	0.30	0.12	0.34	0.07	0.26	1.79	0.48	0.47	0.00	Income Return %
	-16.64	1.94	-6.52	56.04	28.73	38.28	28.66	35.68	-54.12	62.98	20.51	-22.53	Capital Return %
	4	10	54	36	14	16	77	55	34	85	28	42	Total Rtn % Rank Cat
	0.00	0.01	0.00	0.04	0.02	0.09	0.02	0.12	1.03	0.13	0.20	0.00	Income $
	1.13	0.00	0.00	0.42	0.06	0.00	0.00	3.28	0.00	0.00	0.00	0.00	Capital Gains $
	—	1.75	1.75	1.75	1.75	1.68	1.63	1.60	1.61	1.64	1.58	—	Expense Ratio %
	—	0.08	0.19	0.76	0.51	0.87	0.61	0.36	2.10	0.56	0.60	—	Income Ratio %
	28	38	43	58	40	36	59	29	46	48	25	—	Turnover Rate %
	2	3	10	33	137	975	1,646	2,375	963	1,672	2,172	1,548	Net Assets $mil

Performance 09-30-11

	1st Qtr	2nd Qtr	3rd Qtr	4th Qtr	Total
2007	1.25	12.80	12.97	5.36	35.94
2008	-9.90	-0.17	-26.39	-27.99	-52.33
2009	-3.87	32.85	20.07	6.60	63.46
2010	3.63	-7.86	19.93	5.65	20.98
2011	-1.70	0.02	-21.21		

Trailing	Total Return%	+/- MSCI EAFE	+/- MSCI Emg Mkt	%Rank Cat	Growth of $10,000
3 Mo	-21.21	-2.20	1.35	27	7,879
6 Mo	-21.19	-3.45	2.26	26	7,881
1 Yr	-18.16	-8.80	-2.01	53	8,184
3 Yr Avg	3.33	4.46	-2.94	61	11,033
5 Yr Avg	2.77	6.23	-2.10	55	11,464
10 Yr Avg	15.14	10.11	-0.93	44	40,951
15 Yr Avg					

Tax Analysis	Tax-Adj Rtn%	%Rank Cat	Tax-Cost Rat	%Rank Cat
3 Yr (estimated)	2.80	51	0.52	48
5 Yr (estimated)	2.24	33	0.52	17
10 Yr (estimated)	14.78	27	0.31	10

Potential Capital Gain Exposure: 16% of assets

Rating and Risk

Time Period	Load-Adj Return %	Morningstar Rtn vs Cat	Morningstar Risk vs Cat	Morningstar Risk-Adj Rating
1 Yr	-18.16			
3 Yr	3.33	Avg	-Avg	★★★
5 Yr	2.77	Avg	-Avg	★★★
10 Yr	15.14	Avg	-Avg	★★★
Incept	13.46			

Other Measures	Standard Index MSCI EAFE	Best Fit Index MSCI Emg Mkt
Alpha	5.6	-2.7
Beta	1.10	0.98
R-Squared	85	99
Standard Deviation	30.22	
Mean	3.33	
Sharpe Ratio	0.26	

Portfolio Analysis 06-30-11

Share change since 03-11 Total Stocks:79	Sector	Country	% Assets
⊖ Vale S.A. ADR	Basic Mat	Brazil	2.76
⊖ America Movil SAB de CV	Comm Svs	Mexico	2.75
⊖ Samsung Electronics Co.,	Technology	Korea	2.64
⊖ Petroleo Brasileiro SA P	Energy	Brazil	2.34
⊖ OAO Gazprom ADR	Energy	Russia	2.30
⊖ Mtn Group Limited	Comm Svs	South Africa	2.16
Bank Bradesco ADR	Finan Svs	Brazil	2.10
⊖ Taiwan Semiconductor Man	Technology	Taiwan	2.03
⊖ Wal-Mart de Mexico SAB d	Cnsmr Def	Mexico	2.02
⊖ Lukoil Company ADR	Energy	Russia	1.95
Sociedad Quimica Y Miner	Basic Mat	Chile	1.92
⊖ Bank Rakyat Indonesia (P	Finan Svs	Indonesia	1.87
⊖ Synnex Technology Intern	Technology	Taiwan	1.81
⊖ X5 Retail Group N.V GDR	Cnsmr Def	Russia	1.74
⊖ Samsung Fire & Marine In	Finan Svs	Korea	1.70
⊕ CNOOC, Ltd. ADR	Energy	China	1.70
⊖ Arcelik A.S.	Cnsmr Def	Turkey	1.63
⊖ China Merchants Holdings	Industrl	China	1.56
⊖ AmBev ADR	Cnsmr Def	Brazil	1.51
⊖ Tencent Holdings Ltd.	Technology	China	1.47

Current Investment Style

Value Blnd Growth		Market Cap	%
	Large Mid Small	Giant	45.0
		Large	36.7
		Mid	16.0
		Small	2.3
		Micro	0.0
		Avg $mil:	20,255

Value Measures		Rel Category
Price/Earnings	11.99	1.00
Price/Book	2.22	1.11
Price/Sales	1.23	0.99
Price/Cash Flow	4.43	0.77
Dividend Yield %	2.20	0.87

Growth Measures	%	Rel Category
Long-Term Erngs	11.99	0.70
Book Value	9.24	12.32
Sales	7.09	0.89
Cash Flow	9.71	6.07
Historical Erngs	-5.53	NMF

Composition - Net

Cash	1.6	Bonds	0.8	
Stocks	96.0	Other	1.6	
Foreign (% of Stock)	99.4			

Sector Weightings	% of Rel MSCI Stocks	EAFE	3 Year High Low
↻ Cyclical	39.64	—	
🅰 BasicMat	11.39	—	4 0
CnsmrCyc	7.84	—	10 7
FinanSvs	20.41	—	2 1
Real Est	0.00	—	14 6
↝ Sensitive	28.21	—	
CommSrvs	8.57	—	25 20
Energy	12.19	—	19 8
Industrl	5.79	—	17 13
Technlgy	14.17	—	13 7
→ Defensive	32.15	—	
CnsmrDef	16.51	—	4 3
Hlthcare	3.13	—	9 5
Utilities	0.00	—	10 4

Regional Exposure		% Stock
UK/W. Europe	4	N. America 1
Japan	0	Latn America 30
Asia X Japan	45	Other 20

Country Exposure		% Stock
Brazil	15	Russia 9
China	15	Mexico 9
South Korea	9	

Morningstar's Take by William Samuel Rocco 09-15-11

Harding Loevner Emerging Markets still has significant long-term appeal.

This fund remains in great hands. Co-lead manager Rusty Johnson, who has been at the helm throughout this fund's 13-year life, has a fine international-investing resume. Craig Shaw, who became a co-lead manager earlier this year, has been part of this fund's team since 2006 and he had a decade of investment and operational experience in the developing world when he joined Harding Loevner in 2001. Comanager Simon Hallett is the firm's CIO and previously posted strong long-term results running its foreign large-growth fund. And the three managers are supported by the 18 other investment pros at Harding Loevner, including the managers of the firm's successful world- and foreign-stock funds.

Johnson and Shaw are following the same quality-growth strategy that they've always used here and that their colleagues have employed to earn good long-term results at the firm's other

offerings. Namely, they insist that their picks have healthy balance sheets, clear competitive advantages, as well as strong revenue, earnings, and dividend growth rates. And they build distinctive country and sector weightings as they pursue stocks that meet their high standards. For instance, the fund has far more Mexico and consumer-defensive exposure than its average peer as well as higher average returns on assets and equity.

Largely due to its quality bias, this fund has been significantly less volatile than the typical member of its explosive group. That bias has also held the fund back in the 2009 and other extreme rallies, which explains its so-so three- and five-year returns, but the managers' approach has been a success over the longer run. The fund posted a 14.5% annualized return since its inception, in fact, while its typical peer gained 11.5% on an annualized basis. All told, this fund remains more attractive than most of its peers.

Address:	Harding, Loevner Funds, Inc. c/o The Northern Trust Company Chicago, IL 60680-4766 877-435-8105	Minimum Purchase:	$5000	Add: $0	IRA: $5000
		Min Auto Inv Plan:	$0	Add: —	
		Sales Fees:	No-load, 2.00%R		
Web Address:	www.hardingloevnerfunds.com	Management Fee:	1.25%, 0.15%A		
Inception:	11-09-98	Actual Fees:	Mgt:1.25%	Dist: —	
Advisor:	Harding Loevner LP	Expense Projections:	3Yr:$499	5Yr:$860	10Yr:$1878
Subadvisor:	None	Income Distribution:	Annually		
NTF Plans:	Fidelity Retail-NTF, Schwab OneSource				

 Mutual Funds

Fig. 9-8

Section 9.3:   International Sector Mutual Funds and ETF's

Lesson #43: What NOT to own: International "sector" mutual funds and Exchange Traded Funds (ETF's) DO add moderate diversification value, but are somewhat redundant and difficult to use. They also contain a substantial risk of being caught in an investment bubble. So I recommend that you do not invest in them.

Sector funds invest specifically in one unique asset class, such as precious metals or petroleum. The stewpot of available sector funds includes funds across an entire spectrum of potential risks and returns. They are most useful as small allocations to undervalued sectors of the financial markets or as insurance policies against unforeseen change. But diversified funds should invest in these same sectors, and it is impossible to guess accurately what each sector will do. As a result, many investors lose lots of money investing excessively in sector funds, via "competence by proxy." Thus I recommend that you simply avoid investing in them.

When we get to portfolio allocation, you'll see that I DO advocate holding 5% in an energy mutual fund, perhaps 5% in a commodities fund, and perhaps 5% in a health care mutual fund, but that's it. Even then, I'm leery of trying to outguess markets via sector fund investing. I advocate investing in these sectors simply to add unique diversification, not to outperform markets.

Wall Street tends to create sector mutual funds in what is hot, overcrowded, and overpriced now, not what is unpopular, abandoned, and cheap. It's a reverse market indicator: the more new funds you see in any one sector, the more overvalued that sector probably is, and the more you should probably be rebalancing a little money into investments elsewhere.

Energy mutual funds are extremely cyclical, depending largely on the price of petroleum. You need to be very patient, since petroleum cycles tend to go from frenzy to crash and back again. During that process, however, energy stocks tend to provide a bit of inflation insurance. As a result of all this, I am recommending that you invest only 5% at most. Rely on more flexible value funds for additional energy holdings in their portfolios.

Natural resources and **precious metals** funds tend to move in tandem, with precious metals funds likely to skitter off on their own volatile paths. These are other boom-and-bust investments. Again, look for proxy holdings for these within international allocation and domestic allocation or value mutual funds. By doing so, you are likely to hold these stocks when they are cheap and despised, and avoid being caught up in a gold bubble like so many other investors.

Gold especially becomes an international medium of exchange when the world becomes wary. In some countries, currency exchange may be limited by politics or simple access to markets, so gold can rapidly surge as people invest due to economic or geopolitical fears. This can be unexpected, so you want to own your precious metals before the event.

Once again, mostly look to more diversified funds for a precious metal holding. Or, if you are seeking more "inflation insurance", select a mutual fund which holds more than just precious metals, and includes the stocks of the producers of other commodities as well. Then own only 5% of your portfolio or less.

International health care sector funds hold global stocks of corporations which make drugs and provide other health care services. We are in a health-care revolution. Nobody knows what will happen to the health care industry, except that our population will need more of it as our average age increases. Investing 5% of your portfolio in a health care sector mutual fund provides you with a small dab of implicit insurance: these stocks tend to retain value better than most in a stock market decline.

But health care stocks also tend to lag during big bull markets upwards. In addition, health care stocks, and thus health care sector mutual funds, tend to be subject to an unusually high level of political risk, even within the United States. Holding a fund which focuses only on the health care venue should be limited, therefore, to 5% of your portfolio or less.

What not to own: Exchange Traded Funds, known in the world as "ETF's" are artificial computer-created stock baskets which mimic a great variety of indices in stock markets around the world. They have the advantage of trading like stocks, at current valuations. They also have the substantial disadvantage of incurring stock-transaction fees when you trade.

More importantly, they also sometimes serve as hedge funds' vehicles for market manipulation. In the past few years, this has resulted in "flash crashes" in which ETF's in play by hedge funds have gyrated dramatically in the space of a single day, with prices changing 30% or more.

That's unfortunate if you happen to be living life at the moment, instead of keeping your nostrils pressed tightly to the computer screen. In fact, the manipulation in these ETF's is sometimes so overt that I even wonder if this sort of financial instrument should be legal. At any rate, since you are not a short-term trader, you don't need ETF's. ETF's are a product of society's adoration of control. In reality, all these choices aren't needed. But people like to take charge, so savvy marketing Wall Streeters have created everything but the Dachshund Weiner Dog Index. (We could call it the DWI.)

Traditional mutual funds are priced by adding up all the individual investments they hold at the end of the day. You invest in them by adding money directly to the fund after the market closes. You accept whatever the market did that day as your price.

If the market is crashing on any particular day, you can't get out of a traditional mutual fund during the slide. You just have to endure it, and take your money out after the market closes and the damage is done. If the market is booming, you can't get in before the market closes, either.

In other words you can't day-trade a normal mutual fund. You can't sell it in the morning and buy it back in the afternoon. However, with an ETF or a closed end fund you can trade at any time. If you have an ETF which is an index fund of the S&P 500, you can buy that index at any time during the day and that's the price you get.

This is a very comforting feature for active traders. But in the longer term it doesn't really affect the performance of your investments. One day's returns don't really have that much of an impact, and the transaction costs of jumping in and out of the stock market can deeply dent any gains you make.

I have <u>never</u> met an investor whose financial success was influenced by the choice of ETF's versus traditional mutual funds. I HAVE SEEN people who became wealthy selling a plan of investing in ETF's to individual investors.

There are many hundreds of ETF's all of which represent some kind of esoteric index. The original ETF, the SPDR (pronounced "Spider) is an ETF version of the S&P 500 Index fund. From there you may follow a wandering bean stalk of investment choices, from Indian stocks to South African stocks, to global financial stocks, to gold.

ETF's are less valuable in broader arenas where active managers can add genuine values. Thus, in general, you don't really need them at all.

Review: The Lessons of Chapter 9

Lesson #42: Mutual funds which exclude stocks or bonds of the US but invest in the rest of the world are known as International funds. These can operate in any part of the financial markets. It is normal to find international value funds, or international growth funds, or international sector funds. The difference is that all of their holdings are outside the US.

Funds which include stocks or bonds of the United States, but only as a minority of their holdings, are called Global mutual funds.

These funds can be used interchangeably to diversify your portfolio. They should play a major role.

Lesson #43: What NOT to own: most "Sector" mutual funds and ALL Exchange Traded Funds (ETF's). Energy, Commodities, and health care sector funds DO add moderate diversification value, and thus are worth owning in small amounts.

All other sector funds are somewhat redundant and difficult to use. They also contain a substantial risk of being caught in an investment bubble. I would recommend avoiding them.

ETF's are market traded financial vehicles which have all the same disadvantages, and are play-toys for the hedge fund day-traders. So I recommend that you do not invest in them. Just say no to market manipulation.

Chapter 10

Build a Diversified Portfolio of Mutual Funds

Think of diversification not so much as an investment strategy, but rather as a manner of investing -- a way of being in the markets. It can be applied equally well to aggressive, moderate and conservative portfolios.
—John Prestbo, January 16th, 2009

The only investors who shouldn't diversify are those who are right 100% of the time.
—John Templeton, 1983

Section 10.1: The Basics of Portfolio Construction

Lesson #44: To create your portfolio, invest in a VERY wide assortment of mutual fund asset classes.

Like a general contractor, you have gathered all the tools, materials, and skills, and now you are ready to begin work on building your portfolio. To review, the reason your portfolio will be created like this is because of the following realities:

1. In the past few decades, we have experienced several sharp global financial downturns.
2. We genuinely don't know what will happen next. More downturns? Nobody can guess.
3. Unexpected change is a reality of life. We probably need to invest more defensively than we thought.
4. Markets go to both high and low extremes.
5. Irrational behavior on the part of investors is an <u>essential</u> component of financial market behavior. To some degree, we are all subject to irrational behavior as well.
6. You must embrace an investing program which self-limits your ability to behave irrationally. Also, inevitably, you will <u>not</u> be right about market expectations 100% of the time.
7. To meet these challenges and uncertainties, you must invest only in no-load or transaction-fee-only mutual funds.
8. You should invest via a discount brokerage, and rely on the information in your monthly statement and *Morningstar* reports.
9. Instead of burying your head like an ostrich, you will actively diversify using information about each mutual fund.
10. You will use a combination of asset classes to assemble your portfolio.

Although the exact behavioral relationships between asset classes change, they follow general trends. The importance of these is demonstrated in the graph below, which charts the diversification between only US stocks and US bonds. The "up"

Stocks and Bonds: Risk Versus Return
1970–2010

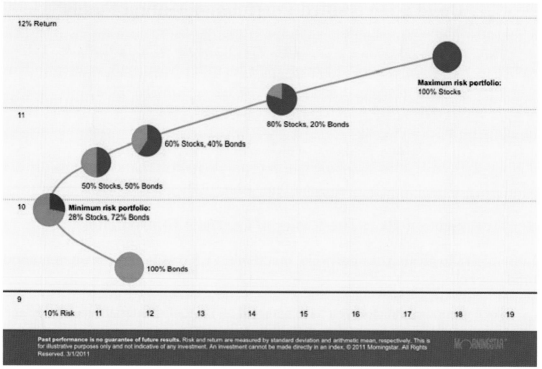

12% Return

Maximum risk portfolio:
100% Stocks

11

80% Stocks, 20% Bonds

60% Stocks, 40% Bonds

50% Stocks, 50% Bonds

10   Minimum risk portfolio:
28% Stocks, 72% Bonds

100% Bonds

9

10% Risk   11   12   13   14   15   16   17   18   19

Fig. 10-1)

axis represents average historical returns. The "sideways" axis represents standard deviation, which in turn represents risk. (Fig. 10-1)

Higher on the graph is a higher return. Farther right on the graph is greater risk. So the ideal investment is in the upper left of the graph. No risk. High return. Dream on.

The line is a gross approximation of real world investment returns relative to risk. Of course in the real world this line floats and changes, but the essential form remains about the same.

What this line represents is what you can actually make in the real world with a simple US stock and US bond mix, as opposed to theoretical world. Investment returns above this conceptual line don't exist for long, if at all, because short term traders, called "arbitragers" quickly obliterate them. Below the line are returns that actually happen. The line itself represents the optimal returns from a diversified stock/bond portfolio. This line is as good as it gets in the real world for a spectrum of risks. In the financial world, this is called the "efficient frontier". When you are offered an investment which is above the 'efficient frontier" in terms of projected return, it may be a rare opportunity, but odds are, it's a scam.

The lowest portfolio on the graph is the all-red 100% bond portfolio. Note that an all-bond portfolio has historically delivered lower returns and does not completely diminish risk. Surprising isn't it? Over the long-term, you actually REDUCE overall risk by adding a modicum of stock mutual funds.

The minimum risk portfolio IS REALLY IMPORTANT! What this is telling you is that over the long-term, risk is <u>lowered</u> and returns are <u>enhanced</u> by diversification, including a small holding in stock mutual funds. An all-bond portfolio is not as efficient.

The rest of the portfolios displayed in the graph show you that as you add stock mutual funds into your portfolio, returns and risk both rise, until at some point the additional return per unit of risk goes down. The law of diminishing returns applies to mutual funds as well as most of the rest of the world. So you make less return per additional unit of risk. In other words, the additional risk beyond an 80% stock/20% bonds portfolio probably isn't worth it, unless you simply enjoy volatility.

Now, stretch your mind. This graph simply represents a portfolio divided between cash, bonds, and the S&P 500 Index. It's very simple. ***But you are going to invest in a much broader spectrum and diversify much more. So imagine that instead of a line, this looks like a blanket, billowing with the turbulence of 50 different financial markets but following approximately the same conceptual curve.*** Like this mental image of a blanket, your portfolio is going to be much more complex than this simple line graph.

You can see this in the following graph, as we add international stocks to the mix. As you can see, most investments by themselves do not historically offer the optimum blend of risk and reward. For example, you can see the dot which represents Canadian stocks on the graph. You can see that Canadian stocks from 1970 to 2010 had an expected volatility of about 20+%, which was greater than both US bonds and US stocks. Canadian stocks also had an expected return which was higher than US stocks or bonds. In other words, Canadian stocks had higher risks and higher rewards. (Fig. 10-2)

Now lay a ruler on this graph horizontally at the level of Canadian stocks, and follow it to the left until it reaches the light blue line. That light blue line represents a global portfolio. As you can see, from 1970 through 2010, a blend of US stocks and bonds and Canadian stocks offered higher long-term returns and LOWER overall risk than US or Canadian stocks! This was possible because the Canadian and the US financial markets were not entirely correlated. In other words, they didn't move together in lockstep.

This is historic data. It is unlikely that this relationship will be replicated exactly in the coming 38 years. But something like it will undoubtedly unfold. If we diversify more than we did in the past decades, we are likely to reap some efficiencies of diversification which aren't currently quantifiable. The challenge is to accept that we don't know what will happen and to simply diversify our portfolio with that in mind.

Later in this chapter I will describe the allocations for a safe money portfolio, a low risk portfolio, a moderately risky portfolio, and a market risk portfolio. These all assume that the financial markets are temporarily fairly valued and that interest rates aren't changing. In other words, these are theoretical allocations which simply get you started. They will work well enough in the long-term. Employing the techniques I will describe in later chapters will make them work better.

If your choice of risk/return exposure is "safe money", you are willing to accept very little risk to get higher returns. In this case, you will go off the reservation with about 30% of your money and buy something other than mutual funds: FDIC insured certificates of deposit. ***These are no-risk, low-return bank deposits which you will buy***

International Enhances Domestic Portfolios
1970–2010

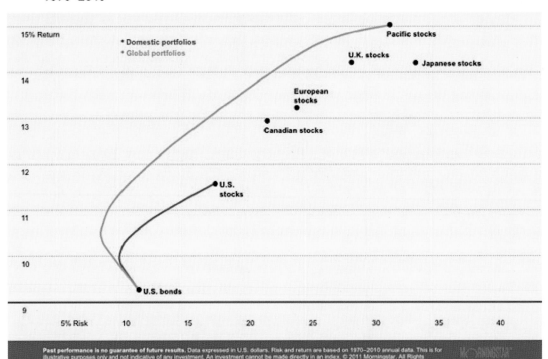

Fig. 10-2)

directly through your discount brokerages. You will then put the remaining 70% of your money in seven other money market or mutual fund investments. You will thus have 10% of your money in each investment.

If you wish to accept somewhat more risk in return for potentially higher returns, in "Low Risk", "Moderate Risk", or "Market Risk" portfolios, then you will want to hold a total of 20 mutual funds, each ideally comprising about 5% of the portfolio. That will provide you with diversification without chaos.

Such broad diversification ensures that you are not dependent upon any one manager for your success. After all, they can't foretell the future any more than you can. This also means that you distribute these funds within larger asset classes. For example if you decide that you wish to have a "Market Risk" allocation, as part of your portfolio you will have four very different growth funds which are correlated as little as possible, and four different value funds, and four different asset allocation funds, and so on. Within each asset class, your mutual funds will be unlike each other, intentionally.

Section 10.2: How to Select "Good" Mutual Funds

Lesson #45: Select mutual funds for your portfolio using a series of selection screens.

I cannot provide you with exactly the right mutual fund for your needs. For one thing, I don't know what your individual needs are. Also, if you are investing in a

Data through August 31, 2011 For internal and/or client reporting purposes only.

Hussman Strategic Total Return

Ticker	Status	Yield	Total Assets	Mstar Category
HSTRX	Open	0.9%	$2,518 mil	Conservative Allocation

Governance and Management

Stewardship Grade:

Portfolio Manager(s)

John Hussman launched this fund in 2002. He holds a doctorate in economics and taught in that field before starting this fund. Although Hussman receives the advice of key personnel on the fund's board of trustees and at Hussman Econometrics, this fund depends heavily on Hussman himself, leaving the fund exposed to some manager risk. He invests all of his liquid assets (outside of cash and money market accounts) in his two funds.

Strategy

Manager John Hussman analyzes price trends and trading volume as well as valuation measures to assess the general market climate and the attractiveness of individual stocks, metals, and bonds. Depending on his market assessment, Hussman may use put and call options to hedge the portfolio.

Historical Profile

Return	Above Avg
Risk	Below Avg
Rating	★★★★★ Highest

Investment Style: Equity Stock %

19% 22% 22% 23% 20% 15% 5% 2% 8%

▼ Manager Change
▽ Partial Manager Change

Growth of $10,000
— Investment Values of Fund
— Investment Values of M* MdTgRk

20.0
17.5
15.0
12.5
10.0

Performance Quartile (within Category)

History

	2000	2001	2002	2003	2004	2005	2006	2007	2008	2009	2010	08-11	
	—	—	10.19	10.60	11.05	11.11	11.05	11.50	11.56	11.97	12.13	12.70	NAV
	—	—	—	9.80	6.50	6.00	5.66	12.61	6.34	5.84	7.03	5.03	Total Return %
	—	—	—	-12.68	-4.98	-1.04	-7.29	3.98	28.53	-15.93	-5.38	0.94	+/-M* MdTgRk
	—	—	—	10.99	-9.49	-2.95	0.73	2.89	-1.67	18.90	-8.39	0.96	+/-Mstr Md Cn Rk
	—	—	—	2.04	2.00	2.69	2.25	3.41	1.22	0.84	1.24	0.32	Income Return %
	—	—	—	7.76	4.50	3.31	3.41	9.20	5.12	5.00	5.79	4.71	Capital Return %
	—	—	—	71	39	4	86	1	1	97	89	3	Total Rtn % Rank Cat
	—	—	0.04	0.21	0.21	0.29	0.25	0.37	0.14	0.10	0.15	0.04	Income $
	—	—	0.00	0.37	0.02	0.30	0.43	0.54	0.49	0.17	0.54	0.00	Capital Gains $
	—	—	—	0.90	0.90	0.90	0.90	0.90	0.90	0.75	0.67	0.64	Expense Ratio %
	—	—	—	1.99	2.34	2.25	2.94	2.86	2.05	0.26	1.59	0.61	Income Ratio %
	—	—	—	151	174	64	55	41	212	36	118	254	Turnover Rate %
	—	—	13	39	121	127	188	206	577	1,396	2,426	2,509	Net Assets $mil

Performance 08-31-11

	1st Qtr	2nd Qtr	3rd Qtr	4th Qtr	Total
2007	0.72	0.18	6.68	4.60	12.61
2008	4.78	0.25	0.67	0.56	6.34
2009	1.38	1.28	3.12	-0.04	5.84
2010	0.42	3.79	3.06	-0.36	7.03
2011	0.16	0.65	—	—	—

Trailing	Total Return%	+/- M* MdTgRk	+/-Mstr Md Cn Rk	%Rank Cat	Growth of $10,000
3 Mo	3.16	5.51	4.05	1	10,316
6 Mo	4.78	1.74	1.51	1	10,478
1 Yr	5.07	-9.67	-6.17	90	10,507
3 Yr Avg	6.64	1.13	0.98	11	12,127
5 Yr Avg	7.59	2.09	1.95	1	14,416
10 Yr Avg	—	—	—		—
15 Yr Avg	—	—	—		—

Tax Analysis	Tax-Adj Rtn%	%Rank Cat	Tax-Cost Rat	%Rank Cat
3 Yr (estimated)	5.31	9	1.25	59
5 Yr (estimated)	5.95	1	1.53	76
10 Yr (estimated)	—	—	—	—

Potential Capital Gain Exposure: 6% of assets

Rating and Risk

Time Period	Load-Adj Return %	Morningstar Rtn vs Cat	Morningstar Risk vs Cat	Morningstar Risk-Adj Rating
1 Yr	5.07			
3 Yr	6.64	Avg	-Avg	★★★★
5 Yr	7.59	High	-Avg	★★★★★
10 Yr	—			
Incept	7.48			

Other Measures	Standard Index M* MdTgRk	Best Fit Index Amex Gold
Alpha	5.5	2.9
Beta	0.20	0.13
R-Squared	15	68
Standard Deviation	7.35	
Mean	6.64	
Sharpe Ratio	0.88	

Portfolio Analysis 03-31-11

Total Stocks:14 Share change since 12-31-10	Sectors	P/E Ratio	YTD Return %	% Net Assets
⊕ Agnico-Eagle Mines	Basic Mat	38.3	-9.25	1.51
⊕ Barrick Gold Corporation	Basic Mat	16.8	-2.15	1.34
⊕ Newmont Mining Corporatio	Basic Mat	13.3	2.26	1.15
⊕ AngloGold Ashanti Limited	Basic Mat	—	-6.94	1.01
⊕ Buenaventura Mining Compa	Basic Mat	18.8	-3.34	0.90
⊕ Goldcorp, Inc.	Basic Mat	24.6	16.62	0.63
⊕ Randgold Resources, Ltd.	Basic Mat	73.0	26.04	0.60
⊕ Harmony Gold Mining Co.,	Basic Mat	—	8.21	0.44
⊕ Gold Fields Limited ADR	Basic Mat	—	-6.62	0.12

Total Fixed-Income:9	Date of Maturity	Amount $000	Value $000	% Net Assets
US Treasury Note 3.625%	02-15-21	300,000	304,313	12.81
US Treasury Note 2.625%	11-15-20	300,000	279,984	11.79
US Treasury Bond 4.75%	02-15-41	250,000	259,883	10.94
US Treasury Note 3%	08-31-16	75,000	77,344	3.26
US Treasury Bond 2.5%	01-15-29	41,023	46,596	1.96
US Treasury Note 2%	07-15-14	29,203	32,078	1.35
US Treasury Note 2%	04-15-12	27,128	28,384	1.20
US Treasury Bond 4.25%	05-15-39	25,000	23,984	1.01
US Treasury Bond 2.375%	01-15-27	16,378	18,278	0.77

Equity Style			Fixed-Income Style	
Style: Growth			Duration: —	
Size: Large-Cap			Quality: —	

Value Measures		Rel Category
Price/Earnings	17.06	1.18
Price/Book	2.28	1.18
Price/Sales	3.51	2.70
Price/Cash Flow	8.56	1.26
Dividend Yield %	0.87	0.34

Growth Measures	%	Rel Category
Long-Term Erngs	9.93	0.98
Book Value	7.59	1.13
Sales	7.77	0.44
Cash Flow	34.78	2.07
Historical Erngs	26.11	4.04

Avg Eff Duration [1]	—
Avg Eff Maturity	—
Avg Credit Quality	—
Avg Wtd Coupon	3.44%

[1]figure provided by fund

Market Cap %			
Giant	24.3	Small	0.1
Large	58.1	Micro	0.0
Mid	17.5	Avg $mil:	17,413

Sector Weightings	% of Stocks	Rel M* MdTgRk	3 Year High Low	
ᔫ Cyclical	95.40	2.60		
🪙 BasicMat	95.40	13.25	0	0
🏠 CnsmrCyc	0.00	0.00	0	0
💳 FinanSvs	0.00	0.00	0	0
🏢 Real Est	0.00	0.00	0	0
⌇ Sensitive	0.00	0.17		
📡 CommSrvs	0.00	0.00	0	0
⚡ Energy	0.00	0.00	0	0
⚙ Industrl	0.00	0.00	95	25
💻 Technlgy	0.00	0.00	0	0
— Defensive	4.60	0.00		
🛒 CnsmrDef	0.00	0.00	0	0
✚ Hlthcare	0.00	0.00	0	0
🔌 Utilities	4.60	1.01	0	0

Composition - Net

● Cash	46.4
● Stocks	8.1
● Bonds	45.5
○ Other	0.0
Foreign (% of Stock)	81.0

Morningstar's Take by Janet Yang 04-08-11

Hussman Strategic Total Return remains poised for a downturn.

Portfolio manager John Hussman uses various assessments of valuation and other market signals to tactically manage this fund's allocation to bonds (mainly U.S. government securities) and other investments (such as currency exchange-traded funds and energy and precious-metals stocks). He made the right call in late 2007 when he warned of a downturn based on signals such as peak price multiples and rising-bond yields.

He's lately been sounding alarms on some commodity prices, and because he believes that investors aren't being adequately compensated for risk, he has defensively positioned the portfolio. The nonbond portion of the fund stands at less than 10% of assets (it can go as high as 30%) and consists mainly of precious-metals miners. Most of the bond holdings are in U.S. Treasuries with an average duration of about 4 years, though this had been as low as one year throughout 2010.

Tactical calls are notoriously difficult to get right. While Hussman has lately made strong interest-rate calls, the size of the fund's nonbond allocation has historically had a greater impact on relative returns. So far, his recent shift into bonds has cost the fund: It lagged most peers in 2010 and is again trailing in 2011. But avoiding downturns, such as the fund did in 2008, can be a boon to long-term relative results. Since its launch in 2002 through the end of March 2011, the fund's annualized 7.3% gain has more than kept up with its goal of beating inflation by 2% a year. (During that time, inflation clocked in at an annualized 2.4%.) The fund has also performed well versus the conservative-allocation competition, which averaged a 5.1% return, while enduring significantly lower volatility.

For investors looking to beat inflation by a bit and willing to forgo some of the upside to protect on the downside, this fund remains a good option.

Address:	5136 Dorsey Hall Drive Ellicott City, MD 21042 800-487-7626	Minimum Purchase:	$1000	Add: $100 IRA: $500
		Min Auto Inv Plan:	$1000	Add: $100
		Sales Fees:	No-load, 1.50%R	
Web Address:	www.hussmanfunds.com	Management Fee:	0.50% mx./0.45% mn., 0.08%A	
Inception:	09-12-02	Actual Fees:	Mgt:0.49%	Dist: —
Advisor:	Hussman Econometrics Advisors Inc	Expense Projections:	3Yr:$233	5Yr:$406 10Yr:$906
Subadvisor:	None	Income Distribution:	Quarterly	
NTF Plans:	N/A			

M◯RNINGSTAR®   **Mutual Funds**   ⓔⓠ

Fig. 10-3)

(Inclusion in this book does not constitute an endorsement of Hussman Strategic Total Return fund. Please do your own research and determine which funds are best suited to your own needs.)

constrained retirement plan or 401(k) menu or something otherwise restricted, you may need to select funds from a very limited selection. Funds change and may become less or more attractive.

To deal with this, I will describe to you which *Morningstar* categories I recommend for each portfolio risk/reward category. Then follow the subsequent search paradigm to select mutual funds. As you can see, it is designed to minimize your emotions.

Here's how to pick a fund.

1. As guided by the *Morningstar* self-help program, find the exact *Morningstar* category for which you seek mutual funds. I will list these for you later in this chapter.

2. **Within the category**, search by *Morningstar* ranking: select funds with as many stars as possible. Pick the top twenty which have three year track records. If there aren't twenty funds, pick as many as possible.

3. Search for the best average annual performance for three years within the *Morningstar* category. Pick the top ten which are not in the same fund family. You want ten independently managed funds, which are traded in your discount brokerage. Be sure you know what trading fee structure the discount brokerage applies to each fund before you trade. In an ideal world, you find ten independently managed transaction-free funds. If you can't find ten funds out of your original twenty, go back and bring in more funds based on *Morningstar* ranking until you have ten funds from which to select. If you have an abundance of equivalent funds from which to choose, select the ten with the lowest expenses.

4. From those ten mutual funds, pick the five mutual funds which differ the most from each other. You are thus seeking maximum independence.

For your final picks, in addition to all the other statistics I have gifted upon you, I also suggest that you use "R^2" aka R-Squared. You can see it on the following *Morningstar* page. For the Hussmann Strategic Total Return Fund, the "R^2" is 15. (Fig. 10-3)

The R^2 statistic measures how much the given mutual fund moves in lockstep with its most relevant index. You can find it on both your discount brokerage website and on any *Morningstar* mutual fund snapshot.

We look at R^2 data because most investors pick a portfolio which looks something like the selections on the left of the following graph. As you can see on that graph, all the mutual funds of Equity Portfolio A have essentially the same holdings. So this investor might have several funds, but they are all so highly correlated that diversification is minimal. This usually happens when an investor buys this year's "hot" funds, so he or she owns the one market sector which is bubbling this year. (Fig. 10-4)

As you can see, T Rowe Price Equity Income fund has an R^2 of 96. That tells you that it moves largely in lockstep with its relevant index, in this case the S&P 500. (Fig. 10-5)

A high R^2 is not in itself bad! It simply tells you will need other funds with lower R^2's to get more diversification. By using the portfolio asset class matrices which are provided later in this chapter, and selecting the lowest R^2's available, you will invest in

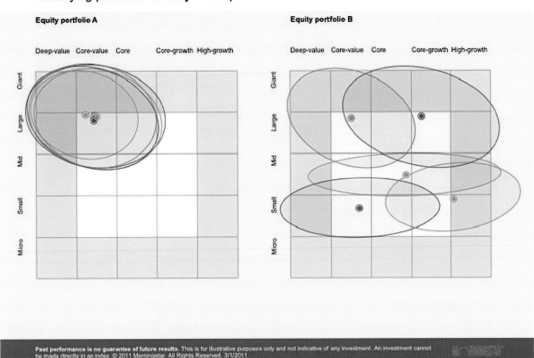

More Funds Do Not Always Mean Greater Diversification
Identifying potential security overlap

Fig. 10-4)

a portfolio which looks somewhat more like the highly diversified portfolio B on the right of the preceding diversification graph. That's good.

Section 10.3: The "Safe Money" Portfolio

Lesson #46: You create the "safe money" portfolio allocation when you simply want to minimize risk, with the highest possible return.

This is a very effective place to be when you are dealing with very short-term investments or other changes in ownership or investment goals. If you will need your money within five years, this may be an appropriate portfolio allocation for you.

Historical returns to a "safe money" portfolio are approximated by the 3-month CD performance portrayed on the following graph. As you can see, such investment mixes deliver a nice smooth pattern of returns. Check out the stock market falling on its face in 2008-2009. The CD returns hardly budge. (Fig. 10-6)

The downside, as you can see, is that relative to other investment classes, the "safe money" portfolio has historically delivered very lackluster returns. Let's look at those returns from a longer term perspective. In this graph, savings account returns are approximated as "Treasury bill" long term gains. (Fig. 10-7)

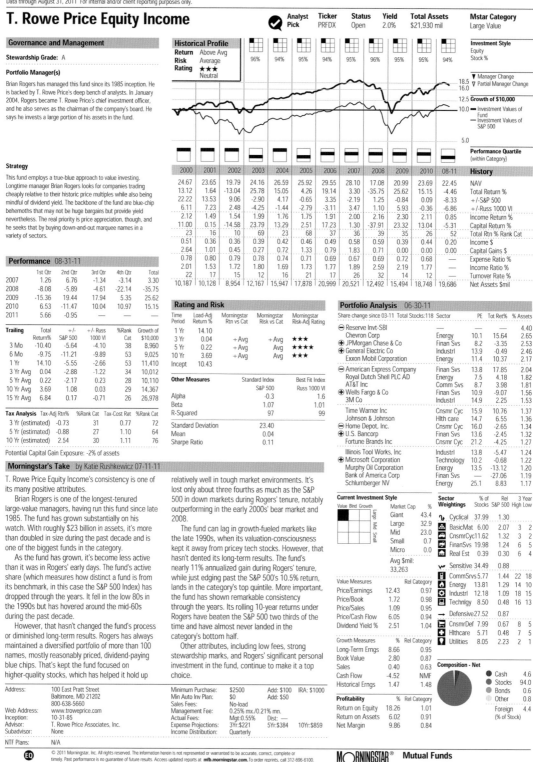

Data through August 31, 2011 For internal and/or client reporting purposes only.

T. Rowe Price Equity Income

Analyst Pick	✓
Ticker	PRFDX
Status	Open
Yield	2.0%
Total Assets	$21,930 mil
Mstar Category	Large Value

Governance and Management

Stewardship Grade: A

Portfolio Manager(s)

Brian Rogers has managed this fund since its 1985 inception. He is backed by T. Rowe Price's deep bench of analysts. In January 2004, Rogers became T. Rowe Price's chief investment officer, and he also serves as the chairman of the company's board. He says he invests a large portion of his assets in the fund.

Strategy

This fund employs a true-blue approach to value investing. Longtime manager Brian Rogers looks for companies trading cheaply relative to their historic price multiples while also being mindful of dividend yield. The backbone of the fund are blue-chip behemoths that may not be huge bargains but provide yield nevertheless. The real priority is price appreciation, though, and he seeks that by buying down-and-out marquee names in a variety of sectors.

Historical Profile
Return: Above Avg
Risk: Average
Rating: ★★★ Neutral

History

	2000	2001	2002	2003	2004	2005	2006	2007	2008	2009	2010	08-11	
	24.67	23.65	19.79	24.16	26.59	25.92	29.55	28.10	17.08	20.99	23.69	22.45	NAV
	13.12	1.64	-13.04	25.78	15.05	4.26	19.14	3.30	-35.75	25.62	15.15	-4.46	Total Return %
	22.22	13.53	9.06	4.17	-0.65	3.35	-2.19	1.25	-0.84	0.09	-8.33	+/-S&P 500
	6.11	7.23	2.48	-4.25	-1.44	-2.79	-3.11	3.47	1.10	5.93	-0.36	-6.86	+/-Russ 1000 VI
	2.12	1.49	1.54	1.99	1.76	1.75	1.91	2.00	2.16	2.30	2.11	0.85	Income Return %
	11.00	0.15	-14.58	23.79	13.29	2.51	17.23	1.30	-37.91	23.32	13.04	-5.31	Capital Return %
	23	16	10	69	23	68	37	36	39	35	26	52	Total Rtn % Rank Cat
	0.51	0.36	0.36	0.39	0.42	0.46	0.49	0.58	0.59	0.39	0.44	0.20	Income $
	2.64	1.01	0.45	0.27	0.72	1.33	0.79	1.83	0.71	0.00	0.00	0.00	Capital Gains $
	0.78	0.80	0.79	0.78	0.74	0.71	0.69	0.67	0.69	0.72	0.68	—	Expense Ratio %
	2.01	1.53	1.72	1.80	1.69	1.73	1.77	1.89	2.59	2.19	1.77	—	Income Ratio %
	22	17	15	12	16	21	17	26	32	14	12	—	Turnover Rate %
	10,187	10,128	8,954	12,167	15,947	17,878	20,999	20,521	12,492	15,494	18,748	19,686	Net Assets $mil

Performance 08-31-11

	1st Qtr	2nd Qtr	3rd Qtr	4th Qtr	Total
2007	1.26	6.76	-1.34	-3.14	3.30
2008	-8.08	-5.89	-4.61	-22.14	-35.75
2009	-15.36	19.44	17.94	5.35	25.62
2010	6.53	-11.47	10.04	10.97	15.15
2011	5.66	-0.95	—	—	

Trailing	Total Return%	+/- S&P 500	+/- Russ 1000 VI	%Rank Cat	Growth of $10,000
3 Mo	-10.40	-5.64	-4.10	38	8,960
6 Mo	-9.75	-11.21	-9.89	53	9,025
1 Yr	14.10	-5.55	-2.66	53	11,410
3 Yr Avg	0.04	-2.88	-1.22	34	10,012
5 Yr Avg	0.22	-2.17	0.23	28	10,110
10 Yr Avg	3.69	1.08	0.03	29	14,367
15 Yr Avg	6.84	0.17	-0.71	26	26,978

Tax Analysis	Tax-Adj Rtn%	%Rank Cat	Tax-Cost Rat	%Rank Cat
3 Yr (estimated)	-0.73	31	0.77	72
5 Yr (estimated)	-0.88	27	1.10	64
10 Yr (estimated)	2.54	30	1.11	76

Potential Capital Gain Exposure: -2% of assets

Rating and Risk

Time Period	Load-Adj Return %	Morningstar Rtn vs Cat	Morningstar Risk vs Cat	Morningstar Risk-Adj Rating
1 Yr	14.10			
3 Yr	0.04	+Avg	+Avg	★★★
5 Yr	0.22	+Avg	Avg	★★★★
10 Yr	3.69	+Avg	Avg	★★★
Incept	10.43			

Other Measures	Standard Index S&P 500	Best Fit Index Russ 1000 VI
Alpha	-0.3	1.6
Beta	1.07	1.01
R-Squared	97	99
Standard Deviation	23.40	
Mean	0.04	
Sharpe Ratio	0.11	

Portfolio Analysis 06-30-11

Share change since 03-11 Total Stocks:118

	Sector	PE	Tot Ret%	% Assets
⊖ Reserve Invt-SBI	—	—	—	4.40
Chevron Corp	Energy	10.1	15.64	2.65
⊕ JPMorgan Chase & Co	Finan Svs	8.2	-3.35	2.53
⊕ General Electric Co	Industrl	13.9	-0.49	2.46
Exxon Mobil Corporation	Energy	11.4	10.37	2.17
⊖ American Express Company	Finan Svs	13.8	17.85	2.04
Royal Dutch Shell PLC AD	Energy	7.5	4.18	1.82
AT&T Inc	Comm Svs	8.7	3.98	1.81
⊕ Wells Fargo & Co	Finan Svs	10.9	-9.07	1.56
3M Co	Industrl	14.9	2.25	1.53
Time Warner Inc	Cnsmr Cyc	15.9	10.76	1.37
Johnson & Johnson	Hlth care	14.7	6.55	1.36
⊖ Home Depot, Inc.	Cnsmr Cyc	16.0	-2.65	1.34
⊕ U.S. Bancorp	Finan Svs	13.6	-2.45	1.32
Fortune Brands Inc	Cnsmr Cyc	21.2	-4.25	1.27
Illinois Tool Works, Inc	Industrl	13.8	-5.47	1.24
⊕ Microsoft Corporation	Technology	10.2	-0.68	1.22
Murphy Oil Corporation	Energy	13.5	-13.12	1.20
Bank of America Corp	Finan Svs	—	-27.06	1.19
Schlumberger NV	Energy	25.1	8.83	1.17

Current Investment Style

Value Blnd Growth — Large/Mid/Small

Market Cap	%
Giant	43.4
Large	32.9
Mid	23.0
Small	0.7
Micro	0.0

Avg $mil: 33,263

Value Measures		Rel Category
Price/Earnings	12.43	0.97
Price/Book	1.72	0.98
Price/Sales	1.09	0.95
Price/Cash Flow	6.05	0.94
Dividend Yield %	2.51	1.04

Growth Measures	%	Rel Category
Long-Term Erngs	8.66	0.95
Book Value	2.80	0.87
Sales	0.40	0.63
Cash Flow	-4.52	NMF
Historical Erngs	1.47	1.48

Profitability	%	Rel Category
Return on Equity	18.26	1.01
Return on Assets	6.02	0.91
Net Margin	9.86	0.84

Sector Weightings	% of Stocks	Rel S&P 500	3 Year High Low
↻ Cyclical	37.99	1.30	
BasicMat	6.00	2.07	3 2
CnsmrCyc	11.62	1.32	3 2
FinanSvs	19.98	1.24	6 5
Real Est	0.39	0.30	6 4
⚡ Sensitive	34.49	0.88	
Energy	13.81	1.29	14 10
Industrl	12.18	1.09	18 15
Technlgy	8.50	0.48	16 13
→ Defensive	27.52	0.87	
CnsmrDef	7.99	0.67	8 5
Hlthcare	5.71	0.48	7 5
Utilities	8.05	2.23	2 1

Composition - Net

	%
● Cash	4.6
● Stocks	94.0
● Bonds	0.6
○ Other	0.8
Foreign	4.4

(% of Stock)

Morningstar's Take by Katie Rushkewicz 07-11-11

T. Rowe Price Equity Income's consistency is one of its many positive attributes.

Brian Rogers is one of the longest-tenured large-value managers, having run this fund since late 1985. The fund has grown substantially on his watch. With roughly $23 billion in assets, it's more than doubled in size during the past decade and is one of the biggest funds in the category.

As the fund has grown, it's become less active than it was in Rogers' early days. The fund's active share (which measures how distinct a fund is from its benchmark, in this case the S&P 500 Index) has dropped through the years. It fell in the low 80s in the 1990s but has hovered around the mid-60s during the past decade.

However, that hasn't changed the fund's process or diminished long-term results. Rogers has always maintained a diversified portfolio of more than 100 names, mostly reasonably priced, dividend-paying blue chips. That's kept the fund focused on higher-quality stocks, which has helped it hold up relatively well in tough market environments. It's lost only about three fourths as much as the S&P 500 in down markets during Rogers' tenure, notably outperforming in the early 2000s' bear market and 2008.

The fund can lag in growth-fueled markets like the late 1990s, when its valuation-consciousness kept it away from pricey tech stocks. However, that hasn't dented its long-term results. The fund's nearly 11% annualized gain during Rogers' tenure, while just edging past the S&P 500's 10.5% return, lands in the category's top quintile. More important, the fund has shown remarkable consistency through the years. Its rolling 10-year returns under Rogers have beaten the S&P 500 two thirds of the time and have almost never landed in the category's bottom half.

Other attributes, including low fees, strong stewardship marks, and Rogers' significant personal investment in the fund, continue to make it a top choice.

Address:	100 East Pratt Street, Baltimore, MD 21202, 800-638-5660
Web Address:	www.troweprice.com
Inception:	10-31-85
Advisor:	T. Rowe Price Associates, Inc.
Subadvisor:	None
NTF Plans:	N/A

Minimum Purchase:	$2500	Add: $100	IRA: $1000
Min Auto Inv Plan:	$0	Add: $50	
Sales Fees:	No-load		
Management Fee:	0.25% mx./0.21% mn.		
Actual Fees:	Mgt:0.55%	Dist: —	
Expense Projections:	3Yr:$221	5Yr:$384	10Yr:$859
Income Distribution:	Quarterly		

MORNINGSTAR® Mutual Funds

Fig. 10-5)

(Inclusion in this book does not constitute an endorsement of T Rowe Price Equity Income fund. Please do your own research and determine which funds are best suited to your own needs.)

Investment Growth

Item(s) from 10-01-1996 to 9-30-2010

Fund	Cumulative Return %	Annualized Return %	Max Front Load %	Max Back Load %	Gross Exp Ratio %	Amount at End of Period $
● Vanguard 500 Index Investor	110.33	5.45	**NA**	**NA**	0.17	21032.80
● Vanguard Total Bond Market Index Inst	140.20	6.46	**NA**	**NA**	0.07	24020.33
● USTREAS CD Sec Mkt 3 Mon	65.73	3.67	**NA**	**NA**	NA	16572.81

Initial Value: $10,000

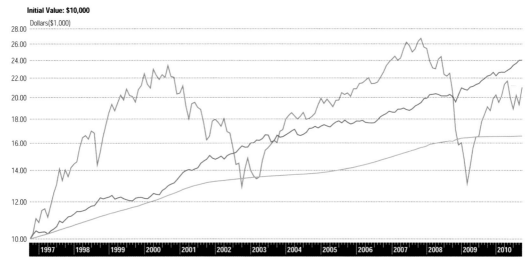

Morningstar copyright 2011

Fig. 10-6)

Bond Market Performance
1926–2010

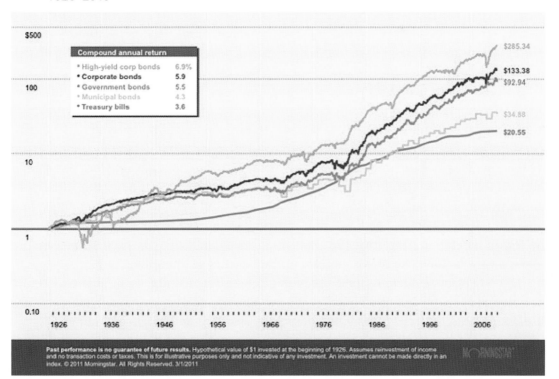

Compound annual return	
• High-yield corp bonds	6.9%
• Corporate bonds	5.9
• Government bonds	5.5
• Municipal bonds	4.3
• Treasury bills	3.6

$285.34
$133.38
$92.94
$34.88
$20.55

Past performance is no guarantee of future results. Hypothetical value of $1 invested at the beginning of 1926. Assumes reinvestment of income and no transaction costs or taxes. This is for illustrative purposes only and not indicative of any investment. An investment cannot be made directly in an index. © 2011 Morningstar. All Rights Reserved. 3/1/2011

Fig. 10-7)

In fact, returns to a "safe money" portfolio are so low that when taxes and inflation are added in, you often find that all increases in spending power have been chewed away. You can see that in the following graph: real returns to a "safe money" portfolio are approximated by the green Treasury bill line. (Fig. 10-8)

When you are seeking to utterly avoid risk, you are talking about bank accounts, money market funds, certificates of deposit, and Treasuries, and that's about it. Two years ago I would have added short-term corporate bond funds, but that was before 2008 when several of the "safest" of these invested in rancid bank and brokerage bonds and fell off the table.

When you select a "safe money" strategy you are seeking the following:

1. Minimum risk in an innately risky world.
2. You are willing to accept increased inflation risk to avoid the short-term volatility of investing in stocks.
3. Whatever returns that may bring.

So your initial asset allocation should look like this:

SAFE MONEY ALLOCATION	Target portfolio
Equity/stock mutual funds	0%
Bond mutual funds	60%
Asset Allocation mutual funds	0%
International mutual funds	0%
Cash	40%
Total	100%

This portfolio is simply one step above cash in terms of both return and risk. It DOES have a modicum of interest rate risk, a dollop of default risk, and a bit of exposure to inflation. Notice that it contains no stock exposure at all. In this portfolio you own literally thousands of individual bonds, mortgages, and other debt instruments. The risk of catastrophic loss is very low.

I would recommend that you are willing to accept the genuine risk of investing in short-term municipal bonds. In that case, you get tax free interest from the municipal bond funds in return for the slight risk of default by municipal bond issuers. Be sure to get short-term single-state bond funds to maximize your tax benefits since bonds issued by the state in which you reside are both Federal and State income tax free. You should only do this if your marginal tax bracket is simply ugly and you have consulted your tax professional about doing so. If you DON'T consult your tax pro, you might find yourself paying onerous "hate the rich" penalties such as "alternative minimum tax". So if you feel the need to invest in municipal bonds, talk to a tax professional first to make sure you can make maximum use of the benefits of muni investing.

DO NOT put municipal bond funds in a retirement account or in any tax exempt or deferred account. In these vehicles, the tax-free nature of municipal bond interest is useless. Instead, simply add to your short-term Treasury or mortgage holdings.

Again, if you have questions about whether or not you should invest in municipal bonds, ask your tax professional.

The "safe money" portfolio is unique in my allocation suggestions because it contains only 10 investments. You shouldn't need more to obtain adequate diversification

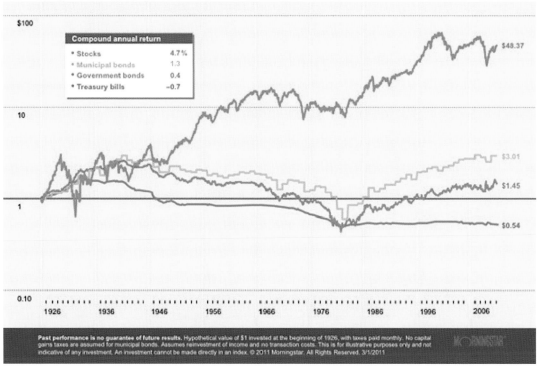

**Ibbotson® SBBI® After Taxes and Inflation
1926–2010**

Compound annual return	
• Stocks	4.7%
• Municipal bonds	1.3
• Government bonds	0.4
• Treasury bills	–0.7

Past performance is no guarantee of future results. Hypothetical value of $1 invested at the beginning of 1926, with taxes paid monthly. No capital gains taxes are assumed for municipal bonds. Assumes reinvestment of income and no transaction costs. This is for illustrative purposes only and not indicative of any investment. An investment cannot be made directly in an index. © 2011 Morningstar. All Rights Reserved. 3/1/2011

Fig. 10-8)

because your investment venues are constrained by your vestigial risk tolerance. Here's a detailed suggested 'safe money" portfolio. As I mentioned before, it still has risks, only the risks are minimized.

Cash allocation for Safe Money Portfolio

Treasury money market fund sweep	10%
Treasury money market fund select	10%
Treasury money market fund select #2	10%
Agencies money market fund select	10%
Bond allocation	
Short-term Muni Bond #1 or stable value bond fund	10%
Short-term Muni Bond #2 or inflation-protected bond fund.	10%
Short-term Treasury Bond Fund #1	10%
CD #1	10%
CD #2	10%
CD #3	10%
Total	100%

In your discount brokerage, you will have a "sweep" money market which is the place cash automatically goes when it is in the account. This will produce interest, but often not much. Ask your discount brokerage representative about "select" or "traded"

Stocks and Bonds: Risk Versus Return
1970–2010

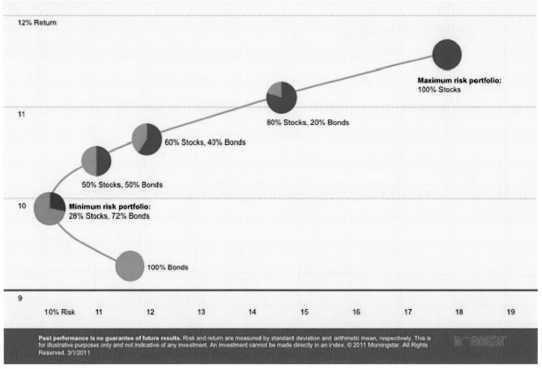

Fig. 10-9)

money market funds. These are money market funds which are essentially ultra-short mutual funds. You have to place a trade to get into them.

Why have more than one money market fund? Remember these are very low risk but not risk free. By having more than one money market fund you diversify and stay below any insurance limits in existence. Sometimes, also, you can find a municipal note money market fund and receive tax-exempt interest.

The "safe money" portfolio is the only situation in which I advise anyone to put money into something other than mutual funds. These are three certificates of deposit within your discount brokerage. Buy them in three different bank-issued CD's in three different maturities: 6 months, 1 year, and 1.5 years. Then when the shortest-term CD matures, roll it out to 1.5 years. DO NOT be lured by your discount brokerage representative into a higher-paying, longer-term CD, since these are vulnerable to changing interest rates. Be sure to stay under the maximum size which can be ensured by the FDIC. If your account is very large, keep adding CD's to stay under the FDIC insurance limits.

If you are using an investment advisor, he or she should be able to embellish this portfolio a bit with a touch more diversification and insured certificates of deposit which have the ability to tap into financial market performances. A good investment advisor can add value to even a "safe money" portfolio.

Section 10.4: The "Low Risk" Portfolio

Lesson #47: The "Low Risk" portfolio allocation provides the possibility of long-term increased returns, with some increased volatility from a small holding in stock mutual funds.

It is designed to put you at approximately the 28% stocks, 72% bond position on the efficient frontier. (Fig. 10-9)

As you can see in the graph of the efficient frontier, a small allocation to equities (stocks) in the form of mutual funds theoretically REDUCES long-term risk. You don't know precisely what proportion is correct, since these risk vs. rewards are always changing. But you DO know that the basic concept is historically proven.

In addition, as you expand your portfolio outwards from bonds, additional diversification can be derived from investing in asset allocation funds. The managers of these will go poking into the worlds of junk and convertible bonds, and can sometimes find terrific bargains. When you own these, your diversification becomes almost incalculable.

If you select this sort of risk exposure, you should expect lower volatility. But you should also expect to lag the stock market during "up" years. People who select this kind of safer allocation often complain mightily when the full volatility of the stock market is driving pure stock portfolios irrationally skywards, while their less risky portfolios are trailing behind. Their portfolios ARE DESIGNED to trail behind a bull market, in return for not dropping like a brick in an outhouse when a crash comes along.

During times when stock markets are surging, investors with "low risk" allocations will respond to this sense of being left behind by unconsciously avoiding rebalancing. (I will discuss "rebalancing" in a later chapter.) They will let their boomer growth funds grow as a proportion of their portfolios until they actually have a riskier portfolio than intended. Then when the crash comes, they are surprised by how much their portfolios drop. If you select a "low risk" allocation, avoid this by scrupulous periodic rebalancing as I will describe later.

A low risk portfolio should look somewhat like this:

LOW RISK ASSET ALLOCATION: Morningstar categories	Target Portfolio
Equities	15%
Bonds	30%
Asset Allocation	30%
International	20%
Cash	5%
Total	100%

Within this allocation, you need to really mix it up. Once again, do your research and select a spectrum of funds. Choose good funds with lower R^2 statistics wherever possible. This is to provide maximum diversification.

You will note that this doesn't completely match the minimum-risk allocation you've seen on graphs. That's because those graphs are two dimensional models, while this portfolio has many more venues for investment. We don't really know exactly what today's minimal risk portfolio looks like in the real world because we can't quantify it. And if we could, it would change anyway. So this portfolio is a reasonable real-world approximation of a lower risk, highly-diversified allocation.

Since you have 15% in equities, an allocation of three funds seems appropriate. It should look like this:

Equity Fund distribution in a "low risk" portfolio	Percentage of total portfolio
Vanguard Index 500 fund or other S&P 500 Index fund	5%
Value Fund (you select)	5%
Growth Fund (you select)	5%
Total	15%

You are diversifying by having the Vanguard Index 500 or another S&P 500 index fund as your stock market proxy mutual fund, one value mutual fund, and one growth fund.

Here is an example of a bond allocation for a "low risk" portfolio inside a pension plan. A 30% allocation means six mutual funds, each holding 5% of your money. If your portfolio is not inside a pension plan, consider replacing some of the corporate bonds with municipal bond funds, both short-term and intermediate term, should your tax environment call for such a change. Be sure to buy both longer and shorter maturities to reduce interest rate risks. Also consider buying a dab of Vanguard Total Bond Index fund, so that you can see the behavior of the bond market index within your own account.

Bond mutual fund distribution in a "low risk" portfolio	Percentage of total portfolio
Vanguard Total Bond Index fund or similar bond index fund	5%
Short-term Treasury fund (you select)	5%
Intermediate Government fund (you select)	5%
Intermediate Term Bond #1 (you select)	5%
Intermediate Term Bond #2 (you select)	5%
Short-term Corporate Bond (you select)	5%
Total	30%

As you can see, these are listed by *Morningstar* category, to help you in your search.

Here is an example of mixing it up inside the 25% of your portfolio which is allocated to asset allocation funds. You can see that first you diversify by apportioning your money into different asset classes, and then you diversify again within each asset class. Again, you are doing this because you don't know what will happen, and you don't want to hang your hat on any one manager or management style. It IS important, however, to select the best funds you can find in each *Morningstar* category. You do this by using the star rating first, then by looking for R^2, and thinking through WHY this fund is doing so well. Emphasize "conservative allocation" funds: they are more likely to be different from each other and have a management style characterized by caution.

Asset Allocation mutual funds in a "low risk" portfolio	Percentage of total portfolio
Conservative Allocation fund #1 (you select)	5%
Conservative Allocation fund #2 (you select)	5%
Conservative Allocation fund #3 (you select)	5%
Moderate Allocation fund #1 (you select)	5%
Moderate Allocation fund #2 (you select)	5%
Moderate Allocation fund #3 (you select)	5%
Total	30%

You will also need to apportion the money in your international mutual funds. Essentially your international mutual fund portion is a mini-portfolio of its own: select a variety of good funds with the best star ratings possible, with lower R^2 and beta statistics where possible.

International mutual funds in a "low risk" portfolio	Percentage of total portfolio
Foreign Large Blend fund #1 (you select)	5%
Foreign Large Blend fund #2 (you select)	5%
World Allocation fund #1 (you select)	5%
World Allocation fund #2 (you select)	5%
World Allocation fund #3 (you select)	5%
Total	25%

"Low risk" portfolios offer reduced risk with potentially lower returns. You should be able to sleep nights even in the toughest times

Section 10.5: The "Moderate Risk" Portfolio

Lesson #48: The "moderate risk" portfolio allocation attempts to optimize your returns while keeping risk somewhat lower than full market risk. In a perfect world, this sort of portfolio lags only slightly during up markets while providing substantial protection in hard times. When you invest in a moderate risk portfolio, you are willing to accept substantial yet hopefully not crushing volatility while seeking market-level gains.

The goal of this portfolio is to gain the risk/rewards position of "Portfolio 3" or "Portfolio 4" shown in this graph. (Fig. 10-10)

This graph shows you that IN THEORY, you are willing to accept about 50% to 75% of the stock market's risk to get almost the same long-term returns. Why can't we be more precise? Again, you are dealing with a much more diversified portfolio while this study addresses only generic "stock" and "bond" portfolios.

20-Year Portfolio Performance
1991–2010

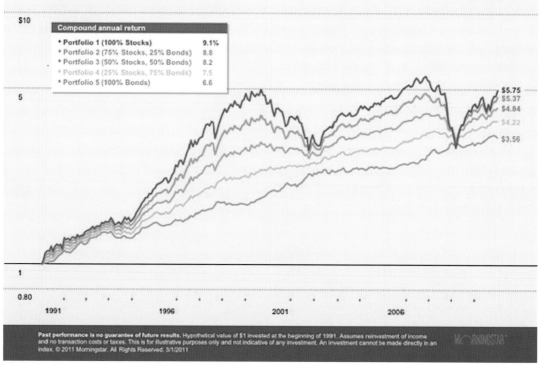

Fig. 10-10)

To me, this is the portfolio "sweet spot". In the Financial Panic of 2008, the stock market itself declined about 37%, which is historically gigantic. "Moderate risk" portfolios under my management were down between 25% and 30%. I consider that a successful genuine real-world test, ugly as it was.

Once again, the key to maintaining that moderate risk exposure is to rebalance periodically. By doing so, you will keep your successful funds from temporarily overpowering your less aggressive performers.

Here's a hypothetical allocation of a "moderate risk" portfolio:

MODERATE RISK ASSET ALLOCATION	Target Portfolio
Equities	35%
Bonds	15%
Asset Allocation	20%
International	25%
Cash	5%
Total	100%

You can see that you have a 5% cash position, to provide for any unexpected cash needs.

Here's your equity allocation for a "moderate risk" portfolio.

Stock mutual fund distribution in a "moderate risk" portfolio	Percentage of total portfolio
Vanguard Index 500 fund or similar S&P 500 index fund	5%
Large Growth fund (you select)	5%
Large Value fund (you select)	5%
Small Value fund (you select)	5%
Small Growth fund (you select)	5%
Growth fund (you select)	5%
Value fund (you select)	5%
Total	35%

When you do your own allocating, WATCH OUT FOR FUND OVERLAP! Keep a close eye on those R-2 statistics. You can see that you are broadening out your exposure to stock markets. You now hold stocks of all sizes and categories, and you are accessing seven management teams with seven different viewpoints, hopefully.

Here's your bond allocation:

Bond mutual fund distribution in a "moderate risk" portfolio	Percentage of total portfolio
Vanguard Total Bond Index fund or similar bond index fund	5%
Short-term corporate bond fund (you select)	5%
Intermediate Government fund (you select)	5%
Total	15%

Your bond portion includes only three funds. The "short term corporate" allocation makes it a bit more exposed to economic risk but also more likely to deliver attractive returns. A "moderate risk" portfolio will rely on its asset allocation funds, which usually carry a lot of bonds, to provide bond market diversification.

Your asset allocation apportionment is about the same as for a "low risk" portfolio but with two fewer funds. We're relying on this portion of your portfolio to serve the role of bond surrogate for diversification, so we don't want to shelter higher risk funds here.

Asset Allocation mutual funds in a "moderate risk" portfolio	Percentage of total portfolio
Conservative Allocation fund #1 (you select)	5%
Conservative Allocation fund #2 (you select)	5%
Moderate Allocation fund #1 (you select)	5%
Moderate Allocation fund #2 (you select)	5%
Total	20%

"Moderate risk" portfolios have the same percentage exposure to international as "low risk" portfolios, but you add more risk via fund selection. This is because, as we have seen, the 21st Century economy will be global. Thus you are willing to accept a bit more risk to garner some of the gains of economies beyond North America. World Allocation funds tend to be cowardly, so they help add diversification. Also an Asian fund pins a bit of your money in the place where most of the growth is happening. But making it an Asian Growth and Income fund assures that you won't be utterly hostage to very volatile Asian markets.

International mutual funds in a "moderate risk" portfolio	Percentage of total portfolio
Foreign Large Blend fund (you select)	5%
Foreign Large Value fund (you select)	5%
World Allocation fund #1 (you select)	5%
World Allocation fund #2 (you select)	5%
Asian Growth and Income fund (you select)	5%
Total	25%

Section 10.6: The "Market Risk" Portfolio

Lesson #49: The "market risk" portfolio allocation is appropriate only if you can genuinely state that you are willing to ride out full-strength market volatility to get at-market or perhaps above-market gains.

If you choose to invest in a "market risk" portfolio, you are saying you are willing to ride the tiger. In 2008, this would have meant that when your portfolio dropped 37%, you were comfortable with it.

The prospect of facing large short-term losses requires some reflection. As you can see on the following chart, most years provide some sort of positive gains. Some years are utterly dismal, and are sometimes followed by equally dismal second years. These wounds <u>do</u> heal over time, however. So as this chart shows you, before you create a "market risk" portfolio, you should be willing to stay invested for a long time, both to heal injuries and to garner maximum gains. If you are able and willing to tough out a rough patch or two, then a "market risk" portfolio can be quite rewarding.

Having said that, I still wouldn't invest in a market risk portfolio with my own money. But then I'm a confirmed coward. I haven't been on a roller coaster in ten years. (Fig. 10-11)

As you can see on the graph below, investing in a "market risk" portfolio means that you are willing to accept more risk for the additional incremental long-term gains that your portfolio might gain versus a "moderate risk" portfolio. This portfolio allocation aims to put you somewhere near the performance of "Portfolio 1 (100% Stocks)" on the following graph. At this level of stock market exposure, additional potential gain sometimes requires taking excessive additional risk. (Fig. 10-12)

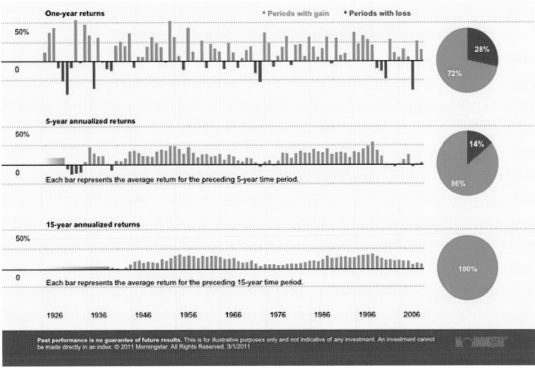

Fig. 10-11)

In order to achieve such market exposure, a whopping eleven out of twenty of your funds will be in US stock venues. Diversification has actually been somewhat reduced overall to give you maximum potential for gains over the long-term. As you can see, your 5% cash reserve has gone away since cash tends to underperform stocks over time.

MARKET RISK ASSET ALLOCATION	Target Portfolio
Equities	55%
Bonds	5%
Asset Allocation	10%
International	30%
Cash	0%
Total	100%

You can see what has happened to the stock allocation: both value and growth styles are represented by funds which invest in small and large stocks. To keep this portfolio a bit diversified, you should still seek low R^2 statistics with at least some of these eleven funds.

20-Year Portfolio Performance
1991–2010

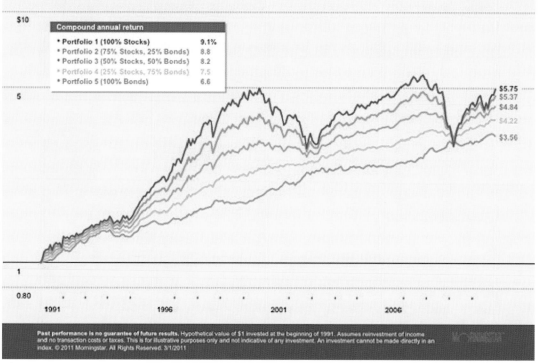

Fig. 10-12)

Stock mutual fund distribution in a "market risk" portfolio	Percentage of total portfolio
Vanguard Index 500 fund or similar S&P 500 Index Fund	5%
Large Growth fund (you select)	5%
Large Growth fund (you select)	5%
Large Value fund (you select)	5%
Large Value fund (you select)	5%
Small Growth fund (you select)	5%
Small Growth fund (you select)	5%
Small Value fund (you select)	5%
Small Value fund (you select)	5%
Blend Fund (you select)	5%
Blend Fund (you select)	5%
Total	55%

Bonds are represented in only one fund in the "market risk" portfolio. You may as well get maximum diversification out of that fund by making it the Vanguard Total Bond Index fund or something similar. At least you will know what the bond market is doing.

Your "market risk" portfolio will contain only two asset allocation funds. My thought is that since you still want diversification, you should pick one "conservative allocation" fund and one "moderate allocation" fund.

You have reduced market risk somewhat by selecting a bond fund for 5% of your money and two asset allocation funds for a total of 10% of your money. You now <u>add risk back into</u> the portfolio in your international allocation. You add one additional Foreign Growth fund, an Emerging Markets fund, and a pure Asian fund.

International mutual funds in a "market risk" portfolio	Percentage of total portfolio
Foreign Large Blend fund (you select)	5%
Foreign Large Value fund (you select)	5%
Foreign Growth fund (you select)	5%
World Allocation fund (you select)	5%
Emerging markets fund (you select)	5%
Asian fund (you select)	5%
Total	30%

Trust me, after a few years watching your Emerging Markets and Asian funds, you will understand why so many investment advisors are bald. But Emerging Markets may be a gigantic venue in the 21st Century. In fact the majority of the global economic growth of the 21st Century may be outside the United States. So this portfolio requires stepping outside of the box. ***It's not for everyone.***

It's also a reality that sometimes even a market-risk portfolio lags the S&P 500. This is usually transient, and takes place because the S&P 500 sometimes moves differently from the global market. With asset allocations to such potential boomers as small stocks, Asian markets, and emerging markets, this portfolio has the potential to outperform the S&P 500 as well. Investing at such a nosebleed-level of risk simply takes patience and a cast-iron constitution. And don't forget to rebalance to maximize gains and diversification!

Section 10.7:

How your Investment Advisor Should Help with Portfolio Construction

Lesson #50: Your investment advisor should pick mutual funds for you using a technique which resembles the system of diversification presented in this chapter. In short, your investment advisor should do your portfolio construction for you.

If you choose to employ an investment advisor, portfolio construction is where he or she can add a lot of value. The first thing your investment advisor should do is assist you to genuinely understand your tolerance for risk.

Almost everybody gets their risk tolerance wrong at first. So your investment advisor should help to modify your portfolio to reflect that. Often when I am helping an uncertain new client, I will invest the portfolio at one less level of risk than I think the client will want, and then move up to that higher level at the first annual rebalancing.

Your investment advisor should also build the portfolio, select all the funds, and present you with a complete package. At that point he or she should have an explanation for every single mutual fund in your portfolio. You'll have more questions as time passes and you watch the markets move your money.

Review: The Lessons of Chapter 10

Lesson #44: To create your portfolio, invest in a wide assortment of mutual fund asset classes.

Lesson #45: Select mutual funds for your portfolio using a series of selection screens.

Lesson #46: The "safe money" portfolio allocation is when you simply want to minimize risk, with the highest possible return.

Lesson #47: The "low risk" portfolio allocation provides the possibility of long-term increased returns, with some increased volatility from a small holding in stock mutual funds.

Lesson #48: The "moderate risk" portfolio allocation attempts to optimize your returns while keeping risk somewhat lower than full market risk. In a perfect world, this sort of portfolio lags only slightly during up markets while providing substantial protection in hard times. When you invest in a moderate risk portfolio, you are willing to accept substantial yet hopefully not crushing volatility while seeking market-level gains.

Lesson #49: The "market risk" portfolio allocation is appropriate only if you can genuinely state that you are willing to ride out full-strength market volatility to get at-market or perhaps above-market gains.

Lesson #50: Your investment advisor should pick mutual funds for you using a technique which resembles the system of diversification presented in this chapter. In short, your investment advisor should do your portfolio construction for you.

Chapter 11

Rebalance your Portfolio Annually

Foul cantankering rust the hidden treasure frets,
But gold that's put to use more gold begets.

—*William Shakespeare, 1593*

So far in this book you have embraced some relatively large concepts, sometimes in some fairly large chapters. The rest of the book involves very important concepts and strategies, delivered in small packages. Smallness does not relate to importance. So far in this book you've learned how to build a portfolio. Now you are going to learn how to manage it.

It's important for you to realize that this entire process will not be perfect for you because, by necessity, you are using data from the past to construct a portfolio for the future. Also you can never know exactly what optimal allocation or fund selection will work best. Simply accept imperfection, and keep at it. Small errors can be mitigated by staying at the job, and not simply giving up.

Each year, the values of the individual mutual funds within your portfolio will probably change. Some mutual funds will increase in value, and some may decrease. You cannot predict what will happen. As this goes on year after year, your carefully constructed portfolio is likely to be gradually undone.

For example, if your portfolio experiences a stock market bubble, and your original allocation was for 15% in stock mutual funds, then that allocation is likely to grow to 30% or 40% of your portfolio as stock mutual funds outperform your other investments. When the downturn finally arrives, you are likely to find that your portfolio is less diversified than you expected, and you will lose more than expected. The way to avoid this is by "rebalancing."

Likewise, if you are living through a profound stock market downturn, your 15% in stock mutual funds may drop to only 7%. Forcing yourself to bring that equity allocation back up to 15% will ensure that when the market inevitably recovers, you will fully participate to the degree your risk tolerance allows.

In this chapter, I will describe how to bring your portfolio back to the original allocation which you decided would best meet your needs. This will intentionally limit your choice set, and create a system which compels you to buy what is a bit inexpensive and sell a bit of what might be bubbling.

Lesson #51: Rebalancing is restoring the appropriate percentages of investments in your portfolio by selling a little of what has done well and buying a little of what is lagging.

Left by itself, simply allocating your assets and walking away will give you at least <u>some</u> benefits. The reality is that as things change in the world, some of your mutual funds will thrive and others won't.

If your portfolio is properly diversified, all your mutual funds will not outperform simultaneously. If all your mutual funds DO go up together, then everything you own is correlating and your risk exposure is probably much greater than you think it is. To counter this, you simply rebalance to keep your booming mutual funds from taking over your portfolio. This by itself adds a lot of value.

Lesson #52: Rebalance in January, using your December 31st statement. Rebalance once a year.

You rebalance after the New Year in January or February, just to create an annual cycle of managing your investments. This should be relatively easy because you will be interested in what your investments did last year. You will also be preparing for taxes by collecting information about dividends and capital gains.

To describe how rebalancing works, let's walk through an example. Let's assume you have a "moderate risk" portfolio. If so, then your market neutral allocation, as indicated in Chapter 10, is as follows:

Equities	35%
Bonds	15%
Asset Allocation	20%
International	30%
Total	100%

You can see that your international holdings represent 30% of this intended allocation. But let's assume that the past year has been a great year for the global economy. The dollar has fallen relative to the rest of the world's currencies. Meanwhile, rising interest rates caused by an overheating economy have caused bonds to decline in value. The stock market was great, even frenzied last year.

You don't have to know the "why" of any of this. You don't have to know why things move as they do. And you don't know what will happen next. Nobody does. You simply rebalance once a year, to avoid reacting excessively to short-term market changes.

Lesson #53: YOU DO NOT have to understand the economy or the financial markets to invest or rebalance successfully.

This is key: you don't have to decipher what is going on to invest wisely. What is wise investing? To buy low and sell high of course! But if you are like most investors, you won't want to do that. As we discussed earlier, you will want to do the opposite: you will want to buy what is going up and sell what is down.

Rebalancing helps you do the right thing, in spite of yourself.

When you get your December 31st discount brokerage account statement in the mail, you sit down in front of your computer and open it. If you have more than one account, add the investments from all the accounts together, and approach it as one large portfolio. You may wish to use your computer to do this, but the back of a napkin also works.

In this example, when you study your allocation as of December 31st, you notice several things. After calculating your total return for last year, you discover that your portfolio made 15%. Your $100,000 investment is now worth $115,000. That's a reason to celebrate. You also discover that your allocation now looks like this:

	Current portfolio Allocation
Equities	41%
Bonds	10%
Asset Allocation	14%
International	35%

In other words, when you do the math, you can see that the following changes need to happen to return to your target allocation:

	Target portfolio	**Current Allocation**	**Changes needed**
Equities	35%	41%	-6%
Bonds	15%	10%	+5%
Asset Allocation	20%	14%	+6%
International	30%	35%	-5%
	100%	100%	0%

So how are you going to do that? As you recall, our target allocation of each mutual fund is 5% of the portfolio. Your equities portion thus has seven mutual funds in it, and your bond portion has three mutual funds in it. You should also rebalance each mutual fund as well. In other words, as much as you are able, take each fund back to 5%.

This is going to be hard to do, emotionally. Some of your funds were heroes last year, and the last thing you want to do is to sell them. But you aren't selling them. You are trimming them.

Lesson #54: Rebalance as much as possible WITHIN EACH ASSET CLASS as part of the larger rebalancing process.

Consider the following nightmare: You own a mutual fund of legendary proportions. It soars to great heights year after year, and you don't sell it. You don't sell it because you don't know what it will do next year. You don't want to pay the taxes on the gains. Also your mutual fund just keeps making so much money!

So you leave it alone for five years. And by the time these five years pass, your equity position is about 50% instead of 35%, and your super-fund takes up about 50% of your equity position. So this one fund makes up about 25% of your portfolio.

You are having a great time telling your friends about this fund which is making you rich. The fund manager is now a celebrity. You sleep well at night, knowing that the fund's incredibly skilled management team is taking care of your money.

Then 2008 happens. The fund drops 57%.

This actually happened. Millions of investors got badly burned.

The lesson here is that we all have to do what we don't like in life. We have to floss our teeth, and we have to get medical exams. We have to pay taxes. And we have to rebalance our mutual funds.

If our portfolio is now worth $115,000, then 5% of that is $5,750. So that is our rough target allocation for each mutual fund. Make it $6,000 if you like round numbers. You don't need to be ruthlessly precise.

First we trim (sell) all mutual funds over $5,750, and then we allocate the cash to the other funds in the portfolio to bring them UP to $5,750. If you rebalance imprecisely, you will still get most of the gains. Don't sweat it. Just do it. For example, you will garner the gains of this exercise if you set the mutual fund upper limit at $6,000 rather than $5,750. If keeping it simple gets it done, then simplicity rocks.

This is when those transaction fee-free mutual funds at your discount brokerage pay for themselves. Some of your funds will be trimmed a little and some a lot. It helps if you don't have to worry about trading costs. If you ARE facing fees, you are welcome to do what I do: fudge. In such a situation I focus on rebalancing the funds which are genuinely overgrown, and leave the tiny trades until next year.

When you are dealing with a fund that charges fees for transactions, feel free to let the fund grow a little bit beyond your normal limits to reduce the per-dollar effect of the transaction fee. You DO NOT want to do a trade which costs $49 for $200 of mutual fund! That's a 24% cost of trading! Instead, let this fund grow to the point where the $49 fee is a relatively small cost: For a $3,000 trade, a $49 transaction fee is 1.6%. Just don't let this fund or its brethren take over your portfolio. Better yet, make sure your discount brokerage has a menu of transaction-free funds, and use those as much as possible. It's your choice. You don't have to be perfect here: you just have to follow the general plan.

It's important not to get diverted into researching for new funds right now. If you chase a magazine's top-performing funds, you will wander off into a forest of mutual fund statistics and anxiety. Let it go. Right now all you need to do is rebalance to the best of your ability.

If you don't know how to deal with the mechanics of buying and selling, feel free to call the discount brokerage and ask them to help you work through this. Politely ignore their suggestions for other possible investments, and gently herd them back to task when they stray. They will be happy to help.

And then don't rebalance until next January.

Think about what you have just done: you have just bought low and sold high. Congratulations.

Review: The Lessons of Chapter 11

Lesson #51: Rebalancing is restoring the appropriate percentages of investments in your portfolio by selling a little of what has done well and buying a little of what is lagging.

Lesson #52: Rebalance in January, using your December 31st statement. Rebalance once a year.

Lesson #53: YOU DO NOT have to understand the economy or the financial markets to invest or rebalance successfully.

Lesson #54: Rebalance as much as possible WITHIN EACH ASSET CLASS as part of the larger rebalancing process.

Chapter 12

Weed the Garden

Goodness is the only investment that never fails.
—Henry David Thoreau

Here is where you are:
1. You have learned that inevitably life brings with it occasional tough times and unexpected events. Most financial and investment plans don't account for these.
2. Like it or not, you need to budget, avoid debt, and save to succeed. The money you will invest is probably going to come into your life through your own discipline and sweat.
3. Your mind will want to follow the herd. To manage these feelings, you will adopt an investment style which confines your choices to proven successful behavior, and includes routines which don't evoke subjective judgment. In other words, you will take your emotions and "guessing" out of the process as much as possible.
4. Part of this system will be to invest only in mutual funds, and to invest only through a discount brokerage.
5. You will follow the asset allocation guidelines to create a diversified portfolio which will provide moderate protection against unexpected market fluctuations.
6. You will rebalance to avoid being caught in investment bubbles.

So far, so good. But you will face one more challenge: how to recognize and cull out mutual funds which are not doing as well as they should.

Because investing evokes such primitive emotions, many investors don't do this. Instead, they sell their winning mutual funds entirely because they are afraid of losing gains. This doesn't work, does it? It involves guessing, which is always problematic. Also it invites the other psychological process of over-commitment, in which the investor tries to wait out a bad performance.

Routinely, I see the result: a portfolio brought in by a prospective client which is full of underperforming funds. The investor is usually waiting for them to break even so he or she can sell them. That happens rarely. So when such an investor shows me his or her investment choices, I often see a portfolio full of dogs.

As a successful investor, you will want to keep your winners, rebalance them annually, and cull your losers. That way you will enlist the best managers to your winning cause. You need to periodically clean out your portfolio. If you don't do this, then as mutual funds change management, become too big, or simply remain wedded to an obsolete management style, you will continue to own the fund and suffer accordingly.

On the other hand, many good mutual funds stay good for a long time. Even good mutual funds have occasional years when they miss a market trend and are temporarily left behind. Usually they catch up later. As a result, a great deal of mutual fund trading is unnecessary. Too much mutual fund trading will hinder your returns because of transaction fees, taxes, and taking your attention off of your long-term plan.

Worse yet, mutual fund selection can become deeply subjective, and thus hostage to all those emotions which cripple most investors. Your system must avoid those emotions as much as possible. This has two benefits. Your portfolio will benefit from your ability to NOT guess. And you will not be caught up by your own pre- and post-decision angst.

Here is how to gently cull out the under-performers from your account. I call it "weeding the garden." You do it once a year, and then return to enjoying your life.

Lesson #55: In July or shortly thereafter, you weed the garden. "Weeding the garden" is identifying the mutual funds which make up the relatively worst-performing 10% of your portfolio and replacing them with funds which are better relative performers. You also replace all mutual funds with a *Morningstar* rating of 1 star.

You do this by engaging in what looks suspiciously like a game of cards. In July you are going to look at the <u>relative quality</u> of your mutual funds, not the <u>percentage positions</u> they hold in your portfolio. Rebalancing is something you will do in January. In July, you focus on owning the top-performing and most diversified portfolio you can find.

It is quite acceptable to "weed the garden" imperfectly. The big picture is what matters here. You should finish this project with a small amount of your least-well managed portfolio replaced by new fresh management. 10% turnover is the ideal number. We are going to do this by winnowing down from a larger selection to a smaller final list of new mutual funds.

Again, the mission is not to find mutual funds which are lagging on an absolute basis. For example, bond mutual funds lag in a strong bull stock market, but they also provide essential diversification. The funds you wish to cull are those <u>which are under-performing relative to similar mutual funds.</u>

The best easy source of information for this is *Morningstar*. So your first July assignment is to find access to *Morningstar*, either via the Internet or in print. Your local library is usually able to provide this access.

You can do this in two ways: either print up the *Morningstar* pages for <u>all</u> your funds, or do it virtually on a spread-sheeting program. I'm going to walk through this process by using *Morningstar* pages. *Morningstar* will always offer a one-page summary of each mutual fund's performance. Your discount brokerage will have approximately the same data, usually using a *Morningstar* rating system.

1. **First print up *Morningstar* pages for all your mutual funds and make piles according to category.** Depending on the size of your portfolio and the risk-reward allocation you have chosen, sometimes you will have a pile consisting of one mutual fund. That's OK.

2. **Set aside all funds which have a *Morningstar* rating of 1 star to replace.** As you know, *Morningstar* ratings are a look in the rear view mirror: they are relatively imperfect at predicting the future. However, in general,

Morningstar ratings for good funds tend to float between 5 stars and perhaps, at the very worst, 2 stars, depending upon the current market cycle. A fund which is currently receiving a *Morningstar* ranking of 1 star indicates a collapsed fund, which indicates flawed management. The future for a 1 star ranked fund is usually bleak. So you want to get it out of your portfolio.

This step gives you an "out" to cull any collapsed funds out of your portfolio regardless of what proportion of your portfolio these may represent. The need to do this is rare.

Set the *Morningstar* pages for these funds aside in the "sell" pile.

3.   Next, set aside your index funds. Of your piles of fund reports, one is composed of the indices you use for comparison. You have only two funds in that pile: an S&P 500 index fund, such as the Vanguard Index 500, and a bond index fund, such as the Vanguard Total Bond index. You will rebalance these funds, but you will never sell them. After all, they ARE the stock and bond markets. Set these aside in a separate "keep" pile.

4.   Seek the 70% of your remaining mutual funds which are performing best in the last 3 years. <u>Judge funds relative to their peers in the same pile, not relative to the market or any absolute return.</u> Set the 70% aside in the "keep" pile. Set the lowest-performing 30% in the "study" pile.

In a 20-fund portfolio, you will be retaining 14 of your funds. You will be studying the 6 funds which are lagging to possibly sell. Now you have one pile made up from all the other piles. Every other fund's page is now in the "keep" pile or the "sell" pile. That makes three piles: "study", "keep", and "sell'.

In your pile to "study" you have your 6 relatively under-performing mutual funds. There are two very different reasons for a mutual fund to lag its peers.

The first reason is that a mutual fund is invested in an asset class which is not doing well. It isn't entirely the fund manager's problem if the financial markets are simply awful. In this case you may have a good mutual fund in a bad market climate. You probably don't want to replace a good mutual fund which is simply caught in a storm. This is why you are comparing funds in the same category only.

The second reason is that the fund management is simply not performing as well as it might. In this case, the fund is under-performing its peers, whatever the market. You may have a less-than-adequate mutual fund. Moving on to another mutual fund may be called for. This is why you are using two criteria for removing a fund.

Find the "3 year average performance" statistic on the *Morningstar* pages <u>of the indices,</u> and circle them in highlighter. You can also do this entire study with "5 year average performance" if you wish, with the caveats stated below in mind.

You are going to use these numbers to compare performance. Why 3 year? Because this year's or last year's numbers are simply too short a time period to compare mutual funds, and anything longer than 3 years washes away recent performance.

With that in mind, find the "3 year average performance" statistic for each of your mutual funds as presented by *Morningstar*. The data may not be entirely up to date: it doesn't matter as long as the profiles are dated within 3 months of each other. You aren't doing exact analysis here. The point is to identify large trends.

Now make two piles from the one. You will need the data pages for stock and bond index funds for use as references. Compare your entire group of stock-oriented funds, domestic, asset allocating, and international, with the statistics of your S&P 500 index fund. You do this because this index mutual fund is a real-world proxy for the Standard and Poor's 500 Index. Of course, different mutual fund categories perform differently. In one pile you may well have your worst-performing fund doing better than the best performing fund of another pile. That's OK: you have already done this culling <u>within each category</u> to preserve diversification.

Compare all bond funds to your bond index fund. This mutual fund is an imperfect real-world proxy for the entire bond market. Once again you should already have this fund in your portfolio, so comparing it is relatively easy. As with the other piles, organize your funds so that the best performers are on top and the less-good performers are on the bottom.

Now, take away the top 70% of each of your piles, based on absolute performance, and set these aside. You will be keeping these funds, so put them in the "keep" pile now.

Here is a chart to guide you in this:

If you have this many funds in your pile…	70% is….	Remove	Leave
7	4.9	5	2
6	4.2	4	2
5	3.5	4	1
4	2.8	3	1
3	2.1	2	1
2	1.4	1	1
1	0.7	0	1

5.   With the remaining lowest performing mutual funds, pick the two funds (10% of the portfolio) which have the HIGHEST R^2 statistics when compared to either the stock or bond index funds. Set these in the "sell" pile.

Go through the *Morningstar* page of each of your remaining funds. Highlight the R^2 statistic.

Do the same for the two index funds. Now study the R^2 statistics for those index funds. You will note that these are "100" or very close. They should be. Since these indices are market proxies, they should certainly correlate with themselves!

However, you don't want to see all "100" R^2 statistics in your portfolio. If you see a mutual fund with an R^2 close to 100, then your mutual fund is tracking its index to the point that it is a stealth index fund.

In fact, when you analyze the 30% of your portfolio which is underperforming, you want to remove the two funds which most correlate.

Think about it: you should pick the two funds which perform the worst and don't add as much diversification as they should. Keep in mind that you want to compare bond funds with the bond index fund, and stock or asset allocation funds with the S&P 500 index fund.

A fund which has low correlation with the indices and simply performs badly will eventually get a one-star *Morningstar* rating and get flushed as well. So this methodology protects your diversified funds, such as your asset allocation funds, from being tossed simply because they are lower risk.

Therefore, you find the two funds which have the highest correlation to their respective index. In other words, pick the one or two funds with the largest R^2 statistics, and put them in the "sell" pile.

The "keep" pile of mutual fund *Morningstar* pages can be set aside for later reading or whatever: these funds are staying no matter what happens next.

Remember, the R^2 statistics for bond funds are calculated against the bond index, and the R^2 statistics for stock funds are calculated against the stock index. Also, we know that R^2 statistics change. But in general, they don't change rapidly or routinely.

Yes, this is a very imprecise, imperfect way to do this. But it's a very imprecise world, and this culling is as efficient a technique as any.

Unless you are dealing with collapsing mutual funds that are receiving *Morningstar* rankings of 1 star, you don't want to sell more than 10% of your portfolio. If you routinely sell more, you will be moving too much money based on what is happening NOW. In other words, you will be sucked into the "buy high-sell low" reactive behavior which so damages most other investors.

On the other hand, if you sell less than 10% you aren't culling proactively. Replacing 10% of your account means that it takes you 10 years to get through your portfolio. You can't be accused of excessive trading.

6.   Now select mutual funds to replace the mutual funds in your "sell" pile, with one fund replacing each fund which is being sold. Replace each underperforming fund with a fund from <u>exactly the same</u> *Morningstar* category.

At this point, you have a "sell pile" of mutual funds you wish to replace. These are funds with 1 star *Morningstar* rankings as well as the 10% you have selected for culling.

To retain your diversification, you want to replace each fund with another mutual fund from <u>exactly the same</u> *Morningstar* category.

For <u>each</u> mutual fund to be replaced, research the mutual fund's category at either your discount brokerage or at *Morningstar* and select replacement mutual funds.

Once again, here is the process:

    o **Stay in the exact *Morningstar* category as the fund you are seeking to replace.**

    o ***Morningstar* ranking: as many stars as possible. Pick the top twenty which have three year track records. If there aren't twenty funds, pick as many as possible.**

    o **Average annual performance for 3 years: pick the top ten which are not in the same fund family. You want ten independently managed funds which are traded in your discount brokerage. Be sure you know what trading fee structure the discount brokerage applies to each fund before you trade. In an ideal world, you find ten independently managed transaction-free funds. If you can't find ten funds out of your original twenty, go back and bring in more funds based on *Morningstar* ranking until you have ten funds from which to select.**

    o **R^2 statistic: pick the lowest 5. Then pick the fund or funds you find attractive, based on that limited choice set.**

What should we see in a replacement fund? Essentially the opposite of the culled fund: in <u>exactly the same</u> *Morningstar* category, with higher *Morningstar* ratings, better historical performance, and <u>absolutely</u> a lower R^2.

Obviously, you should LIKE the fund. But more importantly, to keep your irrational mind from running this, the R^2 has to be lower. Otherwise, during bull markets you will find that you have a portfolio full of very similar mutual funds.

Do these replacement trades, on the computer if possible. If you wait, you will meditate, stew, agonize, and procrastinate. So just do it. Pull the trigger. Replace the entire position of the culled fund, even if it is not exactly 5% of the portfolio. You can rebalance next January.

Study the trade confirmations when they arrive. They should match the trade you placed.

If your account is subject to taxation, immediately contact your tax professional to let him or her know that a trade with tax consequences has taken place. When in doubt, call.

Now go enjoy your life, and leave your portfolio alone until next January, when you will once again rebalance.

7. If you are working with a fee-only investment advisor, he or she should follow approximately the same process.

You might find that your manager replaces a bit more or less of your portfolio annually. You might find that he or she only sells half of failing funds and revisits them a year later. The details may be quite different, but the methodology should be similar.

The manager SHOULD identify funds which are struggling, and assess why the funds are in this condition. Given this imperfect world, there SHOULD be a fund which is struggling, or at least struggling relative to other picks. If the manager can't identify the funds he or she likes LEAST, then ego may be a factor.

The manager SHOULD communicate a general strategy to you which informs you of a continuing long-term plan to weed the garden.

The manager SHOULD make a compelling case for each replacement fund which is brought into the portfolio.

The manager SHOULD NOT be trading based on guesses of what any financial market will do next.

The manager SHOULD NOT be trading large portions of the portfolio.

The manager SHOULD NOT be holding failed funds in the portfolio.

In general, the manager should be doing the vast bulk of all this without your involvement. You should be kept informed, with the ability to track the process on your computer or via statements or confirms. Otherwise, the job of weeding is for the manager to do.

Review: The Lessons of Chapter 12

Lesson #55: In July or shortly thereafter, you weed the garden. "Weeding the garden" is identifying the mutual funds which make up the relatively worst-performing 10% of your portfolio and replacing them with funds which are better relative performers. You also replace all mutual funds with a *Morningstar* rating of 1 star.

Chapter 13

Recognize and Avoid Investment Bubbles

"Look at market fluctuations as your friend rather than your enemy;
profit from folly rather than participate in it."
– Warren Buffett

"The four most dangerous words in investing are, 'This time it's different.'"
-Sir John Templeton

Section 13.1: Investment Bubbles

At this point you have learned how to manage your investments, or at least how to work with an investment manager to manage what you own. This chapter returns to financial market behavior to discuss a true potential life-wrecker: investment bubbles. Then I am going to provide you with an OPTIONAL way to cope with them.

WHAT YOU ARE ARE ABOUT TO READ IS OPTIONAL. The system as it has been presented through Chapter 12 will work just fine. But here's a way to add a little extra performance. We all like that, don't we?

Lesson #56: Markets in all free-traded goods tend to go to extremes, from bargains to bubbles, and then back again.

Investment bubbles deserve their own chapter because they are the cumulative expression of all the irrationality which I discussed earlier. THE BIG mistake I see investors make is to get caught in a market bubble. For some reason most investors are hog-blind to them.

A "free-traded good" is essentially anything which can be turned into cash within a week, at an openly agreed-upon price, without disabling taxation or penalty. That would include tulip bulbs, canned corn, stocks, which are bits of corporate ownership, and bonds, which are simply IOU's put to paper. Houses are free-traded goods. Cars are free-traded goods. So is toilet paper. Obviously, in this book, we're talking about investments.

Another feature of an investment is "liquidity", which measures how QUICKLY you can sell something. Houses tend to be relatively illiquid: they often take a long time to sell.

But the investments we're going to discuss here, such as those packets of corporate ownership we call stocks, and bonds, which are varieties of debt, tend to be very liquid: you just sell them on an open exchange such as the New York Stock Exchange or the NASDAQ, a virtual computer-based exchange. As you have read, I am a committed advocate of conservative and diversified investing. As you have read, that's why I advocate that you buy all your stocks, bonds, and other investments via mutual funds.

However they invest, investors tend to move in herds and create market bubbles.

Market bubbles, aka investment bubbles, are times of extremely high market prices, when everyone wants to buy. They are La Brea Tar Pits for many investors. History tells us that there have been investment bubbles in almost all investment markets. In Holland, in the 17th Century, there was an investment bubble in tulip bulbs. In 1720, in England, great covens of amoral investors were appropriately ruined by the South Sea bubble, speculating in slave trading to South America.

There have been bubbles in almost everything which can be bought and sold, including "Tickle Me Elmo" and "Cabbage Patch" dolls. One year, when my two older children were much younger, a special model of scooter was especially hot. It sold for about $200. The following year, something else was everybody's object of obsession, and the same scooter sold for $30.

Section 13.2: Expectations and Valuation

When I look at the wreckage of the past few decades in the investing world, I can see two big market booms, the technology market bubble of the 1990's, and the real estate/mortgage bubble of 2004-2007. Both of these were shortly followed by market plunges, the Crash of 2000, which lasted 3 years, and the Financial Panic of 2008.

A. Gary Shilling, a noted economist with a substantial record identifying investment bubbles, writes in his book, "The Age of Deleveraging" that he has called a market bubble about every seven years. So, as you can see, investment bubbles are multi-year events which can thrash your investment plan if you don't avoid them.

Market bubbles are always characterized by a radical increase in relative valuation. In other words, people become irrationally willing to pay more for a dollar of revenue. Almost always this is because someone is preaching that "this time is different" and revenues are about to soar to impossible levels.

To explore the concept of valuation further, let's look at owning a rental house.

If you have a home which rents for $1,000 per month, then your annual return is $12,000 per year.

For this example we'll ignore reality and pretend that there aren't any costs of owning a rental property, and that $12,000 represents a net yield. We'll also pretend that housing appreciation isn't part of the valuation. Welcome to fantasy real estate investing.

If you pay $120,000 for that house, you are netting 10% a year, aren't you? That's a good return relative to what you can get elsewhere. So you would say that the house is a good investment.

If the price of the same house drops to $60,000, that $12,000 would represent 20%, and the home would be a bargain.

If the price was at $400,000, the $12,000 would be 3%, and the house wouldn't be that attractive.

Of course, pricing stocks or any other investment in the real world is much more challenging. In a world full of uncertainty, our expectations about the future profitability of the investment shape the price.

For example, if you knew or believed that our hypothetical house sat on an undeveloped diamond mine, what would the price be? One would expect that the price would go up. On the other hand, if the home was located on a flood plain which experienced torrential deluges every five years, and the last big flood was four years ago, how much would the price be then? Much lower, I hope. Expectations ALWAYS shape the price.

To value stocks in the real world, we use a mathematical ratio called "P/E, or "Price/ Earnings ratio". This essentially calculates how much we are paying for a dollar of earnings.

For example, if the stock price is $40 per share, and the company earns $5 per share, 40/5 is 8. Historically, the average stock in the world has a P/E between 12 and 15. So we know that either there is a reason for this low P/E (i.e. the company's product causes disease, they are being sued, they make buggy whips, etc.), or the stock is a screaming bargain. It may be a great time to buy. Likewise, if the stock price is $200 per share, and the company earns $5 per share, 200/5 is 40. Is the stock a good buy? Probably not.

Now here's the clincher. Are you sitting down?

MOST INVESTORS IGNORE VALUATION!

I am not making this up.

Why do they do that?

Because stock prices are shaped by expectations, and most expectations are emotional.

In the late 1990's for example, we were on the cusp of an economic boom. Technology and internet companies were in the news hourly, and it seemed that the world was transforming. So investors looked at the stocks of those technology companies, and decided that "This time is different!" They invested emotionally, not rationally.

The probability that the stock markets were clearly overvalued was obvious to anyone who could read. Yet people kept investing, and various stock market venues--the Dow Jones Industrial Average, the S&P 500, and the technology heavy NASDAQ-- kept soaring to astonishing levels.

As the markets and valuations rose, the emotional need to invest became palpable. One magazine featured a cover with a headline that shouted "Everybody's Getting Rich But Me!" So the money poured into the markets regardless of valuation.

At its height, the P/E of the NASDAQ Index…an average of the entire group of tech stocks trading on the NASDAQ exchange… was 264. People were literally, eagerly paying $264 for $1 worth of current NASDAQ earnings. Seems crazy, doesn't it? But at the time literally millions of well-educated, officially sane people were thinking otherwise.

The historical P/E average for another mainstream stock market index, the Dow Jones Industrial Average, is about 15. In this case, the index is an artificial construct created by the Dow Jones Corporation to provide an average price for US industrial stocks regardless of which exchange is used for trading.

In late 2000, the average P/E for this index was about 44. And people were saying that this time was different and buying ever more. Investors ignored valuation because the story was so enticing, and the social mania was so great. Then, in 2000, the stock markets suddenly collapsed, leaving millions of investors badly damaged.

Expectations changed very rapidly as it became apparent that projected earnings in technology stocks were not going to reach their expected astronomical levels. In fact, most investors in technology stocks lost more than the markets themselves because most investors bought more as the markets rose. Many investors were clamoring to buy at the very top, days before the meltdown commenced.

Now why would they do that? They thought irrationally and invested emotionally. And they paid for their mistakes many times over.

In the late 2000's we had a real estate bubble, on the heels of the tech bubble. Amazingly, the very same investors exhibited the same irrational behavior, within five years of the last meltdown. This time they did it with their homes.

There are several valuation indicators for homes. One is price relative to income. Another is price relative to Gross Domestic Product. Essentially they both measure the same thing: people's ability to pay off a mortgage. Both of these indicators, and others, SCREAMED overvaluation by 2005. Yet more and more people kept buying, and prices kept going up and up until late 2007. At that moment of bloatation, a tiny uptick in interest rates caused variable rate mortgage payments to go up and imploded the entire fantasy.

Section 13.3: Market Cycles

All financial markets tend to follow long-term multi-year cycles punctuated by irrational extremes at the low and high periods. This cycle, from high to low to high, can take up to several decades, but it is a feature of any open market, from bonds to stocks to gold to real estate.

Let's leap on the roller-coaster and take a ride on the financial market bubble machine: In other words, let's walk through the process of a market cycle.

Picture an ideal, generic stock market. We're going to look at the stock market because it is the most common investment platform. If you look you will also recognize market cycles in other investment venues such as bonds, real estate, or race horses, or whatever you select as investments.

As I have written earlier, a share of stock is an equally-divided slice of ownership of a corporation. If we visualize the corporation as a pie, then if you own any shares of the corporation's stock, you own a slice of that pie. The size of that slice depends upon how many shares you own.

The pie gets bigger if the corporation succeeds, and therefore your slice gets bigger. When the corporation doesn't do well, the pie and therefore your slice gets smaller. Unless you buy more, sell, or re-invest dividends, which are cash payouts, your number of shares stays the same, but their value goes up and down.

Historically, the stock market's annual return has been about 10% a year. That includes the Great Depression of the 1930's, and the Financial Panic of 2008. In the long-term, the pie tends to grow. But it grows very erratically: two steps forward and one step back. This is normal. But this up and down movement can lead us to make reactive short-term decisions which are very harmful.

Let's say the stock market is down right now. It may be acting on irrational fears or genuine indicators of a coming financial downturn. In a capitalistic system, economic cycles are normal, so none of this ought to be particular cause for profound panic.

But that's not how investors behave. Usually they stampede to get out, forcing the market down. A sawtooth movement down like this is known as a "bear market", and its hallmark is fear. To repeat, a "bear market" is a market which is going down, and people in general think that it will keep going down.

The reality is that bear markets don't last. But that's not what people think.

As a miasma of pessimism settles upon the investing community, our ideal stock market will normally extend downwards to a place where it is actually undervalued, where there are many genuine bargains. Investors don't see that, because most are sating their need for lemming-like mass destruction, not pursuing a rational hunt for good investments. AT THE TIME OF A MARKET BOTTOM, THE GENERAL CONSENSUS IS THAT DECLINES WILL CONTINUE!

In this kind of investment downturn you tend to see lots of dismal public news. When people discuss a financial market which has crashed, they do so with the kind of disgust usually reserved for dysentery or ex-spouses. If the down market is the stock market, you will also see general market P/E's below 15.

But finally, after some months of low valuation and lots of investor wailing, the market begins to chop sideways. It does this for some time, perhaps months or even in extreme cases for years. Then corporate executives begin seeing their companies recover, in terms of earnings or future orders. They react to this by buying more of their own stock. These insiders buy for two reasons: the stock of their corporation is cheap, and conditions behind the factory door are actually beginning to improve.

This usually happens long before the public can recognize that the economy is beginning to recover. When the first glimmers of recovery begin, the public investing mood usually continues to be morose. As far as the public can see, the economy and the financial markets are still at the bottom of the roller coaster.

As insiders and intelligent investors increasingly buy stocks, the good news spreads, and at some point the investing public begins to buy again. This creates an upward movement of the stock market in general, punctuated by small multi-month downturns.

Since the market consistently recovers from these small downturns, investor caution decreases as the numbers keep building. At this point, the media, anxious for more advertising dollars, will usually stoke the furnace with positive messages about how people are getting rich.

A market with a multi-year sawtooth pattern upward is known generically as a "bull market". It is a world of joy and insanity. A "bull market" is a market which is going up, and everybody knows it.

As you can see on the following graph, in the longer term, the stock market's entire trend is up. Nevertheless there are plenty of downturns along the way. You can see that sawtooth pattern shaped by changing economic conditions and most importantly, changing expectations.

Stock Market Contractions and Expansions
1973–2010

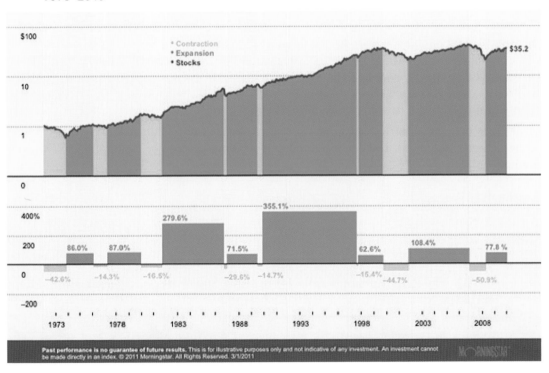

After some years of an upwards market, investors gradually plaster over their old memories of loss and suffering and begin to embrace the "black and white thinking" and the "hot-hand fallacy" previously discussed. They ignore risk, and increasingly buy stocks which are going up simply because stocks are going up.

They forget one of the world's great lessons: *that which is devastating but occurs rarely is neverthless devastating when it occurs.* They forget another, more basic lesson: *big booms are <u>always</u> eventually followed by big transient busts.*

This is where the "bubble" really begins: the conflagration of greed reaches a crescendo of buying, as whatever is in our hypothetical market becomes way too expensive. AT THE TIME OF A MARKET TOP, THE GENERAL OPINION BY EVERYBODY, INCLUDING MEDIA AND EXPERTS, IS THAT THE MARKET WILL CERTAINLY CONTINUE TO RISE. And that, of course, is when that market becomes as dangerous as a rattlesnake.

Section 13.4: Don't Get Caught in an Investment Bubble

Lesson #57: We *need* to decrease our holdings when the investment is expensive…when others are buying. This is the opposite of what we *want* to do emotionally.

You have already learned about "rebalancing". Rebalancing is selling a small bit of what is booming, just as it is booming, and buying a bit of what is undervalued. You have also learned about "weeding the garden", wherein you annually cull out your least-best mutual funds.

Simply by themselves, rebalancing your portfolio and "weeding the garden" will get you through to successful results. If you practice these behaviors scrupulously you will find that your portfolio continues to do well over the long-term.

However, that portfolio will INEVITABLY be caught up in occasional bubbles and the downturns that follow them.

When these downturns take place, YOU DO NOT WANT TO SELL INTO THEM! At that point you may be locking in a loss. So, regardless of the fear which drenches the entire investment community, you want to ride it out.

But you can also practice the <u>optional</u> technique of **"valuation weighting"**. That's when you consciously slightly underweight what is overvalued in the presence of what you think is a bubble. You also buy in a bit more…actually increase your risk exposure…close to long-term market bottoms.

<u>This is optional</u>…but it works, and in reality carrying out "valuation weighting" is less stressful than not doing it. The key is to do it <u>only near market tops or bottoms</u>, and NOT to do it emotionally.

Lesson #58: When:

> **1. The Value Line Estimated Median Appreciation Potential statistic is BELOW 50%**
and/or
> **2. The Price/Earnings ratio for the S&P 500 or its proxy index mutual fund is OVER 20**
then
Move back to the next-lowest risk level in your portfolio allocation, and adjust your portfolio accordingly.

For example, if you have a "market risk" portfolio and you choose to practice "valuation weighting", when you see either a P/E of 20 or higher or a VL-MAP below 50%, you would move your portfolio to a "moderate risk" allocation.

Remember, market price is a function of valuation, and valuation is to a large degree a product of expectations. A HIGH P/E or a LOW VL-MAP indicates that either valuation is excessive, or expectations are about to decline. We've had stock market downturns when P/E's are lower than 20, or VL-MAP is higher than 50%, but they usually haven't lasted. Genuine bone-breaking market crashes require a market bubble to create overvaluations. P/E and VL-MAP are good indicators of that.

P/E is a simple indicator. A. Gary Shilling is an economist with a stellar record of identifying investment bubbles. In his book, "The Age of Deleveraging" he reports a study by Robert Shiller of Yale University, in which P/E's over 20 produced an average annual decline of 2% for the next decade. P/E statistics may be skewed by current interest rates, but the basic verity that a P/E of 20 or higher is a warning sign seems unassailable.

I have always seen a high P/E over 20 at the same time as a low VL-MAP. The two tend to confirm each other.

So now you know when you may wish to cut back on your stock mutual fund positions. You will note that I suggest cutting back to the next-lower risk level, not all the way to 0% stock.

The reason for my advice is that investment bubbles can go on for years. And years. It's almost impossible to call a market top in the short-term. Also, it's very difficult to cut back at all during market bubbles, since all the social pressure is oriented towards buying, not selling. If you practice "valuation weighting", you have to be prepared to live with your chosen risk-averse allocation for multiple years before the market actually declines.

On the other hand, it is at market tops, when values are inflated by the hot air of media boosterism and investor frenzy, that most amateur investors are most aggressive, least conscious of risk, and most likely to move money into the stock market, not out.

The market top is when most people will want to invest. And it is the most dangerous and least profitable time of all. At this point in the market cycle, investors are feeling wealthy and invulnerable. The level of investors' confidence is indescribably high. By now, the average P/E is in the 20's at least. Once again, though, investors are ignoring valuation.

If you are a conservative investor, however, your behavior is intentionally quite abnormal. You can't predict the future. But while others are buying, buying and buying more you are consciously rebalancing and choosing to sell…that is, underweight, the overpriced stock market. You will feel terrible when you do this, because it will seem to you that everybody else is making money…and you are lagging far behind.

The change from a financial bubble to a financial crash tends to happen rapidly and unnoticed. Usually it is only recognized in hindsight. Often it is a small uptick in interest rates, as in 1929 or in 2007. Only a few investors sell out at first because this small downturn looks like merely one more small correction of many in a bull market's upward surge. If you are practicing "valuation weighting" you aren't one of these sellers, because you have already sold enough to feel comfortable.

But then, for some reason, the herd stampedes out of the stock market. This most often happens when prices are overextended. Picture 2000 elephants trying to leave a stadium at the same time. People all try to leave at once. Prices "gap", that is, skip downward in freefall. And the rout begins. Welcome to the new bear market.

Bear markets bring claws to the game. A true bear market will follow a sawtooth pattern downwards, so the incurably optimistic investor will be fooled by small upturns into trying to buy low.

The result is continued punishment as everybody tries to determine where the mythical "bottom" might be. Hunting the bottom is historically a loser's game, but immensely entertaining and profitable for the media. So people keep trying, and the market continues to leave them bloodied.

As a bear market emerges, at first many investors don't sell. They hold onto their stocks and pray that the bottom comes soon. But eventually we reach the stage called "capitulation".

That's when the investing herd moves en masse to finally stop the pain. There is a final rush to get out, as fear and loathing dominate the financial community.

During the capitulation phase of a bear market, most investors are selling, when they should in fact be buying. Most investors are saying to themselves, "Why should I save and invest? I have lost so much in this downturn, and the media says we're doomed, so why buy now?" That's what happened in our perfect storm of 2008, in real estate, oil, gold, and mortgages. And what a mess it was. Of course, at the bottom, most investors were selling.

In fact, the exact opposite is true. This might not be the bottom, but if you are a patient, multi-year investor, <u>now</u> is when you should be gradually buying. And since you are following the guidelines of this book, that is what you do automatically: you rebalance, that is, you sell a bit of that which didn't lose money and buy a bit of what was badly damaged.

And, if you have chosen to practice "valuation weighting", you OVERWEIGHT the stock market slightly.

You will do this trembling with fear and possibly holding your nose. Once again, while all the other investors are moving in one direction, you are gently moving in the other. What you are witnessing is the reality that most investors buy high and sell low. They do this because the mania of bubbles lures them in, and ruins them. And you are doing the opposite.

Lesson #59: When:

    1. The Value Line Estimated Median Appreciation Potential statistic is AT OR ABOVE 90%
and/or
    2. The Price Earnings ratio for the S&P 500 or its proxy index mutual fund is AT OR UNDER 12
then
Move UP TO the NEXT-HIGHEST risk level in your portfolio allocation, and adjust your portfolio accordingly.

Warning: you may not buy at the bottom. In fact, it's normal to buy before or after the historical bottom of the financial market occurs. So you could feel AWFUL for months when you buy in early. If you practice "valuation weighting", you have be capable of enduring your choice to invest early for YEARS!

In fact, the 2008-2009 bear market caused the VL-MAP to reach over 130%. But any purchases I made when the VL-MAP was 90% have been great successes. You simply need to stay the course.

In the long-term, stocks and many other investments make money. As you witnessed, the graph looks like a giant saw, tilted upwards towards the right. The general trend is to grow. The stock market has made about 10% per year on average for centuries. That includes years where the market grew by 40%. It includes years when the market fell more than 40%.

The key is to NOT PARTICIPATE IN BUBBLES, and BEWARE OF OUR OWN IRRATIONAL MINDS! When others want to buy, you should reduce your holdings. When others are cringing in fear, consider investing moderately. You will note my dependence on the P/E and VL-MAP statistics. People have been financially ruined by using emotions to pick market tops or bottoms. Use P/E and VL-MAP instead of your irrational mind and you should come out smiling.

Review: The Lessons of Chapter 13

Lesson #56: Markets in all free-traded goods tend to go to extremes, from bargains to bubbles, and then back again.

Lesson #57: We *need* to decrease our holdings when the investment is expensive…when others are buying. This is the opposite of what we *want* to do emotionally.

Lesson #58: When:

    1.   The Value Line Estimated Median Appreciation Potential statistic is BELOW 50%

and/or

    2.   The Price Earnings ratio for the S&P 500 or its proxy index mutual fund is OVER 20

then

Move back to the next-lowest risk level in your portfolio allocation, and adjust your portfolio accordingly.

Lesson #59: When:

    1.   The Value Line Estimated Median Appreciation Potential statistic is AT OR ABOVE 90%

and/or

    2.   The Price Earnings ratio for the S&P 500 or its proxy index mutual funds is AT OR UNDER 12

then

Move UP TO the NEXT-HIGHEST risk level in your portfolio allocation, and adjust your portfolio accordingly.

Chapter 14

Chapter 14: Time, Discipline, and Consistency

We are what we repeatedly do. Excellence, therefore, is not an act but a habit.
—Aristotle

Practice isn't the thing you do once you're good.
It's the thing you do that makes you good.
—Malcolm Gladwell, Outliers: The Story of Success

Now you know the basics of how to invest and manage your own money.

You have learned that there is no way in the real world for you to invest for decent gains yet avoid all risk.

In reality, what I have described to you will ameliorate extreme risk, provide a buffer even in the worst times, and allow you long-term growth of wealth.

But in doing this you will be unavoidably injured to some degree when the financial system fails, as it did in 2008 and 2009.

The essential reason for using the investment methodology presented in this book is that you will be financially bruised in such a calamity but not ruined. You should even be able to find bargains amidst the desolation.

Diversification works over time. It works only if you have the ability to stay with the program, as discussed earlier in this book. There will be times when your diversified portfolio's performance will lag the performance of key indexes. Does this mean you should stop diversifying and invest only in index funds? Of course not. Now you know that such a contention is hilarious, in reality. True wealth, true safety, is found in AVOIDING excessive concentration of your investments in any one venue.

In conclusion, let's review the key 10 rules of investing. They are all important. And you should review them, and seek to conform to them, every time you seek to manage your investments.

1. **Times of economic and physical hardship are an inevitable part of life. They pass.** Times of economic and physical hardship are PAINFUL! But you've learned in this book that they pass.

2. **Budget, reduce or avoid debt, and save to succeed.** Now you know that there is no magic bullet, no winning lottery ticket, for most of us. We must SAVE to succeed.

3. **Manage your own irrational mind.** "What, me, irrational? Yes. We are all subject to moods and emotions. The key, as you've learned in this book, is to minimize them.

4. **Be cautious with your investments:**
   a. **Use a discount brokerage**
   b. **Select actionable, relevant financial information**
   c. **Select good professional help.**

Success requires keeping the complexity OUT of your investments! You've learned that in this book.

5. **Invest only in mutual funds:**
   1. **Cash and money market funds**
   2. **Bond mutual funds**
   3. **Diversified asset allocation mutual funds**
   4. **Stock mutual funds**
   5. **International mutual funds**

You know now that mutual funds provide you with the ability to hire managers and access markets throughout the globe. And you've learned how to select potentially winning funds.

6. **Diversify through asset classes to reduce risk to your perceived tolerance.**

This means that you'll have money in markets which are underperforming. But you've learned not to guess, right? Stay diversified to stay the course.

7. **Rebalance your portfolio annually <u>between and within </u>asset classes.**

You know now why we do this: to force ourselves to buy low and sell high. And you know now that we aren't guessing when we rebalance. You no longer have to guess what the economy or the financial markets will do.

8. **"Weed the garden" annually to find the best possible mutual funds.**

This will force you to cull your losers, but at the same time you won't exit markets which are temporarily down. It's a winning technique.

9. **Recognize and avoid investment bubbles by recognizing mania and overvaluation.**

Somewhere out there, as you read this, there is an investment bubble growing. Investors are becoming more and more excited. The financial media is writing more and more articles about this amazing new way to get rich quick. And you now know enough to stay away.

All of which leads us to

10. Repeat steps 1 through 9 to succeed with time, discipline, and consistency.

Lesson #60: Properly managing a diversified portfolio requires that you stay the course year after year, rebalance every January despite your emotions, and continue to weed the garden every July instead of waiting for lagging funds to recover. You may also choose to practice valuation weighting. Becoming wealthy and staying wealthy requires time, discipline, and consistency.

This is culmination of all which I have written before. The ongoing application of these investment principles over the span of years, carried out with enthusiastic discipline and consistency will inevitably make you better off. Yes, there will be challenging moments, moments of despair and doubt, but eventually these principles will deliver wealth for you, and create more serenity, and more well-being, for you and for your family.

The choice to succeed is yours.

Review: The Lessons of Chapter 14

Lesson #60: Properly managing a diversified portfolio requires that you stay the course year after year, rebalance every January despite your emotions, and continue to weed the garden every July instead of waiting for lagging funds to recover. You may also choose to practice valuation weighting. Becoming wealthy and staying wealthy requires time, discipline, and consistency.

And one final comment!

Everything in life is a work in progress.
That includes this book.

If you have questions, comments, or suggestions for improvement of later editions, please go to our website at www.andresenassoc.com and let us know! You are also welcome to email me at pete@andresenassoc.com.

Now go be rich….

Glossary

Here are some of the simple financial terms and concepts which have been discussed in this book:

- **1099, IRS Form:** This form is used by vendors or brokerages to report taxable income which is not wages. For us, this means that the 1099 form will report taxable events in your portfolio. You should receive these within a few months of the end of the tax year, in January or February. Save them and give them to your tax professionals. Do not be surprised to receive another revised form 1099 later in the tax season, especially from international mutual fund sources. This can be very frustrating.
- **Active trader:** Someone who changes their investments a lot. This can produce very successful results but more often it simply produces lots of trading expenses. It can also indicate a gambling addiction which is being played out in an investment venue, or simply a person who is seeking emotional gratification from the investment process.
- **Annuity:** a form of investment, usually quite complex, in which the investor trades the possibility of future gains for a sense of security and set monthly income, and often ends up with less as a result. More formally, a financial insurance product sold by well-compensated financial institutions which has special-interest tax protection as it grows. At a future date, the value of the investment is set to pay out in fixed monthly payments. Annuities are routinely used to create a pre-established fixed cash flow for retirees, and to enrich insurance salespeople.
- **Asset Allocation mutual fund:** A mutual fund that routinely invests in both stocks and bonds, rather than simply one or the other. These funds can also participate in fringe markets such as convertible bonds, commodities, and high yield debt. Some of these mutual funds are profoundly successful. Others are simply frenetic.
- **Asset base:** the amount of money which a professional money manager has under his or her control. Also, similarly, the amount of money in the investment pool of a mutual fund, which is managed by a professional manager. This pool tends to grow as the money manager is successful, and shrink as the manager lags. Obviously, market forces also can increase or decrease a manager's asset base.
- **Asset class:** a group of investments which shares key characteristics in common. Most importantly, an asset class is highly correlated. That is, the investments in any asset class tend to move similarly due to market action. They all go up and down together when markets move. Asset classes change based on definition. The simplest are usually stocks, bonds, real estate, and cash. More detailed

definitions are usually applied for mutual fund investing. For example, large cap stocks, energy stocks, etc.

- **Bear market:** A market condition in which the prices of securities are going down and people in general think that the prices will keep going down. Bear markets are characterized by pessimism, and a sense that the bear market will last into perpetuity. In history, all bear markets have eventually ended. The back parts of bear markets are often buying opportunities.

- **Beta:** A statistical calculation to depict correlation also depicted as "ß". Usually beta is depicted as a single number which centers around 1. A "1" beta indicates that the investment in question is perfectly correlated with the index to which the investment is being compared. For example, a stock-based mutual fund which has a "1" beta to the S&P 500 is essentially perfectly correlated with the S&P 500. When the stock market declines $1, that mutual fund should theoretically decline $1 as well. When a mutual fund has a .50 beta, theoretically that mutual fund should increase $ .50 when the stock market increases $1. Beta may be calculated versus any index, so care should be taken that you understand the index for which the beta is calculated. For example, bond funds also have beta statistics, which are calculated against a bond market index. Also beta DOES NOT serve as an indicator of raw risk: that statistic is called standard deviation. So it is quite possible to find a mutual fund with a low beta which actually has very high uncorrelated risk. Also keep in mind that beta is calculated using historical data, and thus is constantly in flux. Beta can also change quickly especially when the mutual fund manager alters the underlying portfolio of the mutual fund.

- **Black and white thinking:** A dichotomous behavior which many people instinctively adopt under stress. This occurs when you see the world from an "all good" or "all bad" perspective, from one extreme to the other, with no middle ground. Black and white thinking tends to dominate in market extremes. Deeply declining markets feature an overall sentiment that "it will never recover" while strongly positive markets incorporate the feelings that "this will never end" and "It's really different this time."

- **Blend Value/Growth mutual fund management.** A mutual fund management style which incorporates elements of both value and growth management techniques. This can be highly individualized, and depends on the investment philosophy of the management.

- **Bond:** Essentially a big, long-term IOU. Also called debentures, credits, bills (for short term issues) and notes (if the maturity is under 10 years). A debt investment in which an investor loans money to an entity (corporate or governmental) that borrows the funds for a defined period of time at a fixed interest rate. Usually the coupon, the amount paid out as interest, does not change. When that coupon DOES change, the bond is known as an "adjustable rate" bond. The "face value" is the amount loaned. When the bond is sold in the secondary markets, the market value of the bond changes relative to current interest rates. Rising interest rates tend to depress bond market prices, and falling interest rates tend to increase bond market prices. However, the bond's face value usually does not change, and remains fixed at the time of maturity, when the bond's face value is repaid to the bond owner. Thus the valuation of a bond over time roughly resembles that of a guitar string: fixed at the date of issuance, fixed at the date of maturity, but vibrating and changing in mid-lifespan.

- **Bubble:** A rising market, usually multi-year, which features extreme public positive sentiment, and extreme overvaluations. Usually bubbles feature a new investment wrinkle which causes public opinion to believe, erroneously, that "This time is different". These are very dangerous, wealth-wreaking events which take years to develop. Usually the market declines which follow are extremely damaging, take years to resolve, and result in market under-valuations.

- **Bull market:** A market condition in which the prices of securities are going up and everybody knows it. Bull markets are characterized by optimism, and mature bull markets are characterized by excessive and unsupportable valuations. An extreme bull market usually becomes a market bubble.

- **Capital Asset Pricing Model:** Also depicted by the acronym CAPM, this model is used to identify the risk premium which should be reasonably expected from a given investment. In other words, this model uses mathematics to deliver an expected rate of return from any given investment within a diversified portfolio. This model was invented in the 1960's and garnered a Nobel Prize in Economics for its creators. Its invention was the beginning of the quantification era of Wall Street, which failed so spectacularly in the first decade of the 21st Century. As a result, its frequent continued use on Wall Street is a bit like applying shoe polish to dog feces: while a superficial shine may be created, the quality of the core remains intact.

- **Capital gains:** Cash profits from selling any investment which has increased in market value, as opposed to profits from cash payouts by the investment. Capital gains are currently taxed at different and often relatively favorable rates when compared to earned income.

- **Capitulation:** This phenomenon takes place when a collapsing market enters a psychological nadir. It occurs when the investing herd moves en masse to sell. There is a final rush to get out, as fear and loathing dominate the financial community. During the capitulation phase of a bear market, most investors are selling, when they should in fact be buying. Bargains are almost always a feature of capitulation.

- **Cognitive dissonance:** Coping with facts which are apparently both true and yet at odds with each other. This creates both mental stress and a mental effort… often subconscious…to bend fact to fit a preconceived reality. If cognitive dissonance drives a person to further rational study, it can also spur greater understanding and more harmonious financial results. The key is to recognize cognitive dissonance when you see it.

- **Competence by proxy:** A normal irrational behavior by which you diffuse your responsibility for making decisions. It leads you to perceive that risk is lower and your control is greater than they actually are. That is, we gather an irrational sensation of security and control by assigning fictional competence to others, and then create a sense of our own competence by our imagined affiliation with them. That's why celebrities so effectively endorse products and talk show hosts sell books. Competence by proxy is why we enjoy meeting famous people. It is also why a prediction of the future by a famous person in the media is so influential. This is also why actors are able to successfully enter politics.

- **Convertible bond:** a bond which at some future date at a specified price may be transferable for a pre-determined number of shares of the bond issuing company. Essentially this is a bond which can become a stock. Convertible bonds can be very profitable yet provide downside protection which isn't present in the stock market. On the other hand, convertible bonds are tricky, have their own rules, are often issued by companies with less-than-perfect credit, and pay a lower coupon relative to their bond price. My advice is to seek out asset allocation mutual fund managers who can deal with these.

- **Corporate Bond Mutual Fund:** A mutual fund managed with the intent of investing in bonds issued by corporations. Such a mutual fund would normally seek to create a portfolio of such bonds instead of selecting mortgages or government bonds.

- **CPI rate:** Also known as the Consumer Price Index, or cost of living index. This is a statistic which measures the monthly change in a fixed basket of consumer goods, including housing, electricity, groceries, and transportation. This statistic thus measures the rate of inflation. Critics contend that it is too inflexible to measure true costs of living increases, especially when one segment of consumer goods is increasing radically. However, CPI is the universal standard by which inflation is measured.

- **Debt instrument:** Another name for bond, debenture, credit, bill, or note. A securitized loan wherein one entity borrows from another and pays interest for the joy of the experience.

- **Diffusion of responsibility:** a natural mental phenomenon which occurs in groups of people wherein the individuals resist or avoid making decisions to escape public responsibility. This is why people in crowds will avoid calling for help or intervening when they are bystanders to a crime or accident. People in crowds will often agree with consensus decisions or interpretations, even when those decisions or interpretations are glaringly erroneous. In history, the phenomenon of diffusion of responsibility is linked to political disasters such as the rise of Nazism, and social phenomenon such as market bubbles, platform shoes, and pet rocks.

- **Discount Brokerage:** A company which provides transaction services for the buying and selling of investments at relatively low cost, does not provide explicit investment advice, and which does not compensate employees via commission. These are usually computer-based platforms.

- **Diversification:** A risk management technique that mixes a wide variety of investments within a portfolio, so that the individual risks of investments are diluted by the individual risks of other holdings.
- **Dividend:** A distribution of a portion of a company's earnings, decided by the board of directors, to a class of its shareholders, usually in the form of cash. This cash payout is currently taxed at less advantageous rates than capital gains.
- **Domestic Stock Mutual Fund:** For our purposes, a mutual fund which seeks to invest in stocks which are domiciled within the US. This gets blurred a bit: if an international corporation has its headquarters within the US but gets most of its profits internationally, the stock of this corporation is usually regarded as a domestic stock.
- **Efficient frontier:** The curve on a risk-reward graph which plots optimal portfolios that provide have the highest expected return possible for the given amount of risk. Conversely, we might also define the efficient frontier as a plot of the least amount of risk for a given return. This theoretical construct is much harder to plot in the real world but repeated studies have indicated that it clearly DOES exist.
- **Ego extrapolation:** Ego extrapolation takes place when an expert in one specialty psychologically extends his or her perception of mastery to other areas of life. For example, a highly skilled surgeon might extend her perception of competence to flying an airplane, with disastrous results. A lawyer might extend his valid perception of his own mastery of the legal profession to repairing his own car, and obtain mediocre results. Ego extrapolation is why highly competent professionals sometimes make extremely unsuccessful investors.
- **Equity:** The portion of real estate which a homeowner owns beyond the bank mortgage. Also, another term for stocks, or shares of stocks, issued by a corporation. For example, an "equity-based mutual fund" is a mutual fund which specializes in investing in stocks.
- **Exchange traded funds, (ETF's)** Aggregates of investments very similar to mutual funds which are issued by brokerages and traded like stock. These ETF's are usually based on indices of some sort, computer-generated, and can be traded throughout the trading day, whereas conventional mutual funds are traded once a day at the closing price. This offers advantages to short term traders, but appears to deliver a very modest or negligible advantage in the long term. ETF's are also very subject to hedge fund manipulation and trading costs for frequent turnover are high. As a result, I don't usually recommend ETF's.
- **Fed funds rate:** A very short term interest rate which banks and the Federal Reserve, the national bank of the United States, charge each other for overnight inter-bank loans. The Fed Funds Target Rate is set by the Federal Reserve as a feature of national economic policy. A rising rate is used to decrease the velocity of the money supply and reduce an overheated economy. A declining rate is applied to effectively increase the money supply and stimulate the economy.
- **Growth Mutual Fund:** A mutual fund which is managed to select equities, AKA stocks, based on the expected growth of profitability of those stocks.

Growth fund managers will often pay a relatively high price for the shares of especially attractive, fast-growing companies. Thus growth fund managers tend to produce torrid, smile-inducing results when markets are booming. They also tend to ride stock market bubbles until they crash.

- **HELOC (Home Equity Line of Credit)** a loan without a preset repayment plan, usually using one's home as collateral, or security in the event that the loan is not repaid. HELOC's may be created in addition to mortgages, and usually feature an interest rate which is adjusted based upon current short term interest rates. HELOC's are often Satan's bargain: easy to create, very challenging to repay. Thus they are best avoided except in cases of dire necessity. A conservative philosophy of personal wealth suggests that home equity is best left in the home.

- **Inflation:** An increase in the cost of goods and services in day to day living. Inflation takes place (theoretically) when too much money chases too few goods, and thus a currency unit buys less goods and services over time. Often but not always the result of profligate governmental monetary policy, inflation is a major risk to investors since it corrodes the spending power of fixed income. This rate is calculated by the US government's Bureau of Labor Statistics on a monthly basis and expressed as the Consumer Price Index or "CPI".

- **Index (indices):** A mathematical method of measuring the value of an overall market's valuation by using a smaller sample than the overall market. Indices are created by media or investment companies which seek to determine the valuation of a given financial sector or market. They use a variety of sampling methods. For example, the Standard and Poor's Corporation creates a variety of indices, most famously the S&P 500, which is mathematically weighted and measures the valuation of the stocks of 500 large corporations domiciled in the United States. The Financial Times newspaper and the London Stock Exchange work together in Great Britain to create the FTSE 100, known as the "Footsie", which measures the valuation of the stocks of 100 large companies based in England. Essentially an index can be created for any traded investment. And, of course, when an index can be created, then computer geeks can make an investment vehicle which can actually be traded. These actual investment vehicles are known as "Index mutual funds". Most of them are unnecessary.

- **Interest Rate:** The amount of money paid out to borrow, paid by the borrower to the lender. This is usually expressed as a percentage of the amount borrowed, often on an annualized basis, and can be for any debt, for any length of time.

- **International Mutual Funds:** Pools of money managed by professionals which seek to invest outside the country in which they operate. For us in the US, that means that international mutual funds invest everywhere BUT the United States. In recent years some international mutual funds have been profoundly successful, and should be considered for any investment portfolio. GLOBAL mutual funds are able to invest outside the US but may also invest inside the US when the managers consider domestic stocks attractive.

- **Investment Bubble aka Market Bubble:** A stock market phenomenon which occurs when the stocks in a particular sector are inflated out of proportion to their intrinsic value in response to exaggeratedly high expectations of resale value. The bubble is said to burst when stock prices suddenly decline which is then compounded by panic selling of shares. Picture a herd of rhinos attempting to leave a movie theater.

- **Investment grade bond:** A bond or debt instrument which rating agencies have determined has a low risk of failure or default. However, rating agencies have very flawed histories. Diversification is essential when purchasing bond mutual funds.
- **IRA (Individual Retirement Account):** Picture a bag. Some people, depending upon income, are allowed to put money into this bag and invest it to let it grow. You put money into the bag, and perhaps take a delightful tax deduction for that money. The money is able to grow tax-deferred while it is in there. You can buy and sell a variety of investments inside that bag, and there are no tax consequences. When you take some money out, as you MUST beginning at age 70 ½, it may be subject to taxation as ordinary income. Removals from Roth IRA's are NOT usually subject to taxation. IRA's in general are a VERY GOOD THING, and deserve your full attention! Keep in mind, however, that IRA's are NOT investments. They are instead accounts in which to invest.
- **Kleptocracy:** The kleptocracy model…proven throughout history…posits that the elites in power within any society siphon off a certain portion of national economic output for their own agenda. They inevitably place their own needs first. This produces cycles of leadership. Absolute power REALLY DOES corrupt absolutely.
- **Large-cap mutual fund:** A mutual fund which is managed with the intent of buying the stocks of large corporations.
- **Liquidity:** The ability to convert an asset to cash quickly without excessive transaction costs. For example, a check from your checking account is almost perfectly liquid. Stocks and bonds are relatively liquid. Fine art, cars, or real estate are usually much less liquid.
- **Low Risk Portfolio Allocation:** Appropriate for those who want the possibility of long-term increased returns, with some increased volatility from a small holding in stock mutual funds. This allocation tends to lag the stock markets over the very long term.
- **Market Bubble aka Investment Bubble:** A stock market phenomenon which occurs when the stocks in a particular sector are inflated out of proportion to their intrinsic value in response to exaggeratedly high expectations of resale value. The bubble is said to burst when stock prices suddenly decline which is then compounded by panic selling of shares.
- **Market capitulation:** At the bottom of a market collapse following an investment bubble, when investors are willing to sell at any price.
- **Market correction:** a market decline within an overall upwards-moving market. Media and professionals usually regard a decline of at least 10% a "correction", whereas a decline of greater than 20% is usually regarded as a genuine downward-trending or "bear" market. Corrections happen frequently,

often yearly, as investors seek accurate pricing based on earnings. Thus mild corrections are a feature of healthy, reasonably efficient markets.

- **Market Risk Portfolio**: Appropriate for those who are willing to ride out full-strength market volatility to get at-market or perhaps above-market gains. Long term these portfolios have historically done relatively well for time periods of 20 years or longer. However, most people can't handle the volatility, and thus many market-risk portfolios tend to be abandoned.

- **Market timing:** Buying and selling investments based on what we think will happen in the short run. This tactic doesn't get the Good Investing Seal of Approval since it is very hard or impossible to guess right all the time.

- **Maturity:** The time period for a debt or bond. A bond's "maturity date" is the date upon which the bond principal is scheduled to be repaid to the lender. A bond mutual fund's "average maturity" is the average time to repayment of bonds in the mutual fund portfolio. This is important because bond funds with longer maturities have more interest rate risk

- **Moderate Risk Portfolio:** Appropriate for those who are willing to accept substantial volatility while seeking optimal gains. These portfolios tend to theoretically lag market risk portfolios over time periods greater than 20 years. But in the long term, since they are psychologically less punishing for investors, moderate risk portfolios seem to prosper more often in the real world.

- **Money Market Fund:** a mutual fund, a pool of money, managed by professionals with the intent of deriving income from very short term debt instruments. Money market funds tend to operate as cash or bank deposit substitutes, and usually are characterized by extreme liquidity and safety. However, they are usually NOT insured and can carry unexpected risk when managers stray into financially dangerous places searching for higher yield. For this reason I usually recommend that investors confine themselves to money market funds which invest only in Treasury bills.

- **Morningstar:** An American corporation which provides universal mutual funds data to investors. The most commonly used media source for measuring the performance of mutual funds.

- **Mortgage-backed Security:** a tradable investment which has as collateral a specified mortgage, or pool of mortgages. Some of these are quite safe, but others are the lycanthropes of the financial world, capable of turning into wolves and eating investors. They were a major cause of the Financial Panic of 2008. Approach these only in mutual funds, and then with caution.

- **Mutual fund:** A mutual fund is a pool of money managed by professionals for a specific investment goal.

- **Over-commitment:** When an investor becomes emotionally bonded with an investment or a course of action, to the extent that he or she accepts risks and losses which a more rational person would avoid.

- **Perfectionism:** The belief that investors can manage their portfolios without ever experiencing downturns or making flawed choices. The reality is that even the best investor encounters declining financial markets which are utterly beyond his or her control. Perfectionists tend to over-manage their portfolios and agonize over short-term market declines.

- **Ponzi scheme:** A fraudulent scheme whereby the fraudster pays back early investors with the money from later investors, creates a fake high return by providing large cash flows to investors, and draws in new money. These are actually more common than we would like to admit. Usually these feature the promise of exceptionally high gains, or display unusually consistent and attractive results. Avoid by investing only in mutual funds, in a discount brokerage venue.

- **Price/Earnings ratio:** how much we are paying for a dollar of earnings.

- **R^2:** a statistical measure of correlation, sometimes stated as the "coefficient of determination" or "squared correlation coefficient". An R^2 statistic is always expressed as a number between 1 and 0. An "R^2" statistic for a mutual fund measures how much of a mutual fund's volatility is theoretically correlated with the index to which the fund is compared. A "1" R^2 indicates perfect correlation, which suggests that the mutual fund under study may be an index fund, or close to it. And a lower R^2 indicates less correlation. Thus a .05 R^2 would indicate that 5% of the fund's volatility can be theoretically explained by the movement of the compared index. Keep in mind, however, that all statistics thus calculated are historical, "look-back" calculations, and thus to some unknown degree flawed as a future predictor. In fact, in times of crisis, R^2 tends to increase as all investments tend to correlate more. That's why we seek to keep R^2 as low as possible during normal times.

- **Risk:** In the real world, the likelihood that you will permanently lose money on an investment. In the world of theoretical finance, the volatility of an investment's market value.

- **Rebalancing:** Rebalancing is restoring the appropriate percentages of investments in your portfolio by selling a little of what has done well and buying a little of what is lagging. This causes you to "buy low" and "sell high". Doing this with your portfolio annually is adequate.

- **Recession:** A period, shorter than a depression, during which there is a decline in the growth of economic trade and prosperity. Usually recessions feature a decline in growth of the economy, not a genuine, long-lasting decline in economic output. However, a recession can feel very much like a depression when unemployment remains high and economic growth remains stagnant. It's best to keep in mind that recessions always end. And there is always a recession in our future, even in the best of times.

- **ROTH IRA:** A kind of IRA wherein an individual may save earned income in a tax-free retirement account. Taxes are paid on contributions but withdrawals are tax-free. This is a major advantage, but access to a Roth IRA is limited by your income. Check with a tax professional to see if you are eligible, because a Roth IRA is a very good thing.

- **Safe Money Portfolio Allocation:** Appropriate for those who are willing to accept very little risk and who are also willing to accept profoundly below-market returns. In fact this sort of portfolio is going to lag long term investment returns like a banana slug lags a cheetah. This sort of portfolio makes you feel safe, and is a superb venue for money which you will need in the short run, in up to 5 years. However, for anyone investing longer than a decade, returns are often relatively dismal.

- **Simple Total Return Before Taxes** (STRBT) This is totally an in-house concept: I use it in my business to get a quick view of what a client's money is doing. You need it to know what your own money is doing. STRBT = ((portfolio value this month + money you took out – money you put in) – (portfolio value last month)) / portfolio value last month. If this boggles you, it's an indicator that hiring a fee-only investment advisor is possibly a good idea.

- **Specific risk:** When you invest in an individual stock or bond, you genuinely face the risk that the stock or bond will simply cease to exist, and that your money will literally vanish because of the SPECIFIC risk of that unique corporation. Specific risk is risk uniquely associated with that investment: the risk of a unique event which is restricted only to the issuer of the stock or bond.

- **Stagflation:** The combination of inflation and stagnation, wherein prices rise relative to income, while economic stagnation takes place at the same time. This is the worst of all worlds financially: rising prices corrode fixed incomes, but economic stagnation in the form of a recession or depression keeps incomes from rising.

- **Stock:** An ownership position in a corporation, allocated in the form of shares. A claim on its proportional share in the corporation's assets and profits.

- **Systemic risk:** The unavoidable risk which confronts any single financial market, and thus the asset class of investments involved in that market. The only way to reduce systemic risk is to diversify widely both between and within asset classes.

- **Taxable Investment Account:** A brokerage account which is not a retirement account, and thus exposes all profits or losses from transactions to taxation. While this kind of account does not provide a tax benefit for assets contributed, it DOES offer the benefits of taking potential tax losses, favorable capital gains taxation on assets held long-term and then sold, and holding assets for your lifetime and beyond with no taxation at all.

- **Valuation:** The price of a stock relative to earnings. People frequently invent new ways to do this, especially during market bubbles. In reality, plain old current P/E, (price divided by current earnings), and relative dividend work just fine. The goal here is to find investments which appear to be bargains, and avoid investments which appear to be richly priced.

- **Valuation Weighting:** This is an optional tactic. When you consciously slightly underweight what is overvalued in the presence of what you think is a bubble.

- **Value Line Estimated Median Appreciation Potential statistic:** also named by me "VL-MAP", this is the averaged appreciation potential expectation of the analysts working for the Value Line Corporation. Historically, this statistic has been a rather accurate indicator of potential future returns in the 3 to 5 year time horizon, but does not accurately indicate market direction in less than 3 to 5 years.

- **Value mutual fund**: a pool of money managed by professionals which seeks to find "undervalued" investments, based on techniques which may be universally known or proprietary. Good value mutual fund managers tend to be "bean counters" who buy stocks based on current value, NOT on expected future returns.
- **Vulture investing:** extreme value investing, in which managers attempt to find bargains in stocks or bonds which are currently in bankruptcy or in some sort of financial distress.
- **Weed the garden:** Identifying the mutual funds which make up the relatively worst-performing 10% of your portfolio and replacing them with funds which are better relative performers.
- **World allocation mutual fund:** a pool of money which is managed by professionals, which has as its goal investing throughout the world, including the U.S. This kind of mutual fund also invests widely in stocks, bonds, hybrid investments, commodities, and any other liquid investment which seems attractive. This category of mutual fund includes some stand-out mutual funds which have delivered superb performances. However, world allocation mutual funds also have an occasional tendency to lag bull markets profoundly since they are so diversified.

Appendix One:
Investing for Income

We are now in an era of historically-low interest rates. That may change soon: we simply don't know what interest rates will do. Meanwhile, people who are seeking to manage their portfolios for income are feeling the pain of low bond coupons.

Long-term investing for income requires particular time, discipline, and consistency. If you are investing for income, you must remember always that Total Return = Income + Capital Change. This means that your portfolio should stretch beyond bond mutual funds to embrace equity mutual funds with a possibility of providing inflation-beating capital growth. So the old idea of investing for income by investing only in bonds is WRONG. You need to stay committed to your program of investing in a very diversified portfolio of mutual funds.

I am often approached by people who want to invest totally in bonds for income, because they are older and perceive that they should have a shorter time horizon. Actually, while embracing lower risk may be appropriate, an older person may not be as old as he or she thinks. The most rapidly growing demographic sector in the United States is the group of centenarians, people 100 years or older. When you look at it from that perspective, an eighty year old investor may need income from his or her investments for another twenty years at least, which would make anyone a long-term investor. (Fig. 16-3)

When you look forward to living and investing for the next twenty years, you find that you need investments with the ability to retain value and beat inflation. Despite all the hyperventilating which we reserve for stock market fluctuations, inflation is probably the biggest long-term threat to your income stream. Even a 2% rate of inflation, the rising cost of living, over twenty years will reduce a dollar's worth of purchasing power to only about sixty cents.

As I wrote earlier, bonds don't grow. You will be investing in bond mutual funds, not bonds themselves, so you won't witness this firsthand. It will be concealed by the mutual fund's overall performance. But it is happening nonetheless.

A bond is simply a glorified IOU, and the money you put in provides you periodic interest until the bond matures. Then you are supposed to get the money back.

Picture a bond's value like a guitar string: fixed tightly at each end, but flexible in the middle. What makes a bond's total return fluctuate is a change in interest rates. In bonds, as in all investments, **Total Return = Income + Capital Change**.

Imagine you buy a shiny brand-new $10,000 US Treasury bond which yields 5% and has a maturity of thirty years. This means that you are loaning the US government $10,000. The US government is giving you a paper IOU…the bond…and paying you 5% a year until they give you your $10,000 back in thirty years.

Retirees Should Plan for a Long Retirement
Probability of a 65-year-old living to various ages

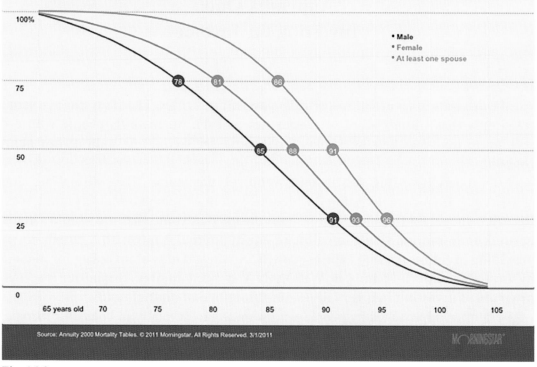

Fig. 16-3

That 5% is a fixed $500 annual payout. It will not change. Inflation will probably be about 3%. So you are netting 2%. And that 2% is taxable. You can already see that you aren't making too much money on this deal.

Let's imagine that next year's shiny new bonds yield 6%. And let's imagine that you decide to sell your one-year old 5% Treasury on the used-bond market. What will you receive? Essentially the market will price your bond so that your 5% coupon yields 6% for the new buyer. That means your bond will lose value on the used-bond market. Of course you can always wait 29 more years and get your $10,000 back when the government repays you. But what happens if you want the money now? Of course it works the other way too: if interest rates go down, your bond will have a positive capital change in the used-bond market.

One result of the mechanics of bond investing is that when yields drop as they did in 2011, investors become frustrated searching for higher income. So they begin to invest in higher and higher risk bonds or bond mutual funds, which are ever more volatile to interest rate or economic changes. Even allegedly sophisticated investors such as hedge funds and banks sometimes become stymied as they search for yield. They act just like uninformed individual investors as they load up on higher and higher risk investments.

The ultimate in risky income investments are dangerous artificial bond derivatives with strange names like "Collateralized Loan Obligations" and "Collateralized Mortgage Obligations". These were the primary triggers of the Financial Panic of 2008.

These bond market Frankensteins allow investors to artificially absorb risk and thus increase returns. In a nutshell, they don't work.

Many of these risky vehicles for income conceal their hidden dangers through "guarantees" and "re-insurance". This makes income investors turn into goldfish. That is, they think all is well, and become soporific. I once had goldfish in my backyard pond. They were quite serene. They were all eaten by raccoons. <u>This is why I recommend keeping maturities short and credit quality high when you buy bond mutual funds</u>.

I also strongly advise that you don't chase yields like a dog yapping after a garbage truck. The higher the relative yield on a bond or mortgage mutual fund, the higher the risk. Low risk funds, like those which invest in Treasuries, play a role in your portfolio because they serve as a parachute in hard times. That's all they do. If you want more income or higher returns, I suggest you avoid high-risk bond mutual funds and turn to the stock market.

Instead of investing in bonds for income, I tend to select asset allocation mutual funds, which are a combination of stocks and bonds. I know this violates the traditional standard of pure income investing, but the numbers are simply too attractive, especially if you examine "Conservative Allocation" funds in *Morningstar.*

If you still need more income from your portfolio, consider selling some shares of your asset allocation or stock funds. If you do your calculations right, you won't invade your original investment. And your sales will probably be taxed at the advantageous capital gains rate.

Investing for income requires a diversified portfolio. You may wish to employ low risk bond mutual funds which invest in low volatility short term bonds such as Treasuries to reduce risk, but I would not rely on them for your core income needs. I would suggest that asset allocation and other stock-oriented funds may provide an attractive alternative to meet your income needs. Thus a "low risk" or "moderate risk" model allocation may be the best choice for you.

If you have a family trust which is providing you income, you may wish to keep the portfolio growing and not invade the principal. To do this, it is helpful to make an annual pre-calculated payout. If you wish to have the principal grow during your lifetime, you will historically do well by taking out no more than 5% of the year-end portfolio value after taxes. Take it out in one lump sum after annual taxes have been paid. Move the money to your checking account so that you can budget it out throughout the year.

If you are relying on a retirement plan, IRA, or other nest egg for your income, and you are willing to deplete it to nothing by the time of your death, it is safest to plan on a lifetime of 105 years. Ask your tax professional or investment advisor to amortize your money out from your current age until you reach 105. DO NOT buy an annuity to do this. Just manage your own portfolio and budget your own income.

And stay with the program!

Appendix Two:
Do You Need an Investment Advisor?

After all you have read, are you still considering hiring an investment advisor? It's a big decision. You should base your decision on what most favors your devotion of time, discipline, and consistency to create a lifetime of savings and wealth.

You have read and learned enough to begin managing your own money. Or, you have learned enough about yourself to know that managing your own money is befuddling and anxiety-producing.

If reading this book was a torment, bored you to hallucinations, or was simply too low on your priority list to finish, then you will probably find that a good fee-only investment advisor is worth the cost.

We all have skills in different things. I am good at managing money. I can't fold my socks, match colors, or repair my own car. I have learned in my life that it is at least socially dangerous for me to attempt any of these things. It took me years to learn this. I agonized, I took classes, and I struggled. I berated myself for my lack of discipline, for my imperfection. All of that didn't change the reality that a wrench in my hands is potentially a tool of mass destruction, even if only that I find it uncomfortable to learn anything different. Meanwhile, I still had to get dressed every day and drive a car.

That's how it is with managing money. If you haven't been able to do the tasks described in this book, stop pounding yourself and get help. That includes budgeting and spending. If you can't save, get help and change. Otherwise the reality is that if you do what you've always done, you will get what you've always gotten. In my case, that means a blue sock on one foot and a brown sock on the other. In your case, it might mean poverty.

If for any reason you can't perform the tasks I have described in this book, or you simply don't wish to do so, you need to hire an investment advisor. If you choose to hire a professional, you will still need to watch over his or her performance, and to follow your own long-term plan.

Out in the big wide world of finance are many people eager to help you, for a commission. "Commission" means that she or he is compensated based on what is sold to you. Because this creates a giant conflict of interest, I can't recommend paying commissions for financial advice.

Likewise, I do not recommend enlisting the advice of any financial planner who receives commissions, for the same reason. He or she has a conflict of interest. It doesn't matter if the individual is loaded with prestigious initials after his or her name: CPA, CFP, CLU. If the person is selling you something via commission the initials are simply advertising and have diminished bearing on the quality of advice you will receive.

Yes, advisors are expensive. But the results of bad choices, being caught in a bubble market or diversifying inadequately, can be catastrophic. It is my opinion that an advisor is probably worth the cost if you wish to employ one.

As I have said earlier, avoid commission-based advice. Even if it is good, as it often is, you are never sure that you are getting unbiased counsel. Your investment advisor should be paid either by assets under management or by the hour.

The advantage of paying by assets under management is that the investment advisor's interests are caught up with yours. He or she gets richer when your assets go up and less wealthy when your assets go down. Since there is no advantage to trade unnecessarily, you may be more confident that changes are motivated by a genuine search for investments which will thrive. Unnecessary expenses will also be avoided.

The disadvantage of paying by assets under management (AUM) is that it is expensive. The average fee is 1% of assets under $1 million. This means that you will pay $10,000 for a year's management of $1 million. In genuine terms, this is less than the expenses of a normal portfolio of individual stocks under the control of a commission-based stock broker.

It should also be worth it: your investment advisor should provide ongoing monitoring and proactive management. If you receive that service, your portfolio should be better off than similar unmanaged portfolios by at least 1% a year. At the very least you should buffer the consequences of market catastrophes which sweep over us all occasionally. 1% a year is much cheaper than losing your money due to bad investing. Sometimes the job of a GOOD manager is to LAG a surging, upward moving stock market or other investment bubble.

The other way of compensating a fee-only investment advisor is hourly. This is often much cheaper than the percentage of asset compensation plan, but it all too often results in less effective management. The advisor is put into the position of either racking up the hours spent on your account, in which case your costs rapidly approach those of AUM billing, or ignoring your account and focusing on the billable tasks at hand, in which case you are not receiving proactive management. Your financial interests are not aligned with the manager's.

As a professional manager, I do most of my business on an AUM basis. I am not alone. The reasons are that I prefer to share the same boat as my clients financially, because their money literally represents my cash flow. I prefer ongoing monitoring and proactive management. Also hourly advising makes me nervous because I can't see the results, and I dislike such a lack of control. Most advisors share my preferences.

Whatever fee structure you prefer, there are some solid guidelines for selecting an investment manager.

   1.   He or she should be registered with either the SEC or your state. There should be a document known as an "ADV" on file and online, and a copy should be made available to you. An ADV is a bit hard to read, but it indicates at least a willingness to disclose.

A REGISTRATION AND AN ADV DO NOT INSURE COMPETENCE, QUALITY OF MANAGEMENT OR EVEN HONESTY. But they do open the door for auditing and disclosure, and somewhat lessen the chances of fraud. At least they show you that the manager is aware of professional requirements.

2.   Your investment advisor should always use a third party brokerage with SIPC insurance. You should NEVER give your investment advisor custody of your money, and he or she should NEVER be a gatekeeper who determines if you get access to your cash. Well-known discount brokerages include Charles Schwab, TD Waterhouse, and Fidelity. He or she should not be an employee of these brokerages: once again, you are trying to avoid conflict of interest. ALWAYS give your investment advisor a LIMITED POWER OF ATTORNEY, not a FULL POWER OF ATTORNEY. A limited power of attorney allows your manager to observe your account on-line, trade within it, transfer money to you only, and collect fees from your account. A full power of attorney gives your manager full access as if she owns it. Let's not go there.

3.   Your investment advisor should invest in only liquid investments. That means that you can sell them and get the money from them within a week. Information about them should be available from places other than your investment advisor. You should be able to gather information about them on the Internet and in periodicals. This vastly reduces the potential for fraud, and ensures that you have full awareness of where your money is now. For me, this means mutual funds. Stay away from limited partnerships and hedge funds. They may sound cool but they are a financial blind man's bluff.

4.   You should receive a periodic report from your advisor detailing what is in your account and what your overall portfolio's performance has been over a recent time period. Almost always this will be a "Year To Date" (YTD) statistic which you might then compare to alternatives. It should also be after all fees and expenses. Surprisingly few investors actually know how their investments have performed over time.

5.   You should also know what you are paying your advisors. Some unscrupulous advisors will tell you that they are providing no load funds when in fact they are providing funds with large 12b-1 fees. That means that you are paying your advisor a secret annual fee, and if you get out of the funds you pay an egregious back-end penalty. Small 12b-1 fees are normal for mutual funds traded on a no-load basis within the structure of a discount brokerage. These should be paid to the brokerage for providing the platform, and your independent investment advisor should receive none of them. Your investment advisor should charge you one periodic clear cut fee.

6.   It is relatively common for Wall Street to dream up a new sexy method of investing which is so complex that literally nobody really understands it. Timing and options strategies might be attractive within one or two mutual funds in your portfolio, but as techniques for managing your entire nest egg, they are

historically loser's games. If you can't understand it, it is entirely possible your manager can't understand it either. Your strategy—and that of your manager— should be simple, robust, and inexpensive. That means mutual funds.

To work with an investment advisor or not is your choice. The bottom line: what choice will reinforce your plan, so that you carry on with time, discipline, and consistency for decades? And which choice do you simply find most attractive?

Appendix Three:
A Basic Reading List

These are probably better than most college textbooks at preparing you for the real world of investing. The goal here is to provide you with an overview of what is happening in the world, to prepare you for your life-long wealth-growing efforts.

You will note that there aren't any formal basic economics or investing books here. What you need to know is what you've read in my book. Also, mental preparation and an overall knowledge of our financial situation are more important than knowing about the arcane details of Wall Street. After all, that's not where you will invest, is it? Likewise, there's no need to rehash the politics of why we are in whatever may be our current financial environment. We are where we are.

The first six books deal with developing and managing a successful mental system for your life. Believe it or not, this is where most of us need the most coaching.

1. ***With Winning In Mind: A Mental Management System*** by Lanny Bassham. This is a small book about competitive rifle shooting. What does competitive rifle shooting have to do with successful investing? Lots. Both require mental discipline and a plan. The lessons of this book are easily adapted to investing. Skim this and learn the basics of the mental habits which lead to success.

2. ***The Top 10 Distinctions Between Millionaires and the Middle Class*** by Keith Cameron Smith. This book is tiny! But it provides you with the specifics to add to your mental plan. Successful people…the individuals who thrive financially…do it differently. Read how they do it here.

3. ***You Can Be Happy No Matter What***: *5 Principles For Keeping Life In Perspective* by Richard Carlson. Yet another small book, packed with wisdom. As I wrote in my book, I have found that many of the most spectacular wealth-busting mistakes people make aren't about money at all. How to maximize your own life is the message of this book. I also deeply recommend the audio version of this book so you can learn while driving.

4. ***The Millionaire Mind*** by Thomas J. Stanley, PhD. Anything by Thomas J. Stanley is worth reading. That said, this is a bit of a textbook, long on genuine data as well as themes for winning. Now that you are firmly on the path to a successful life, I'm guessing you are up to the challenge. I found that the audio version of this book was also worth a listen. In fact, I bought both paper and CD versions, and went through both. People who make themselves rich THINK differently, as you will discover.

5. *Blink The Power of Thinking Without Thinking* by Malcolm Gladwell. Here's another author whose every publication can be devoured with confidence. Malcolm Gladwell deals with the myriad ways we make decisions unconsciously. Unconscious pressures cause investors to make the wrong choices far too frequently. In my book you've read <u>how</u> to master the irrational mind. This book shows you <u>why</u> you need to master it. You'll want to understand how the mind works both rationally and irrationally to invest successfully.

6. *Freakonomics A Rogue Economist Explores The Hidden Side Of Everything* by Steven D. Levitt and Stephen J. Dubner. Our final book about the mental aspects of investing helps us look into the reality that economics control everything, even sometimes unintentionally. In fact, the unintentional results of social and political decisions are all too often just as great as whatever result was originally sought. This book will help you examine why governmental decisions won't necessarily save you. You'll also discover what Sumo wrestlers and teachers have in common, and some disturbing realities of what makes a perfect parent. And you'll also learn why so many drug dealers live with their parents.

7. *All Your Worth* by Elizabeth Warren and Amelia Warren Tyagi. I can't find any of my five office copies of this book. I'm sure I loaned them out to clients and friends. This book is that good. And yes, this is a book about basic budgeting. Not very exciting, perhaps, but it's a crucial read. You need the paper version of this, because there are useful exercises. Perhaps the details won't work for you, but the central aspects of all-important budgeting are very important. I would especially recommend this book to anyone just graduating from college or contemplating buying a home.

8. *The Next Decade: Where We've Been and Where We're Going* *and* **The Next Hundred Years, A Forecast for the 21st Century** by George Friedman. Both books have a lot of politics, which are interesting but as far as investments are concerned, irrelevant. The discussions of demographics, social change, and technology are very important. This book will give you insights into the changes we will face while you are busy trying to create wealth. It's mind-blowing. At least skim these books to get the big picture. You will have a deeper understanding of why you are investing as you are.

9. *The Ascent of Money* by Niall Ferguson. OK, I snuck an economics book into the mix. I prefer the audio version of this so your expectations of eye-glazing boredom never emerge. In fact, this is a fascinating history of our financial system. It's a centuries-long saga of heroes, villains, fools, geniuses, and struggle. And it's never boring. At least not to me. This one is essential because it will show you the high adventure of finance, and the long, long road we have traveled to get to where we are now.

10. Devil Take The Hindmost A History of Financial Speculation by Edward Chancellor. In my book, you've read that investment bubbles are a giant influence for investors. They can be financially catastrophic. This is the best book I've found which provides a history of 400 years of financial bubbles, all the way from Tulipomania in 1630's Holland to the roaring 1990's. If you can get a more recent edition, snap it up. I have read, and re-read, only the paper version of this. I imagine it would be a terrific audio book as well.

11. The Black Swan: Second Edition: The Impact Of The Highly Improbable by Nassim Nicholas Taleb. My take on this book may be a bit unique. Nassim Nicholas Taleb is a very highly educated college professor and successful Wall Street quant. And in this book he's saying that a great deal of that quantification, indeed, the number-crunching which defines the Wall Street ethic, is wasted. These realities are a key aspect of why you and I invest as we do: with the ultimate awareness that we really don't know what will happen. You would think that since we know that already, there's no need to read the book. You'd be wrong. The book's deep understanding of why quantification doesn't work will help you invest correctly.

12. The Age of Deleveraging Investment Strategies for a Decade of Slow Growth and Deflation by A. Gary Shilling. Having said that we don't know what will happen, we can now turn to A. Gary Shilling to learn what is most likely to happen. For despite the reality of "black swan" events, A. Gary Shilling has been a superb professional predictor of financial crashes. Since he has a fine track record, his wisdom is worth reviewing. The reality is that we don't really know what will happen. But A. Gary Shilling will help you understand why we need to stay diversified, flexible, liquid, and cautious. This book is quite dense. I chose to read it one chapter at a time. But now I find that I keep coming back to it to review his thoughts on the next decade or so. It's very worth the read.

I have a veritable plethora of additional books at my website at *www.andresenassoc. com*. Check it out, and please recommend any books which you feel are essential. Meanwhile, learn, and be rich.

About the Author

After several years as a cowboy, military linguist, and U.S. Marine infantry officer, Pete Andresen returned home to Salinas, California. With a bachelor's degree in agricultural economics and a master's degree in international development and finance, his career plan was to manage the family cattle ranch. But local farmers requested his assistance managing currencies for overseas trade, and this quickly transformed into managing their pension plans. In 1988 Pete left ranch management and launched a fee-only investment advisory firm, Andresen and Associates.

As a result of his disenchantment with investing strategies based on uncertainty and speculation, Pete successfully implemented an asset allocation model based on the perennially-honored virtues of time, discipline, and consistency.

Twenty-five years later, Pete's conservative management style and unique financial perspective have grown his little start-up into a firm entrusted with millions of dollars.

With the 2008 financial disaster as motivation, he wrote this book for you, to put real financial control of your money into your hands.

Visit the author at www.dollarsandcommonsensebook.com.